ETHICS and the INVESTMENT INDUSTRY

ETHICS and the INVESTMENT INDUSTRY

EDITED BY
OLIVER F. WILLIAMS
FRANK K. REILLY
& JOHN W. HOUCK

ROWMAN & LITTLEFIELD PUBLISHERS, INC.

ROWMAN & LITTLEFIELD PUBLISHERS, INC.

Published in the United States of America in 1989.
by Rowman & Littlefield Publishers, Inc.
8705 Bollman Place, Savage, MD 20763

Library of Congress Cataloging-in-Publication Data

Ethics and the investment industry / edited by Oliver F. Williams,
Frank K. Reilly, & John W. Houck.
p.   cm.
Includes bibliographies and index.
1. Business ethics.   2. Securities industry—United States.   I. Williams, Oliver F.
II. Reilly, Frank K.   III. Houck, John W.
HF5387.E83   1989   174'.9332—dc20   89-34176 CIP

ISBN 0-8476-7612-9
ISBN 0-8476-7613-7 (pbk.)

Printed in the United States of America

Dedicated
to
All those faithful men and women in the financial community who see
their life and work as a vocation, serving the Lord and all humankind by
helping to make a better world.

Contents

8   *Contents*

Preface

Ethics and the Investment Industry was the subject of the 1987 Symposium of the Center for Ethics and Religious Values in Business. Committed to affirming and improving the role of business in society, the Center sponsors a biennial symposium on some aspect of the theme.

The 1980 Symposium resulted in the book *The Judeo-Christian Vision and the Modern Corporation*, which includes such scholars as James Gustafson, John C. Bennett, Michael Novak, Kirk Hanson, Denis Goulet, Christopher Stone, James Schall, S.J., Edward Trubac, Burton Leiser, William Sexton, Kenneth Jameson, Charles Wilber, Catherine Cleary, and Elmer Johnson. Of the conference, *The New York Times* reported: ". . . there would be no facile resolution of the conflict between the values of a just society and the sharply opposing values of successful corporations."

The 1982 Symposium examined John Paul II's encyclical letter *Laborem Exercens*. The meeting brought together eighteen distinguished scholars and corporate and labor leaders. In a lively and fruitful three days, some 150 persons shared in the discussions, which *Newsweek* characterized as a "free marketplace of ideas" exploring a religious vision of business power. The 1982 conference resulted in the volume, *Co-Creation and Capitalism: John Paul II's Laborem Exercens*, which includes essays by Michael Novak, Stanley Hauerwas, David Hollenbach, S.J., Bernard Murchland, Joseph A. Pichler, J. Bryan Hehir, Denis Goulet, Ernest Bartell, C.S.C., Andrea Lee, IHM, Amata Miller, IHM, George C. Lodge, Mark J. Fitzgerald, C.S.C., and Elmer W. Johnson.

In December 1983, the Center assisted the U.S. Bishops' Committee charged to write a pastoral letter on the economy by convening a three-day symposium, Catholic Social Teaching and the American Economy. More than 250 people attended that symposium, including the five bishops who were to draft the letter. *The Los Angeles Times* observed that "About one-third of the major speakers represented conservative viewpoints, the remaining voiced moderate-to-liberal positions." *The*

New York Times reported that ". . . contentiousness is commonplace here at Notre Dame, the home field of the Gipper. And when dozens of business leaders, theologians and academics lined up against each other at the university this week, the debate over the economy was fought as hard as any gridiron encounter."

In April 1986, a conference was convened to explore whether the concept of the common good might be retrieved and become central in contemporary religious social thought. That meeting resulted in a volume titled *The Common Good and U.S. Capitalism* which includes essays by Charles C. West, John J. Collins, Ralph McInerny, J. Phillip Wogaman, Charles E. Curran, Richard John Neuhaus, Dennis P. McCann, Ernest Bartell, C.S.C., Michael Novak, Charles K. Wilber, John W. Cooper, Gar Alperovitz, Richard DeGeorge, Gerald F. Cavanagh, S.J., William J. Cunningham, Peter Mann, Bette Jean Bullert and David Vogel.

The Center for Ethics and Religious Values in Business is under the co-directorship of Oliver Williams, C.S.C., and John Houck, both of the Department of Management, College of Business Administration. It evolved from the University of Notre Dame Joint Committee on Business, Theology and Philosophy founded in 1976.

The Center seeks to build bridges between business, business studies and the humanities. Its programs are designed to strengthen the Judeo-Christian ethical foundations in business and public policy decisions by fostering dialogue between academic and business leaders and by research and publications.

Publications developed by the Center include: *Full Value: Cases in Christian Business Ethics, A Matter of Dignity: Inquiries into the Humanization of Work, The Judeo-Christian Vision and the Modern Corporation, Co-Creation and Capitalism: John Paul II's Laborem Exercens, Catholic Social Teaching and the U.S. Economy: Working Papers for a Bishops' Pastoral,* and *The Common Good and U.S. Capitalism.* Articles have appeared in *California Management Review, Business Horizons, Theology Today, Harvard Business Review, Business and Society Review* and *The Journal of Business Ethics.*

We wish to thank Michael J. Collins for his assistance in preparing this manuscript. Father Austin I. Collins, C.S.C., Department of Art, University of Notre Dame, deserves special recognition for his sculpture photographed on the cover.

For the conference, *Ethics and the Investment Industry,* and the publication of this volume, we are most grateful for the encouragement and financial support provided by the Olin Foundation, Dean Witter, the Hershey Foods Company and the General Electric Foundation; and at the University of Notre Dame, the College of Business Administration and the Center for Continuing Education.

Finally, it is our pleasure to dedicate this volume to all those faithful men and women in the financial community who see their life and work as a vocation, serving the Lord and all humankind by helping to make a better world.

Oliver F. Williams, C.S.C.

John W. Houck

Frank K. Reilly

University of Notre Dame

Notre Dame, IN 46556

December 1988

Introduction[1]

Oliver F. Williams, C.S.C.

It is commonplace to assume that there is an inherent antagonism between the intellectual class and the business world. Intellectuals celebrate the heroic, the saintly, the noble, and the virtuous. The great intellectuals of the world—Aristotle, Thomas Aquinas, the fathers of the church, for example—had a certain disdain for commerce. Business was never considered to be a noble profession. Consider Aristotle's definition of "noble."

> . . . those actions are noble for which the reward is simply honor, or honor more than money. So are those in which a man aims at something desirable for someone else's sake; actions good absolutely, such as those a man does for his country without thinking of himself; actions good in their own nature; actions that are not good simply for the individual, since individual interests are selfish.[2]

Adam Smith in *The Wealth of Nations* supposedly captured the dominant motivation of business people. For Smith, business is motivated by economic self-interest, the acquisitive impulse, and hence it is not a virtuous or noble endeavor. It is, however, a respectable occupation, he argues, because the aggregate of "self-interests" results in great benefits for the whole society. If each person pursues his or her own self-interest, then the common good will be enhanced, according to Smith. He saw that the sum total of individual self-interests resulted in a market economy that allowed all to better their own condition. A market economy is moral because it raises the level of living for all—even though it is based on acquisitiveness. In Smith's words:

> In civilized society he stands at all times in need of the cooperation and assistance of great multitudes, while his whole life is scarce sufficient to gain the friendship of a few persons. Man has almost constant occasion for the help of his brethren, and it is vain for him to

13

expect it from his benevolence only. He will be more likely to prevail if he can interest their self-love in his favour, and show them that it is for their own advantage to do for him what he requires of them. Whoever offers to another a bargain of any kind proposes to do this. It is not from the benevolence of the butcher, the brewer, or the baker, that we expect our dinner, but from their regard to their own interests.[3]

After observing and listening to many in the financial world, I am convinced that some people can and do participate in the market without being *solely* motivated by economic self-interest. The profit motive, that is, economic action based on self-interest, is not their single-minded concern. I suggest that business is a noble occupation when it is consciously concerned to enhance the common good, and not simply to make money. One can live a noble vocation in the world of commerce; it is not easy, but it is possible.

The role of business is changing in American society, expanding to encompass a wider role of service to the common good. For example, some corporations have resisted moving plants from the inner city to the suburbs because of a commitment to the community. Some suggest that Adam Smith assumed that God would work to transform self-interested behavior to a good end. Thus, his view of God's providence was naive; he seemed to think that God would override human freedom and by a "hidden hand" make things come out for the common good in spite of bad judgment. Believers, as an imperative of their faith, must consciously and deliberately work for the common good.[4] Workers who are not needed, pollution control, and the quality of life in the community as well as the workplace all need conscious care. We must make God's work our own; managers are called to embody the fidelity and the compassion of God, and by their free decisions to make the world a more humane place. The hope is that some in the financial community are called to be leaders in this challenging work. After reading the essays and following the careers of some of the authors, I believe that there are good reasons for that hope.

NOTES

1. These pages are modifications of those previously published in my essay, "The Professional Disciplines: Business and Management," *Justice and Peace Education: Models for College and University Faculty*, ed. David M. Johnson (Maryknoll, N.Y.: Orbis, 1986), pp. 153-154.

2. Aristotle, *Rhetoric*, 1, chap. 93

3. Adam Smith, *The Wealth of Nations*, ed. Edwin Cannan (Chicago, Ill.: University of Chicago Press, 1976), p. 18.

4. Some interpreters of Adam Smith, citing his earlier work in ethics, argue that Smith assumed that the good citizen would promote the common good. Cf. Adam Smith, *The Theory of Moral Sentiments* (Indianapolis, Ind.: Liberty Classics, 1976; originally published in 1753, twenty years earlier than *The Wealth of Nations*).

Part I

The Industry Speaks

As the revelations of illegality and excesses in the financial community begin to be exposed, those of us who are part of this community have to face a hard truth: a cancer has been spreading in our industry . . . The cancer is called greed.

Felix Rohatyn
The New York Review of Books
March 12, 1987

Not since the reckless 1920s has the business world seen such searing scandals. White-collar scams abound: insider trading, money laundering, greenmail. Greed combined with technology has made stealing more tempting than ever. Result: what began as the decade of the entrepreneur is becoming the age of the pinstriped outlaw.

Stephen Koepp
Time
May 25, 1987

Many on Wall Street regard insider trading as nothing more serious than exceeding the 55-mph speed limit—a law nobody believes in or follows.

Bruce Nussbaum
Business Week
June 16, 1986

The Justice Department is considering almost doubling the office's securities fraud staff . . . there is enough business there to support doubling the current effort.

Robert Taylor
The Wall Street Journal
January 19, 1988

In an effort to promote ethical reflection within the investment industry, the first task is to understand the complexity of that world. This suggests the need for intellectual caution by ethicists when questioning the values or intent of something as dynamic as the investment community. Ethical reflection will be greatly enhanced if one first gains an understand-

17

ing of the function and state of the marketplace as seen from the perspective of persons who actually participate daily in this forum.

Given this thought and following a brief synopsis of the developments within the industry, this section presents the views of five respected persons from various segments of the investment industry, including the Chairman and Chief Executive Officer of the New York Stock Exchange. Following the opening paper by the NYSE official, articles by major figures in the financial world are included; authors are the Chairman of the Board of the Midwest Stock Exchange, the President of the Institute of Chartered Financial Analysts, a senior member of a major investment firm, and the President of the National Futures Association.

Developments in the Industry

Over the last twenty years, the investment industry has experienced unprecedented growth and transformation. Table I illustrates the dramatic expansion in the volume and value of trades completed solely on the New York Stock Exchange as well as the increasing number of securities industry personnel. In slightly over twenty years, both the total volume and value of securities traded has expanded more than twenty-five fold to record levels of nearly fifty billion shares and two trillion dollars respectively. The value of funds entrusted to securities industry personnel in 1987 averaged more than four million dollars per person. Add to this the values of the bonds and commodities, and it is easy to visualize the magnitude of the impact of the decisions made by investment industry people upon the economic and social well-being of all. To be sure, the

TABLE I
TWO DECADES OF GROWTH

Year	Total Volume-Shares (millions)	Total Value-Dollars (millions)	Securities Industry Personnel (thousands)
1987	48,142.8	1,888,707	453.5
1980	11,561.5	382,447	243.7
1975	4,839.4	131,705	171.3
1970	3,123.5	102,494	—
1965	1,809.4	73,200	—

Source: NYSE Fact Book (New York: New York Stock Exchange 1988 issue.)

public has legitimate concerns about sound and ethical judgements within this arena.

With the advent of this market growth, change has developed in three ways: institutionalization, deregulation and technology. As illustrated in Table II, there is evidence of a movement from a market composed mainly of small investors to one driven in large part by major financial institutions such as banks, insurance companies, pension funds and various other investment companies. In fact, "Almost all changes (in the financial markets) have been prompted by the significant and rapid growth of trading by large financial institutions . . . The changes were prompted by this new, dominant clientele with requirements that were substantially different from those of the original clientele."[1] The impact of these institutions has affected commissions and quantity of trades and, further, some argue that it has created a tiered market and volatile stock prices.

TABLE II
EVIDENCE OF INSTITUTIONALIZATION

Year	Average Shares Per Transaction	Average Number Block* Transactions Per Day
1987	2,112	3,639
1980	872	528
1975	495	136
1970	388	68
1965	224	9

*Block—10,000 shares or more.

Source: NYSE Fact Book (New York: New York Stock Exchange, various issues.)

With the growth of the institutions' role in the markets and the onset of deregulation, there has been a corresponding loss in the moral intimacy between client and firm. The relationships that were fostered in the past have evolved so that today they are often viewed as merely transactions. To quote Felix Rohatyn:

The explosive growth in financial services, and the huge rewards they bring, have caused obvious strains on the ability to maintain relatively old-fashioned standards and traditions while adjusting to the pressures of the new, deregulated environment and the technologies that allow ceaseless development of new products . . . Long-term relationships are no longer valued; this is the age of the free-wheeling financial samurai.[2]

In addition to these developments, there is the increasing use of technological expertise in decision making. With nearly 90,000 transactions a day completed at the New York Stock Exchange and the development of such techniques as programmed trading, the effect of technology can be most dramatic and swift as was witnessed on October 19, 1987—Black Monday.

Keynote Presentation

In the opening paper, "Ethical Leadership and the Investment Industry," John W. Phelan, Jr., Chairman of the New York Stock Exchange, begins by listing what he feels are the three temptations that must be resisted by ethicists when addressing the investment industry: the hippocratic, the regulatory and the adversary. By a hippocratic temptation, he means the misplaced desire of many parties to have guidelines for action in the form of a "crystal clear" set of rules for the financial community. He contends that to do this would invite failure and commit the sin of pride; "wisdom will lie somewhere between a definition of business ethics that is too precise and one that is too lax, somewhere between the hippocratic fallacy and the legalistic one."

By the regulatory temptation, he writes of the deception in believing that ethical answers lie in the form of more strict laws and regulations: "those that succumb to this regulatory temptation unfortunately would turn the proverbial ounce of prevention into a ton . . . of regulatory mish mash." He states that business efficiency would be "sacrificed at the altar of regulatory purity." He sees a structured self-regulatory system with more accountability as the desirable option; at the same time, he rejects the notion that deregulation means no regulation.

Lastly, he mentions the temptation for some to be adversaries of business. He states:

Adlai Stevenson once said of politics that we, as Americans, get exactly the public servants we deserve. By that, he meant if we honor public service as a calling, we are more likely to attract and keep the best people as public servants. What is true of public life is true of business, and I would ask the question, "Do you believe in your hearts that business can be a worthy profession, a calling in which it is possible to have the highest standards and do the highest good?" If you answer "no," I am afraid your adversary stance towards business is likely to become a self-fulfilling prophecy.

After discussing these temptations, Mr. Phelan tells of a three-year study done by the Exchange that culminated in identifying four "key values" that are necessary for the marketplace to properly serve and perform: integrity, excellence, respect for people and sensitivity to customers. These values must permeate all levels and operations of the investment industry and become part of the system, whether in performance evaluation, job reviews, training or corporate takeovers. He further believes that "a truly ethical person observes a stricter set of standards than merely legal ones."

Phelan then focuses on two areas of ethical concern in the investment industry: insider trading and corporate takeovers. He observes that insider trading is a complex problem: define it too narrowly and the market would not function; define it too widely and you will cause more leakage and manipulation. On the topic of takeovers, he contends that "a cure might be worse than the illness" but at least in a takeover situation there must be a serious effort made to respect the people who might be dislocated and to accord them decent treatment. In concluding, Phelan suggests that the solution to the many ethical issues confronted by the investment industry may be found in hiring men and women of character who know the meaning of leadership. Business leaders must adhere to the highest set of moral principles and encourage their employees and their organizations to follow suit.

Some Reflections By the Experts

Following John Phelan's essay, four brief articles by leaders from differing segments of the investment industry are presented. The first article is by John G. Weithers, the Chairman of the Board of the Midwest Stock Exchange headquartered in Chicago. Given the media accounts of numerous violations of legal and ethical principles, it is interesting to read his balanced assessment of the men and women who work in the industry:

> . . .they are similar to other successful and talented people in business and the professions generally. . . They have had the benefit of education, they are intelligent, energetic, hardworking and . . . law abiding people capable of making the distinction between right and wrong conduct.

He further identifies the main objectives of the securities industry: to raise capital, to provide fair and efficient markets, to provide efficient valuation and to provide services that reduce the risks of investing. He underscores the vital role that markets play in society: "the market should . . . be the major factor in deciding which businesses . . . and governments receive capital and which products or services are funded. If all works well, society's objectives for employment, fairness in allocating capital, stability and opportunity for gaining wealth in conjunction with the right of private ownership are preserved." This crucial social role undoubtedly demands a high degree of ethical sensitivity and commitment.

The second author is Alfred C. Morley, the President of the Institute of Chartered Financial Analysts, a private industry "watchdog" group. The ICFA has a "basic mission that stands to enhance the professional and ethical standards of the members and others in the investment community." Mr. Morley argues that there are sufficient rules, ethical standards and policing bodies to maintain and insure proper conduct by those within his organization. He offers two examples uncovered by the press that, in the final analysis, illustrated the adequacy of the present system. However, he recognizes that "without enforcement, the regulations are meaningless."

The third article is by William Smith, a senior executive of Dean Witter Capital Markets. Mr. Smith discusses four questions: What does Wall Street do? How does it operate? How well does Wall Street do its job? What changes are needed? He questions the performance-oriented environment of Wall Street and notes that often "Wall Street does its own thing without a lot of social conscience."

The last author is Robert Wilmouth, President of the National Futures Association. The National Futures Association, located in Chicago, is a self-regulatory body within the futures market of the investment industry. Wilmouth acknowledges that his industry often suffers from an unfavorable public image. In spite of intense competition and the unique characteristics of the futures marketplace, he believes that the futures industry has done a better job ethically than is generally recognized. He ends on a realistic note, stating that his association must send a clear message: "those who do business unethically ought not be in this business. . ."

NOTES

1. Frank K. Reilly, *Investments* (Chicago: Dryde, 1986), p. 100.
2. Felix Rohatyn, *The New York Review of Books*, "The Blight on Wall Street," March 12, 1987, p. 21.

One

Ethical Leadership and the Investment Industry

John J. Phelan, Jr.

Introduction

Brooks Hayes, who served for many years as a congressman for Arkansas, often told of a particularly memorable campaign. He went from farmhouse to farmhouse through the backhills of the Ozark Mountains. In one of these houses, he was shocked to see a large, color portrait photograph of Pope Pius XII over the mantel in the parlor; the folded hands and the rimless spectacles were unmistakably those of Pope Pius. In those days, 99 percent of the Ozark Mountaineers were Baptists, and the other one percent were Protestants of other sects. Catholics were never to be seen or heard of in the Ozark region. But there it was, larger than life, a portrait of the Pope framed in gold. The congressman was intrigued. He talked with the farmer about the weather and the crops, and then he decided to inquire about the photograph over the mantel. "Farmer Brown," he said, "I'm wondering how you happen to have a very handsome portrait there, that fine likeness of the Holy Father?" After seeing the look of total confusion upon the poor farmer's face, Mr. Hayes pointed to the mantel and repeated his question. "That beautiful photograph there, is it of His Holiness the Pope?" The farmer jerked his head around indignantly. "The Pope? The Pope! The man who sold me that picture said it was Harry Truman in Masonic robes."

The ethical lapse committed by the clever salesman was a simple one; he failed to make a full and accurate disclosure. The ethical issues of today, especially on Wall Street, are not so straightforward or simple as the issue in the above Brooks Hayes story. There is no easy answer to the many questions. What are the moral implications of takeovers in a controlled economy and a free economy? What are the ethical problems in spinning off companies? How can the federal government help and to what extent? What do you do with inefficient companies that are protected from raiders? What about redundant jobs that are protected? What about the towns and families relying on the well-being of one company?

My own conviction is that the vast majority of those who work in the nation's investment industry today are honorable, decent people who are guided by high principles and a concern for the well-being of our industry and the economy as a whole. Outside commentators believe ethical lapses are prevalent in the investment industry. With regard to ethical matters, I argue that the bad apples are in the minority, not the majority. There is a significant need, however, for essays such as the ones in this volume where the ethics of the investment industry can be more fully discussed. The past few years on Wall Street have been years of incredible change and turmoil; the size of companies and the size of transactions have grown enormously. This greater size has encouraged an anonymity that is attractive for those who would cheat in this industry. It is of the utmost importance to preserve an atmosphere conducive to trust, and uphold the values of decency and honesty on Wall Street during this period of change. We simply cannot do business in any other fashion.

Three Temptations

When we discuss business ethics, there are three temptations that must be avoided: the hippocratic temptation, the regulatory temptation, and the adversary temptation.

The Hippocratic Temptation. Eric Hoffer, the San Francisco longshoreman, writer and philosopher, once observed that the particular genius of Americans is their ability to organize. "A truckload of day laborers," he observed, "who pulled into the California wilderness to build a highway, piled off the truckbed and instinctively began organizing themselves, dividing tasks, assigning roles and writing rules. Anywhere you gather a few Americans together," Hoffer said, "they start writing rules; they invent a constitution." The hippocratic temptation for academics, politicians and other outside commentators is to write a set of crystal clear rules for the investment community, the hippocratic oath of American business. To attempt this would be to invite failure and to commit the sin of pride, for things simply are not so easy. Our friends in the medical profession live under an oath whose fundamental requirement is "first, do no harm." While this is an excellent rule for physicians, business people, even those with the highest of ethical standards, must live with an uncomfortable knowledge that in the marketplace many transactions have winners and losers. In these transactions, some players will risk harm.

The world in which even the most ethical businessperson lives is a world of considerable moral ambiguity. In such a world only two kinds of people find things simple: dishonest operators who choose the simple course of corruption, and moral purists who choose the simple course of making judgements from somewhere above the fray. The real world of business is akin to the complicated world of law. In that world ethical judges and ethical lawyers live with the reality that the pursuit of justice with a capital "J" sometimes creates tragedy with a capital "T" and irony with a capital "I." Innocent people are sometimes convicted; guilty ones sometimes go free. By the rules of the world, an ethical lawyer can represent a guilty felon in a criminal case, an unfit parent in a custody case, and an undeserving plaintiff in a lawsuit.

Defining business ethics is far from simple, but it is not impossible. The wisest observers of the investment community will approach this topic with humility. Imagining that we can define and codify business ethics in a precise, neat list of commands would be as dangerous a mistake as thinking we can define ethical conduct as mere adherence to the law. Politicians and businesspeople faced with complaints about their conduct consistently defend themselves by insisting that what was done was within the law. Rabbis of old taught that a righteous man builds a fence around the law. This meant, of course, that a truly ethical person observed a stricter set of standards than merely the legal ones. One finds that moving the legal fence to that outer limit will merely begin to extend the boundaries a little bit further. We live in a society where we have expert lawyers who find loopholes in a law even as it is being written. No matter how much one extends the law, a sense of judgement beyond the law is needed about what one should do. That judgement not only extends to the ethical questions but also to the practical ones. Wisdom will lie somewhere between a definition of business ethics that is too precise and one that is too lax, somewhere between the hippocratic fallacy and the legalistic one.

The Regulatory Temptation. There is a second temptation for those who hope to encourage a high standard of ethics in business. In attempting to provide this ethical standard, they draw an even tighter web of laws and regulations around the investment community to govern it. Those who succumb to this regulatory temptation unfortunately would turn the proverbial ounce of prevention into a ton, or perhaps ten tons, of regulatory mish mash. They would nail the barndoor shut before the horses get out. There is a point of moral hazard, as in the insurance business, for example, where a fire policy is so cheap and generous that people commit arson to gain from it. Similarly, in the investment industry there is a point at which dependence upon regulations to enforce ethical conduct becomes more of a hazard than a help. To define this point of moral hazard is difficult; regulation ensnares the just as well as the unjust; business efficiency is sacrificed at the altar of regulatory purity.

In Washington one result of the wave of post-Watergate reforms is a set of ambitious rules, investigative hurdles and financial disclosure requirements for senior government officials. This implies that the typical presidential appointee is not so much a public servant as a potential crook. Such burdensome ethical requirements have caused honorable and highly qualified people to refuse high government posts rather than submit to the disruptions that are required.

One of the strengths of this country, particularly in the last ten years, has been the experimentation again in a freer, more open market economy. Historically, free markets have gone to an extreme where the people operating within that free market have refused to discipline their freedom and, in fact, have created an atmosphere of speculation and volatility that is difficult to abide by. Society cannot thrive in this environment, and begins to discipline and take away the freedom of the marketplace. In our own individual lives and in the market, part of freedom requires that one not exercise his or her freedom indiscriminately and at a great disadvantage to others. Self-regulation is the only kind of regulation that works, but it might be done in partnership with a government overseeing group. Ninety percent of the time self-regulation works, but in the other ten percent there are economic interests of participants that are so great that these interests require a neutral outside force to impose a discipline upon them. An oversight and partnership is needed between our industry and government regulators such as the Securities and Exchange Commission (SEC) in partnership with the self-regulators. Over the last five to six years, we have not had excessive regulation in many areas. "Deregulation" has been interpreted, in fact, as "no regulation" by many people. They have felt that to struggle free from the regulatory underbrush that has grown up would be most beneficial. As the underbrush is being uprooted, one must not break down the structural retaining walls; eliminating some of the rules and regulations that make business expensive and cumbersome does not make the ethical decency of the business community an open field for prey. I am not a foe of regulatory doctrines. Commonsense regulations are as important to the securities industry as they are to any general business. I might say parenthetically that structural regulation is needed in any business, and our problem today is not that we have too much regulation but that we are in the process of removing too much.

Something else is needed as well—accountability. Accountability involves condemning those who violate the standards of ethics and the requirements of the law that decent people uphold. High standards of accountability mean that boards of directors will "throw the book" at senior managers who show contempt for ethical and legal norms. Senior managers must, in turn, "throw the book" at middle management who take ethical and legal shortcuts. Accountability means that the courts will impose severe penalties on law breakers, not just slaps on the wrist. Perhaps in the misguided effort to show compassion and mercy, society too often has allowed the lines of accountability to go slack. It may seem compassionate to derail the machinery of accountability and may seem harsh to make the business world culpable, but strict accountability serves a vital purpose in society and in other institutions. Strict accountability, accountability with strict sanctions, underscores the values of the community. It helps recompense victims who suffer unjustly. It punishes the wrongdoer without handicapping those who do right. Most importantly, strict accountability deters future offenses by sending a warning to the weak and the tempted. This is true in every aspect of society, including business.

The Adversary Temptation. The adversary temptation is the notion that we can look down on commerce as a profession, that we can denigrate businesspeople as morally unworthy and business as an inferior calling, and still hope that good people will take up that calling. Adlai Stevenson once said of politics that we, as Americans, get exactly the public servants we deserve. By that he meant that if we honor public service as a calling, we are more likely to attract and keep the best people as public servants. What is true of public life is true of business. I would ask the question, "Do you believe in your hearts that business can be a worthy profession, a calling in which it is possible to have the highest standards and do the highest good?" If your answer is "no," I am afraid your adversary stance towards business is likely to become a self-fulfilling prophecy. If leading thinkers and moralists of our society believe that business is unworthy, they send a signal that only the unworthy need bother to take it up and, perhaps unwittingly, they will assist in the abandonment of business to the sharp operators and fast-buck artists. If, on the other hand, we hold up a vision of business as an honorable profession, an affirmative career path in maintaining a capitalistic free market, we are more likely to attract individuals with morals and firm ethical standards. Do not yield to the adversary temptation, the temptation that denigrates business while demanding that it behave itself.

Values of the New York Stock Exchange

One is constantly being told that New York City is crime-ridden and that one is certain to get hit over the head at any time. What is amazing is not the fact that crime exists, but rather that there are so few people committing crimes. Contrary to popular belief, there are not police officers on every street corner in New York City. People continue to go on with their everyday business; there is an accepted standard for the common good that allows for this security and prevents rampant abuses. The same is true in our industry. A lot of attention has been focused on the unethical part of the investment industry but most of the time we operate not by rules, not by regulations, but by discipline. On the trading floor we do not have a policeman, yet only twice in ten years have we had acts of violence, somebody swinging at somebody else. While walking on the trading floor it is amazing to witness the discipline amongst the madness; they have accepted a non-policed regulatory structure of their own peers to settle agreements and disputes.

There is an incredible amount of ethical conduct in our business; people with high ethical standards are handling other people's money because they have a reputation of trustworthiness. The customer will dictate what is acceptable and not acceptable in our trading practices, money management and investment banking. Investment bankers are incredibly disciplined and hard-working, regardless of the restrictions imposed on them. It is only when the whole system begins to break down and a laxity of one form or another is tolerated that you do not have this control. Most investment activity is covered not by law but by good business practice.

Just as charity begins in the home, ethics and moral principles are reinforced by a company's culture and leadership. Companies should have a written code of conduct explicitly requiring obedience to all laws that affect its operations, but this is not enough. A statement of the values that a company expects its employees to abide by is also necessary. At the New York Stock Exchange (NYSE), one hundred and fifty senior people spent two to three days each quarter at a conference center over a two to three year period, assessing and identifying the ethical standards of the NYSE. As a result, four values which guide the Exchange and its member companies were identified.

It was felt we could not operate nor serve the marketplace properly without:

1) Integrity,
2) Excellence,
3) Respect for people, and
4) Sensitivity to customers.

Drafting values on paper is just a preface to an ongoing process; all members of the firm, division, department, group or room must believe in these values so that these people can fully participate in implementing them. Such values must become part of the system in performance evaluation, job reviews, training, corporate takeovers and all other facets of corporate activity. At the NYSE we use these four identified values as a benchmark to measure our ethical reaction to situations, whether it be a six hundred million dollar share trade, a five hundred point loss or an insider trading scandal.

Because the NYSE is not a monolithic institution but rather a competitive arena, it is difficult to impose an ethical standard on listed companies and near impossible to reach a solid consensus on shareholders' rights among all the listed members. The NYSE upholds what is referred to as "just and equitable practices of business," which covers a wide range of activities for member companies. Listed companies on the Exchange must meet a minimum basic requirement in shareholders' rights and financial performance. We have expelled, disciplined, suspended and censured members for a long time under that rule itself. In the late 1970s the SEC tried to impose an ethical standard when dealing with payments to foreign companies and similar transactions, but it ran into a storm of opposition. There is only a minimum consensus on ethical standards.

Insider Trading

Insider trading is a very complicated issue. It stems basically from its definition. Being a regulator, I like to be precise, but other people think that precision is perhaps limited in some ways. There is little problem at the extremes. Corporate employees clearly are prohibited from profiting from their special access to information about their company. On the other hand, what about the person who merely overhears an indiscreet executive in a restaurant or elevator pronouncing as yet unknown news about a merger or an acquisition? Maybe it is not illegal for that person to trade on that information he or she overhears, but is it ethical?

There also is a matter of the size of the transactions that are going on today. Even with the best efforts at secrecy, the number of people with some knowledge of pending mergers or acquisitions may vary from fifty to two hundred, including not only corporate officers, lawyers and accountants, but also printers, secretaries and messengers. The issue today is how to define these so-called groups. What responsibility does a group have, how much information can be shared within the group, and how much information can be shared outside the group? As a result of this complexity, the distinction between who is and who is not an insider and who can trade on nonpublic information can become blurred both from a legal as well as an ethical standpoint.

At one level, the cleaning woman who picks up something out of the waste paper basket at night, takes it home and shows it to her nephew who says, "My God, X is going to merge with Y, we all ought to buy some," is a somewhat clear example of this problem.

We are all at a board meeting and make a decision that is not going to be announced for several weeks, but we walk out and buy some stocks in that company for ourselves or for somebody we know. That is a reasonably easy case. The Texas Gulf Sulfur case was one of these.

Dennis Levine also illustrates a very simple case. While there was considerable money involved, Levine was basically panhandling for gold on the side of a great muddy river that was flowing by, and he got a little leakage that fell out in some way. The Levines are down looking for little drippings and droppings that come their way. Even the Boeskys of this world are really operating on the periphery, not in the mainstream of what is happening.

It is said that if Martin Siegel had gone to trial the jury would never have known whether he had had inside information or not, and the only thing that would have convicted him was the fact that he ran around the park with a suitcase full of money. Any juror there not understanding the question would at least have understood that Siegel *thought* he was doing something wrong, no matter what he actually did.

True insider trading involves market manipulation where enormous amounts of monies change hands; it is somewhat similar to the pool operations of the twenties. The operations are not carried out on exchange floors, but rather over the phone, through computer terminals and by way of offshore deals. This "market manipulation" is, in essence, testing the outer limits of the insider trading definition, testing how far you should allow that group to operate. If you make the definition too narrow then the market does not function. If you make it too wide, you get more leakage and more opportunity for manipulation. There have been very few insider trading cases forthcoming because the culprits are in this upper group, a group that has difficulty deciding what is right and wrong.

Many people in this country have spent a lot of time trying to interpret what they think the law is and then trying to skirt the rim of the law. Many of the problems we are experiencing today are because people try to reach the outer limits of the law when investing and do not consider whether it is right or wrong. In my view, the main problem is to keep people within not only the letter, but the spirit of the law. Certainly in our industry, over the last seven years, we have seen an enormous decline in the willingness of senior people to say, "Do not skirt the law, stay within the spirit as well as the limit of the law, and do not exceed that."

More and more in our industry we have an attitude that says, "Do it now and we will explain later," and this is a major problem. Insider trading at the group level is a very complex issue: the narrower you make the definition, the easier it is to define but the more difficult it is to raise money to do some of the things that should be done; the wider the definition, the more problems you have and the potential exists for market manipulation.

Takeover Ethics

A large investor leads a hostile takeover of an established, profitable but undervalued company. He and his fellow investors take the company private, drastically reorganize it and sell several of its units. Some people are winners, for example, the new owners of the company and the original shareholders including, perhaps, a fair number of widows and orphans. These players profit handsomely from the sale of their stock. But some people are losers, big losers perhaps, such as the original managers of the company and long-time employees who may lose their jobs and their pension benefits, and be deeply resentful about what has happened.

Now what are the ethics of corporate takeovers? Some people will argue that these questions are mainly questions of business efficiency, that takeovers generally enhance business efficiency and public well-being. Others argue that the people they call takeover artists are economic sharks, that there are ethical questions involved, including whether or not the quest for short-term gains is destroying institutions and people in the long term. The answers will depend upon to whom you talk or the particular yardstick by which you measure ethical conduct, and also will depend upon those whose ox has been gored.

The problem with takeover ethics is that the cure is worse than the illness. Do we really want to legislate and prevent what is going on in our businesses in the United States? We are trying to make business more efficient; we are trying to restore a new order of efficiency; we are trying to create new jobs while losing old jobs; and we are trying to upgrade both in manufacturing and in production facilities. Much of this reorganization is causing dislocations and hardships.

Anyone who owns a corporation has a certain number of obligations. The poorest management occurs when fulfillment of these obligations is neglected and somebody, either existing management or a new management, comes in and "throws people out the window." It may be necessary over time to retrench that company, to begin a shifting and sorting process, but throughout, the management has an obligation to those people who have worked there. Management has an obligation at least to sit down and find some way to try to work out some of the problems, and not just "dump people out the door" and say it is in the economic interest of the company and the shareholders that half the work force be eliminated. One might argue that the company cannot afford this sort of obligation to its employees; for if half the workers are not let go, the company might well go bankrupt and all would lose their jobs. Yet any new buyer of a company should have worked out before he or she took over that company what was going to happen with the redundancy force, how the new management was going to treat the employees in some decent way, particularly with regard to the handling of pension funds. We are talking about people's futures; pensions are the cushions for employees when they get to an age where they are not as productive. There ought to be a legal obligation that protects the pensions of employees when moves are made to increase efficiencies of companies. We must respect our employees and part of that respect is to treat them decently whether one is an old owner or a new buyer.

Conclusion

There is indeed a need to encourage higher ethical standards in business, but also I believe we need to encourage higher standards in religion, in politics and in every enterprise throughout our society. Religion, after all, has had its Elmer Gantrys and its Jimmy and Tammy Bakkers. Politics has had its Watergates, Abscams and Irangates. Not long ago in an undercover investigation in New York, 106 bribes were offered to public officials, and 105 were accepted. I would like to be able to tell you that the one who declined was a man of honor, but no, he turned down the bribe because he thought it was too low. Such amusing stories should not make one cynical.

Americans are by nature optimistic people who believe there is a solution for every problem. There *is* a basic solution for the problems that have been discussed in this paper—leadership. That leadership must come from the homes, schools, churches and government, but primarily, it must come from those of us who are responsible for running our small and large financial institutions and enterprises. Businesspeople must set up and adhere to the highest set of principles and encourage individuals and organizations to follow suit. Believing and adhering to a code of conduct and a set of ethical values is the answer to all the ethical problems we see in our industry.

If one is to find fault for the failures in the securities industry, the yuppies are not to blame nor are the bright young people whom we have hired and trained. It is my generation, and perhaps your generation as well, who have failed to carry on the tradition our parents and our grandparents taught. Because of changes in environment and increases in temptation, we have begun to let a little slip here and a little slip there. Because of changing environments, deregulation, free markets, and international markets, we sometimes gave the impression that the basic values and fundamentals which guide individuals and their organizations were themselves no longer valid. These basic values have only been obscured and fogged; the basic propositions of business and of life remain the same. So, if indeed there is a failure, it is a failure at the top. It is the failure of all of us to instill in those young people who have come before us what we know to be true.

As leaders we must return, once more, to the fundamental values and norms of business if it is to be viewed as a decent and honored profession. More important, if business is to accomplish its fundamental and most important goal—producing necessary products and services, providing employment for people and providing opportunities for future generations—we must stress the fundamentals such as integrity, excellence, and respect for people. Moreover, these generations include not only the educated but also the uneducated, not just the rich but also the poor, not just the successful but also the unsuccessful, so that they might find their part in this great American dream of ours. Business, in achieving these goals, can continue to be responsible for raising the standard of living in the United States and giving all a better quality of life. First, however, we must gain the confidence of those citizens who will spend their lives in business, by managing our institutions with the ethical and moral values that are cherished by our people. If we do not accomplish this then, to paraphrase John Donne, "Do not ask for whom the bell tolls, it tolls for thee, and it certainly tolls for me."

Two

Ethics Within The Securities Industry

John G. Weithers

Ethics in the securities industry is a subject that is not only timely, but also critical to the successful attainment of the industry's objectives. This is at a time in history when the industry's performance will have a profound impact on global society.

Before pursuing this point, however, I would like to briefly mention a few reasons why I will refrain from discussing insider trading even though it is the subject that most frequently comes to the forefront when ethics within the securities industry is mentioned. The most visible and widely discussed insider trading activities have been criminal acts committed by people who knew they were committing acts that society and the securities industry had deemed illegal. Notwithstanding this knowledge, these individuals committed these acts and went to great lengths to conceal them. A discussion of their activities might properly draw focus to the surveillance and enforcement practices of the securities industry. There will be other acts committed by both insiders and outsiders that may, after analysis, debate and court action, be found illegal and unethical. The question is so full of complexities that a discussion would inevitably get bogged down in legal technicalities rather than ethical issues. The remarks here will focus on the ethical structure of the industry and the larger society and how both of these ought to have a decisive influence on the behavior of individuals working in the financial community.

The People of the Securities Industry

The securities industry in the United States is made up of several hundred thousand people, including account executives, stock brokers, traders and investment bankers, special products people, operations people, corporate and administrative staffs, top management, and exchange and other regulatory personnel. It is a much more complicated and heterogeneous group than it was when I joined the group twenty-nine years ago. I, of course, do not know everyone in the industry, although over the years I have had the opportunity to work with many of the people in management at the brokerage firms. It should come as no surprise that these managers are similar to other successful and talented people in business and the professions generally. They have had the benefit of education, they are intelligent, energetic, hardworking, and although I have no scientific means of measurement, they are law abiding people capable of making the distinction between right and wrong conduct. As managers, they face a difficult task and they perform it relatively well, in my view.

Investment industry managers take the same risks as other business people in a competitive society, and in some ways our industry takes on risks on a daily basis that are well beyond those taken by the typical management in business. It is an industry where liabilities can be enormous, whether they come from mistakes, poor performance or bad judgement. As managers, investment industry people have proven themselves to be innovative and on that score I believe that they compare very well with people in the wider business community. With very few exceptions, managers think of the securities industry as a profession where the participants are required to have a high level of educational background, advanced training and experience in their given roles. In my view, managers in the securities industry understand themselves to be ethically responsible.

Changes in the Securities Industry

The industry has grown in total size and complexity at a rapid rate throughout the Seventies and Eighties. It has many products, each with its own distinct characteristics, and each is regulated within a fairly well defined system. Most of the products have very technical aspects and therefore each specialized area in a securities firm has its own unique concerns about performance and ethics.

The industry formerly was composed of small firms that were generally partnerships and management was actually located in the same office with most of the account executives. In most cases, management personally knew all investment banking clients of the firm and would strive for an ongoing relationship with these larger clients as well as individual customers. Employee loyalty to firms in the past was high and employee movement between firms was low. Top management was experienced in all areas of the firm. They were the owners of the firms and participated in the hiring and training of key employees, thereby transmitting expected standards of conduct, both by example and by anecdotal and formal training presentations. Industry thought of itself as highly regulated; it thought of itself as competitive for long-term relationships with clients. A special note of professionalism that was always preached, if not always practiced, was that there must be an alignment of the interests between the firms' professionals and the clients. Fifteen years ago the products were simpler, the markets were less complex and life was easier, although there certainly were some conflicts and ethical dilemmas.

Since the mid-Seventies, the rates that were at one time fixed and pricing mechanisms that were regulated became competitive and deregulated. The advent of public ownership of brokerage firms generated large capital pools for many firms. Professional managers who had never had hands-on experience were brought into the industry. The home offices and top management became distant from the customers. Competitive rates put new burdens on production, as did the high cost of market information devices and advanced technology necessary to conduct business. Turnover increased for key people. New products were developed in an innovative spirit to meet the demands of the time. In-house products began to shift the alignment of the professional from that once special relationship with the client; more and more there was a move away from the traditional agency role. The focus shifted from relationships to transactions. Because of the complexities and the specialization of new products, separate units have been set up with much autonomy delegated to given individuals; individuals often must make split-second decisions without the time and availability of group interaction and sometimes with only technical input. The bottom line now tends to become the principal unit of evaluating management's performance.

What our industry has done nationally is now being done internationally. We are providing capital to overseas businesses and governments. The Japanese and financial centers in other countries are doing the same. As we all know, Japan is supplying debt capital to the U.S. government in great measure. Historically, issuers such as corporations and governments used to be in the controlling position. In recent years, intermediaries—sometimes brokers or takeover artists—have had great influence in the markets. Emerging now is the international institution. Money knows no boundaries to these people, and it has no allegiances. While many people in this world, who will be players, have the same basis for judging moral conduct as we do, some do not! Many of the players have a legal approach to the securities business that is extremely different from our own. Most have little or no concern about subjects like insider trading; even those that show some concern have no audit trails for effective surveillance and enforcement.

These changes that have come to the investment industry have some beneficial aspects. I have tried to provide some insight into the tensions and complexities that have been introduced into the business along with enormous growth in size and total activity. If you asked the questions: Did the securities industry of twenty years ago have those who committed criminal acts? The answer is: yes, it did. Did the acts of those criminals adversely affect the customers and the market place? Yes, they did. Was there a larger number of people, in a relative sense, incapable of making the distinction between right and wrong conduct? Probably not. The industry today, I think, is reflective of society in much the same degree as it was when I started.

Ethics and Objectives

What, then, of the ethics within the securities industry? The securities industry is extremely important to our country, to our economy and to attaining many of the goals of society both nationally and internationally. I cannot stress enough how much it affects directly and indirectly the economies of the U.S. and the world. For these reasons alone, those who participate in the industry and make its decisions must have the ability to make the distinction between what is right or wrong. They must strive to develop a code of morals for the industry and they must be willing to evaluate and take action in the light of these standards of conduct. This reform will be extremely difficult in our society; we are living in an era when people are too frequently measured in the first instance by their ability to gain and display wealth, where television teaches and conditions both children and adults to the "me and now" philosophy, and where society in general is so litigious that behavior is measured by what can be gotten away with legally instead of what is right or wrong. In my view, ethics is not stressed enough in business schools. Add all this together with the complexities of global markets and it becomes clear that there is a major challenge at hand that will not be met by a re-issuance of a firm's neglected code of ethics.

Ethics must interact with the objectives of the securities industry. The objectives are fourfold:

(1) To raise capital, both equity and debt, for business corporations in a most efficient manner; capital is needed as well for governmental units from the smallest school districts to national governments;

(2) To provide fair and efficient secondary markets for those who invest in equity and debt, thereby providing and encouraging investment;

(3) To provide an efficient pricing mechanism for stocks, bonds and asset valuation;

(4) To provide services that reduce the risk of investing, such as investment advice and risk transfer vehicles.

The market should therefore be the major factor in deciding which businesses receive capital, which governments receive capital and which products or services are funded. If it all works well, society's objectives for employment, fairness in allocating capital, stability and opportunity for gaining wealth, as well as the cherished right of private ownership, are preserved.

To realize these important objectives in an atmosphere such as I have described, several questions will need answers. Will good regulation and high ethical conduct be driven out of existence by some corollary to Gresham's Law where bad regulation drives out good? Can right and wrong conduct be brought more sharply into focus in such a diverse atmosphere? Can social goals become a factor in the allocation of capital? Will investors cooperate with a global ethic that has yet to be formed? Will governments, societies, and investors take long-term views and forego maximum short-term gain? Obviously, cooperation, correct moral judgment and ethical behavior are critical to answering these questions.

Three

Nuturing Professional Standards in the Investment Industry

Alfred C. Morley

Some fifty years ago a group of investment professionals in Chicago decided to gather occasionally for lunch and share ideas about their profession. They decided to formalize this organization, and thus was formed the Investment Analyst Society of Chicago. This was followed by similar organizations in New York, Toronto and Boston. Forty years ago these founding fathers thought that it would be a sensible idea to have an umbrella organization to aid them with their common services, but primarily to institutionalize the basic mission of these societies. That basic mission stands today: to enhance the professional and ethical standards of the members and others in the investment community. The Financial Analyst Federation (FAF) today is composed of fifty-six societies located across the U.S. and Canada; the FAF is now even more broadly based with the recent addition of an international society. The FAF has approximately 16,000 members who have the direct or indirect responsibility for managing trillions of dollars.

Twenty-five years ago, the FAF thought that it was a vital necessity to keep those in the membership aware of what was transpiring in this dynamic industry so they formed, as a separate entity, the Institute of Chartered Financial Analysts (ICFA). This organization was given the responsibility to develop and to keep current a body of knowledge applicable to investment decision-making; it was also charged to prepare examination procedures to insure that only those passing a rigorous test could be designated a chartered financial analyst (CFA). A very important part of that body of knowledge involves ethical standards.

With respect to the ICFA, since its formation slightly over 10,000 charters have been awarded, and there are some 8,000 candidates in various phases of our program today. One of the requirements for a CFA is the passage of three six-hour examinations over a minimum of three years. No less than 10 percent of each of these examinations deals with ethics, with the remainder dealing with economics, accounting, law, equity analysis, fixed income analysis, and portfolio management.

Not Fit To Print

All the news that is "fit to print" appears on the first page of each edition of the *New York Times*. This phrase has become the policy hallmark of that paper over many decades. Of course, implementation of the policy depends on the definition of the word "fit" by the editors of that newspaper; in varying degrees of interpretation, the same applies to editors of all newspapers, magazines, as well as to all of the press.

Generally speaking, much of what is printed about the investment industry, and especially about the people in the investment industry, tends to be controversial or turbulent, if not downright derogatory. I realize that writing articles about motherhood, patriotism and being a good citizen obeying all laws and regulations does not sell many newspapers or magazines. However, I would like to share with you several examples of what I think was "fit to print," but which did not appear in the public press.

Several months ago a rather prominent analyst working for a broker dealer on Wall Street received some adverse publicity in an article appearing in the *Wall Street Journal*. In essence, the article alleged that when the company refused to enter into an underwriting agreement with the analyst's employer, the analyst threatened to force down the price of common stock by issuing an adverse research report. A few days after the article appeared, I had a telephone call from a *Wall Street Journal* reporter who asked if I had read that article. I answered in the affirmative. He also asked whether I knew that the analyst was a CFA. Again I answered yes. He then went on to inquire about changes that the ICFA and the FAF were going to make in their code of ethics and standards of conduct in light of the alleged infringement by the analyst, as well as in light of all the other publicized unethical behavior going on on Wall Street. With little hesitation, my response to the reporter's question was "none." Momentarily the reporter, I think, smelled a real story. The headline might read: "ICFA and FAF Falling Down on Their Responsibilities; Can't or Won't Enforce Ethical Behavior of Their Members; Will Lose Their Self-Regulation Status." But upon questioning me further about my response and what I meant by "none," his interest waned. For what I meant was simply that we were planning to issue no additional standards. After several telephone calls and my sending him considerable material about our code and standards, as well as the rules of procedure pertaining to their enforcement, he called and told me there would be no story. "You appear to be doing everything right. There is no need for you to change procedures and that is not newsworthy."

Some weeks ago, the top management of a major industrial company invited some 180 analysts from both the sell and the buy side of the street to a meeting and announced, with certain caveats, that "the company expects to report double digit growth and earnings per share in each of the next couple of years and the outlook is quite favorable." The market responded very favorably, rising two to three points the afternoon after the meeting and another two to three points on the following day. Soon thereafter, an article appeared in the *Wall Street Journal* criticizing management for making such an announcement to a privileged few who presumably benefited significantly from having attended the meeting and having obtained material inside information. Again I was called by the press and asked whether the ICFA and the FAF would charge its members attending the meeting with violations of our code and standards.

After appropriate investigation, I called back the reporter and stated that, in my judgment, there were no violations of our code and standards. My decision was based on the following: (1) management clearly provided caveats to the forecast which the analysts may or may not have agreed with; (2) the 180 analysts represented, directly or indirectly, a very large part of the company's total share of ownership and thus could not be classified as a "privileged few"; and (3) the information announced added considerable liquidity to the market place in that it provided both buy and sell opportunities. On this point, I emphasized to the reporter that I could not believe that all 180 analysts left the meeting with exactly the same conclusion. Had they, the price of the shares theoretically would have skyrocketed. With the increase in price and liquidity that did develop, the opportunity was present to those who might have left the meeting with reserved judgment to execute orders in that very liquid market.

Again, after several telephone calls between myself and the reporter and the reporter's examination of the copy of our code and standards, he reached the same conclusion that there was no story, at least one that was "fit to print" that would capture reader interest.

What are we doing right or wrong in terms of perception or the reality in the minds of the press, public, employers and peers in regards to ethical behavior and enforcement of ethical standards of individual investment professionals? The answer to this question is fairly simple, at least in my view. We are doing a lot of things right, but unfortunately, they are not recognized. Thus, what we are doing wrong is not getting the story across very well. Obviously from the two examples, the press will not be of much help, but there are other avenues and these must be pursued to enhance the public awareness of our program and its success.

Maintaining Ethics

The efforts of the FAF and ICFA to enhance professionalism take several courses: the holding of seminars and conferences and the writing and distribution of literature for the changing body of knowledge applicable to the investment process. It was recognized early in the history of the FAF and ICFA that application of the body of knowledge to the investment process must be made on technical and on ethical grounds—given the responsibility of investment professionals to their clients and customers.

C. Stuart Shepherd, the first executive director of the ICFA, in a talk given in 1964, said that the moral element of a profession is of equal importance with the mastery of a complex intellectual discipline. Later, he said that investors are entitled to some public warranty that those entrusted with their resources are individuals who possess not only technical competency, but also a moral and ethical sense of responsibility. These comments proved to be the seeds from which developed a code of ethics and standards of professional conduct, including appropriate enforcement provisions, which were adopted by the ICFA in 1969 and soon thereafter by the FAF.

The code and standards are administered and enforced independently by the FAF and ICFA and by a joint committee of the two organizations having the responsibility of continuously reviewing their effectiveness. The comprehensiveness, currency and enforcement of the code and standards have been recognized and accepted by national and state regulatory agencies and were given recognition in 1984 by a special citation by the President of the United States.

It is well recognized that enforcement of regulations is more difficult than drafting of the regulations themselves. Without enforcement, the regulations are meaningless. There is also the danger of our organizations losing their self-regulating status if the enforcement process is lax or inadequate.

In the case of the FAF and ICFA, the enforcement process has been and continues to be quite effective. The key mechanism is the annual professional conduct questionnaire which is sent to every member of the FAF and ICFA, as well as to ICFA candidates, who also must abide by the code and standards. (There are approximately 25,000 individual investment professionals.) Members and candidates are well informed through various communications about the seriousness of completing and returning the questionnaire; the response rate typically is well over ninety percent each year from the first mailing. If a member or candidate does not respond for two consecutive years, he or she is subject to membership suspension, which is, in effect, taking away a union card. Around eighty-five percent of the possible violations of the code and standards are brought to the attention of the FAF and ICFA by the annual professional conduct questionnaire. To put it in another way, the members are telling on themselves, which can be regarded as positive evidence of self-regulation.

Other sources of possible violations come through various means, including communications from a member addressing the behavior of another member, and review of actions by the SEC, NASD, and other regulatory agencies against persons who are members.

If a member is charged with violations of the code and standards, the case is investigated under precise rules of procedure. If evidence supports the violation, sanctions provided under the rules range from private censure to revocation of membership. Over the life of the code and standards, hundreds of cases have been investigated and sanctions have been imposed on well over a hundred of those cases.

Conclusion

Alleged unethical and criminal behavior of a few on Wall Street may be news that is "fit to print." My intent has been to tell other news. The ICFA/FAF professional conduct program is taken seriously and guides over 20,000 investment professionals, the vast majority of whom, in my opinion, are quite ethical. Yet the typical American knows little about it.

Four

A View from Wall Street

William B. Smith

My perspective on Wall Street is derived from twenty years in the investment banking industry, fifteen of which were with Paine Weber and five with Dean Witter. I would like to relate this perspective by taking a more traditional Wall Street approach rather than focusing exclusively on the ethical aspects. My remarks are designed to be provocative by discussing four subjects: What does Wall Street do? How does it operate within its environment? How well does it do its job? And lastly, what changes are needed?

What Does Wall Street Do?

Wall Street acts as a middleman, generally as an agent. Ninety to ninety-five percent of the time, Wall Street is an agent. It primarily attempts to accomplish three things. First, it raises capital. This has been the traditional function: to underwrite and sell securities. Second, it trades in securities, makes markets, and provides liquidity. Third, the area of much controversy, it manages mergers and acquisitions. Generally its role is as a financial adviser, but more recently it has been as a merchant banker.

How Does Wall Street Operate Within Its Environment?

There are five characteristics of Wall Street. First, the main reason we are in business is to make money. Right or wrong, this has been the primary motivation—to make money.

Second, some of the buzz words that we use—performance, competition, efficiency—indicate clearly that it is a performance oriented environment. The measure is profitability whether it is individually or as a firm. The time frame is one day. At the end of a trading day, a person turns to the next person and asks: "How did you do today? Were you a winner or were you a loser?"

Third, among the firms there is intense competition and, on the horizon, more is expected from banks and the Japanese. It is highly competitive among individuals not only for pay, but for jobs. People are marked to market on Wall Street; one big mistake, one big trading loss, and you have no job. I must also add, however, one illegal action and you have no job on Wall Street *forever.*

Fourth, there is much risk on Wall Street. Underwriting and trading is a risky business; the risk is higher today than at any time in the past, and it is much more so since Black Monday. With very volatile markets, part of it created by Wall Street, the last twenty years have been a very interesting time on the Street. There were many casualties among firms. I would estimate that half of the people are not there today that were there when I came into the business twenty years ago. The reasons are mismanagement, too much risk taking, loss of money and lack of competitiveness.

Lastly, I must admit Wall Street does its own thing without a lot of social conscience. I wish I could tell you that when someone comes to our Mergers and Acquisitions Department with a takeover proposition that the first questions we ask concern how many plants are going to be closed, how many jobs are going to be lost. The reality is that we look at those with whom we are doing business, the risk involved in the transaction, the difficulty of completing the transaction, and the expected profit from the transaction.

When I first joined the industry twenty years ago, I went to a new company listed on the New York Stock Exchange. The CEO of the newly listed company came in, bought the first one hundred shares printed on the tape, toured the exchange, and had lunch in the governors' room with several of the exchange governors. One of the governors remarked how fortunate it was to have the company listed on the New York Stock Exchange. I was clearly the most junior person in the room, and next to me was an empty chair. Midway through lunch, a specialist came in. He had his tie loosened, his coat half on, and he sat down and started eating his lunch. Whereupon the CEO interrupted and said: "Sir, you're very busy, it's obvious." The specialist said: "Yes, markets are terrible." The CEO responded: "But I would like to tell you a little bit about my company and make sure you get on my mailing because you are very important to me as my specialist." The specialist looked up, kept eating, and responded to the CEO: "Listen, I am very busy, markets are really lousy, and I do not really want to know much about your company, and, to be frank about it, I really do not want to hear any annual reports." The CEO was stunned by this display of halfheartedness toward his company and he said: "Sir, why are you so disinterested in my company?" The specialist replied: "I do not think you understand my job. My job, pure and simple, is when there are sellers, I am a buyer. When there are buyers, I am a seller." In essence he was saying that the company is nothing more than a piece of paper. He buys it if somebody wants to sell it and he sells it if somebody wants to buy it. The whole point of the story is that this is typical of Wall Street. We trade pieces of paper for profit. I would question whether it is really Wall Street's responsibility to set public policy on each and every transaction.

How Well Does Wall Street Do Its Job?

In the first three areas, I would say they do a great job: they are very good at raising capital, making markets and providing liquidity. However, turning to Wall Street's role in mergers and acquisitions, because that is the area of controversy, particularly during the '80s, I would say that there are some difficulties.

Mergers were prevalent in the '60s and '70s. We put together two companies and merged them. Many times they were equals, typically with equity securities and with a shareholder vote. The reason for the consolidation was diversification: one and one made three. We put together shareholder votes and securities that made those two companies come together. Our biggest concern was clearly whether a deal would be acceptable from an antitrust standpoint or whether it would be turned down by the government.

Acquisitions during the '80s are a very different matter. Today we are acquiring companies primarily for cash rather than securities; often shareholders do not have the opportunity of voting on the transactions. Yes, they turn in their piece of paper, but the shareholders do not get together and vote on the transaction as a class. These deals often are done by individuals or small companies with little equity. Often the targets are the conglomerates of the '60s or the '70s; the acquirers of the '60s and '70s are now the targets in the '80s. The much discussed restructuring has happened largely in response to takeovers or acquisitions.

Why has this acquisition trend developed? There are four reasons listed in the order of their importance. First, we have had a change in the legislative environment with a significant trend toward government deregulation. Without this change, we would not have had this acquisition phenomenon.

Second, there is a concentration of stock ownership. It is very important for anyone taking over a company to know who owns the stock. Because of institutionalization, one can look up in a manual and identify who holds half or more of the stock; therefore, one knows that once that company goes into play, if an institution does not hold the stock, the arbitragers will. The corollary of these points is the lack of ownership by management. You do not see many takeovers, or attempted takeovers, of companies whose managements own substantial stock.

Third, a key ingredient to this acquisition trend is the development over the last three or four years of the junk bond market. (Some would prefer to call them high yield securities.) This has created the ability of raising large amounts of subordinated debt with very little equity. Before the October 19, 1987 fall, the current state of the art for a leveraged buy out (LBO) was as follows: capitalization consisting of 60 percent bank debt—senior debt, 35 percent junk debt—senior subordinated may be 25 percent, junior subordinated may be 5 percent, and zero coupon, or pay-in-kind subordinated debt of 5 percent. This is very creative financing which clearly did not exist in 1986. The whole structure did not exist five years ago and is made possible by the 35 percent junk bonds or high yield securities; of course this can be very risky.

Fourth, market prices have been significantly below the true worth of the companies; stated simply, this is the much discussed undervaluation of equity securities.

What Changes Are Needed?

If the acquisition trend is wrong, how do we solve it? Do we legislate our way out of it? Do we create new laws or regulations? Do we draft tougher antitrust laws? Many people have proposed that we tightly regulate how one buys a controlling position in a company; for example, regulation could be in play for anything in excess of 20 percent, and then for the process of going from control, which is 50 percent, to total ownership, 100 percent. We could do what we typically do, which is change the tax code. We could take deductability of interest from being deductible to non-deductible; we could tax short-term gains at 100 percent. In my view, more government involvement is not the answer. The government is doing a poor job with its own balance sheet.

I propose two simple solutions: better valuations of companies and more shareholder democracy. They are fundamental and are easy to do but I am not sure they can be implemented. First, we ought to create better valuations for our companies. This can be accomplished through more detailed disclosures by management. All the takeovers, all the LBOs, all the restructurings are orchestrated with two factors in mind: the breakup values of the company and the cash flows. Lenders want to know how they will get paid back. They want to know if assets can be sold to pay back the debt. The breakup values are very important. In my view, if Hilton, Hertz and Westin International, the components of United Airlines or Allegis, were truly worth in the 90 to 100 dollars a share range, then the shareholders of that company should have known. If that were the case, the stock would not have sold at 50 dollars.

The name of the game today in valuations is cash flow, not earnings and not net income. By cash flow I mean pre-tax, pre-depreciation with cost reduction, with efficiency brought to bear by that restructured company that must repay significant debt. This leads to a more streamlined company, which is more efficient, and requires less necessary capital expenditure. That is what counts in valuing a company. You never see cash flow discussed in an annual report and you never hear management conversing about cash flow.

Second, we have to return decision making to the shareholders, for they are the owners of a business. We have to have them vote on more of the action. We have annual meetings and proxy statements to approve two things: the existing board of directors and the accounting firm that provides what are often deficient financial statements. Every year shareholders check the same boxes, but the important actions are not voted on by the shareholders. Let the shareholders vote on cash acquisitions as well as securities mergers.

To conclude, perhaps an example of this need for shareholder rights will be helpful. If I am going to merge two companies and, let us assume, issue a new security to create this new company, the shareholders of both companies must approve that transaction. If Corporation A is going to acquire Corporation B for cash, no one has to approve that transaction. What is the difference between my issuing common stock worth fifty dollars for a company, in which case my shareholders and their shareholders must approve that transaction, and my issuing cash for that stock where neither shareholders as a class must approve the transaction? In my view, shareholder votes on green mail, poison pills, golden parachutes, and all other such issues would act as a cleansing process and eliminate a lot of these questionable schemes.

Five

Futures Market and Self-Regulation

Robert K. Wilmouth

I have been in the futures business for ten years. My mentor during these years was a fellow named Phillip Johnson. He was formerly the chairman of the Commodity Futures Trading Commission (CFTC), which is the governmental agency that oversees all futures regulation. He once observed that the futures industry is a magical and mystical world, but still a legitimate business where transactions are made by persons who work in pits or rings.

Now, would an ethicist want to work in a "pit" or trust someone that does? Would anyone want their hard-earned money to flow into a ring with all that conjures up—thoughts of carnival barkers and animals in the ring?

Would business professors appreciate the fact that our markets are inhabited by "speculators?" Many attempt to create a great distinction between speculators and investors. What perplexes me: why do I speculate if I buy a contract on silver in a futures market but someone else invests if he or she buys IBM stock? Do we not both pursue the same goal—the appreciation of the funds that we have invested?

Would not a philosopher run to the nearest exit if the talk turned to the topic of "scalping?" Day traders in my business engage in scalping, buying and selling a commodity within a few minutes or so.

Would anyone approve of "spreaders" in our business? Most think of spreaders as agricultural instruments that disperse indelicate material, yet we have spreaders in our business whose daily job is to arbitrage contract price differentials.

Lastly, I am certain that theologians would not approve of "hedgers" in the market. After all, politicians hedge their statements, gamblers hedge their bets, and indecisive people hedge their actions. Honest theologians do not hedge!

Well, Phillip Johnson may have been incorrect when he made these remarks eight years ago, but our industry has had a continuing determination to maintain a bad image.

Unfortunately, too many people, like evening newscasters or news analysts, seem to make the assumption that futures markets are wild and woolly laissez-faire institutions that go unregulated and are incapable of dealing with sophisticated financial instruments. My response on both counts is emphatically—not so!

Phillip Johnson, one of the best lawyers in the commodities futures business, states: "The fact is that the regulatory structure of the commodity industry is as pervasive as any in existence and, for the most part, the regulatory coverage, powers and penalties surpass nearly all other regulatory schemes."

To the suggestion that futures markets should adhere solely to the practice of trading in commodities such as corn, cattle and coffee and remain isolated from the likes of bonds, currencies and stock indexes, I would simply state that the principles of hedging to achieve price protection in volatile and uncertain markets are the same. A pension fund, bank trust or portfolio manager should have no less opportunity for the responsible use of these investment tools than anyone else.

Bad Ethics Is Bad Business

The futures industry is unique. The industry has grown rapidly (more than five-fold in ten years), particularly in the financial sectors: Treasury securities, currencies and stock indexes. Today, futures are very much an integral part of the investment group. As in any other sector of the investment community, people in our business are subjected to the same highly competitive work-place pressures to perform, to make money, yet they also have the same ongoing concern about how best to achieve and maintain a high level of ethical conduct. As a businessman, a regulator, and therefore somewhat of a pragmatist, I must say that, in my view, any perspective on ethics must also realize that ethics has an economic dimension.

Futures markets have two principal functions: price discovery and price risk management. The transactions involved are made rapidly and the sums involved are generally substantial. For example, a U. S. Treasury Bond contract alone can amount to twenty to thirty billion dollars a day. For the market to properly perform these functions, one of the absolute requisites is the presumption of ethical conduct.

It is a requisite for two reasons. First, public and investor participation in the market can occur only when there is trust in the market. Take away trust and you take away customers. Secondly, price discovery and price risk management can be accomplished effectively only if the market is truly competitive. Uncompetitive activities (manipulations, if you prefer) produce price distortion and render the market inefficient and ineffective and, eventually, will put them out of business. Simply said, bad ethics is bad business. Whether for this reason or for moral reasons (we would hope for both), the vast majority of people in the futures industry regard unethical behavior to be clearly unacceptable conduct that is not to be tolerated.

But what is the reality? Someone once said that while honesty pays, there are those who think that it does not pay enough. These people exist in every business, ours included. There are brokers who engage unethically and illegally in prearranged, non-competitive trades that exceed allowable position orders or limits. There are occasionally people, particularly if they are fortunate to be billionaires, who seem to think they can power or squeeze the market. Some people might make an allusion to silver back in 1980. There have been people at various times who fraudulently sought to cash non-existent commodities, like salad oil sometime in the late sixties. We have had those who trade without adequate capital, jeopardizing the security of a client's funds, as well as the financial integrity of the market. There have been those who confuse a client's money with their own, some who peddle phony investments, share an account, falsify records, bucket orders, and otherwise engage in any other wrongful activity that the human mind could conjure up in the pursuit of short-term profits.

Obviously, we have had, do have, and will have our problems. There are always those who are unwilling to make do with the wages of honesty. When we have our problems the world hears about them, and I have no quarrel with that. I do sometimes have a quarrel with the implication that regulators are not getting the job done, particularly when some wrongdoing is "exposed" by the efforts of investigative reporters. I suggest that this is a bad and often undeserved criticism.

Let me relate a case in point. Two years ago, our organization and several other regulatory bodies were conducting intensive investigations of four firms in the industry. These kinds of investigations, to be fruitful, take much effort and time. In this case they were allegedly "churning" customers' accounts. It involved developing quantifiable, objective yardsticks of what exactly "churning" is; this being very tedious work conducted over a period of months, it was difficult to keep secret. As a result of the work, a network Chicago TV station rushed in, airing its own expose of the firms under investigation, and wondered aloud why regulators, especially self-regulators such as ourselves, were not vigilant. Legal sanctions against that firm were, as the reporter was well aware at the time, in the process of being finalized. There is much evidence to support the fact that self-regulation can and does work.

A Zero Sum Game

Let me first briefly assess where the futures industry is today and give some reasons why I think we are at this point. While this may smack of heresy coming from a regulator, I believe that I can say, possessing some knowledge of the business and of the people in the business, that by and large, serious violations of ethical conduct are exceptions to the rule and, as I earlier pointed out, widely publicized when they do occur. This being the case, the question that begs for an answer is—how so?

Certainly it is not because people in the futures business, in the front offices, in the back offices, or the trading floors, are under any less pressure to deliver financial performance. Unfortunately, success is something that is too often demanded and too rarely questioned. It is not that ours is an industry lacking in patience; nor do I suggest that the people in the futures industry who make decisions, buy and sell, and handle other people's funds are innately more or less ethical than similar people in analogous circumstances in other industries or other sectors of the investment business. Our industry, in this regard, is not unique. But there are ways in which the futures industry is unique, at least different. These differences may have nothing whatsoever to do with ethics in a moral sense, but are reflected in ethical conduct.

Some of these differences can be loosely described as indigenous to the structure and nature of futures trading. All this is related to the regulation of futures trading. Just as there may be pressures to cheat, there are also, in this business, some very strong countervailing pressures not to do so. Unlike other areas of investment activity where certain kinds of unethical conduct might be foreseen by the perpetrators, be it incorrectly, as victimless crimes, that is clearly not the case with futures. To use an economist's phrase, futures is a zero sum game. Every dollar someone gains, there's a dollar someone else loses. While trading in those pits and rings, the futures markets are fully accustomed to the risks of losing money. They are not people who look kindly to having money taken from them through unethical conduct. Suffice it to say, the trading floors tend to have self-cleaning mechanisms. These mechanisms are not likely to show up in a journal of law or economics. Swindlers on the trading floor have short survivability.

Another difference is that in the futures industry, we have what is known as daily mark to the market and daily cash settlements on all open positions. Consequently, every dollar of gain in the market that day is immediately credited to the customer's account and is available to the customer. Conversely, every dollar of loss is daily debited to the customer's account. This sharply limits opportunities to the kind of long-term unethical schemes you sometimes read about in other sectors of the investment business.

In addition, unlike most other investment forms, futures contracts themselves are inherently short-term. Stock certificates can remain outstanding indefinitely and bonds can have long-term maturity, but futures contracts generally expire in a matter of months. If the contract approaches expiration, exchanges closely examine who holds the position, the size of the position, and the deliverable cash market to buy. We also have very strictly enforced position limits in futures, all of which are designed to make any effort to squeeze or corner the market a futile exercise.

Because of the pace and the competitiveness of futures trading, because of the centralized market structure, open outcry requirements, and the position limits I mentioned, so-called insider trading abuses are not really a major or frequent problem in futures. The markets are prodigious consumers of information and secrets.

All this may come across sounding like a matter of ethical conduct by default, but I think the fact is that it is something more than that. Futures markets and the self-regulation of futures markets have been in process for over a century, and as they have evolved, they were designed with the intent specifically to discourage unethical conduct. The commitment to establish, to exercise, and to enforce high standards of ethical conduct is reflected rather clearly in the regulation of futures trading.

Self-Regulation

The two key points about regulation are (1) that the regulation of this industry is extensive and (2) that it is predominantly self-regulation. For those of you who would like to know how well self-regulation has performed on an industry-wide basis during the past five years, in the organization that I began five years ago, I would refer you to a recent report by the Congress of the United States; it provides a report card on the ethics of the National Futures Association (NFA), which, in my view, amounts to an A minus (REPORT AS OF 9/30/85 TO HOUSE OF REPRESENTATIVES COMMITTEE ON AGRICULTURE, AND SENATE COMMITTEE ON AGRICULTURE, NUTRITION, AND FORESTRY).

In terms of an economic importance, economic benefits or any such similar yardstick, futures is big business and rapidly getting bigger. In terms of the number of people involved, we are not a large industry. The

NFA requires every person engaged in the futures business with the public to be a member; they have no choice. Technically, you have to belong to a self-regulatory futures organization. But our total membership, firms and individuals alike, is less than one hundred thousand. We are relatively minuscule in relation to other investment sections.

Futures probably has more per capita regulations than any other industry in this country. There is virtually no aspect of this business, and certainly no aspect that has to do with ethical conduct, that is not regulated, and often multiply regulated. There is regulation by the member firms in terms of internal auditing compliance, regulation by the exchange in which the futures contracts are traded, regulation by the NFA which is an industry wide self-regulatory organization, and an oversight of all tiers of regulation by the Federal Commodity Trading Futures Commission. The thirteen licensed exchanges each have their own audit and investigative staff. They continuously monitor all trade, conduct surveillances and investigations, and refer evidence of infractions to exchange business-conduct committees for appropriate disciplinary action. Perhaps unethical conduct cannot always be prevented, but it certainly can be discouraged.

The NFA was created by the futures industry with authorization from Congress in 1982. Our purpose has been to insure that all sectors of this industry are subject to regulation, including those not subject to exchange regulation, those that are perhaps more prone to have problems. As of now, the NFA has approximately 350 employees in Chicago and New York. By far the majority of these employees are in the compliance department. The next largest group, being registration, has as one of its functions the screening of prospective members in an effort to keep bad actors out of our industry in the first place. If, however, they do get in, we have the ultimate weapon to get them out, and we have used it on numerous occasions: expulsion. By law, no person may conduct a futures trading business with the public unless they are currently an NFA member, so expulsion from the NFA means expulsion from the industry. It is worth noting that about 75 million dollars annually is spent by the industry to enforce ethical conduct. Thus, our commitment to self-regulation is reflected in our expenditures for this purpose.

The bottom line, I suggest, is that we are sending a clear message, that message being that those who do business unethically ought not be in this business. It is a message we intend to keep on sending because, like any other industry, we do have those people who have not always understood the message.

Part II

Takeovers and the Common Good: Efficiencies, Markets, and Law

On Wall Street, the talk of big money, of big deals and easy money is back . . . The hardy firms that survived October's dark days and the tribulations of insider-trading investigations now find themselves in a charmed world: there seems to be a new deal every day, and there are fewer arbitragers in the race, which means their profits can be greater.

William McBride
The New York Times
March 27, 1988

Top managers must learn to understand the use of moral language and ethical analysis, not only to protect their companies but also to expand the horizon for decision making. Knee-jerk responses, either from the left or the right, poorly serve the church and business, and society as a whole.

Oliver F. Williams
The Harvard Business Review
September-October 1984

Federal prosecutors want to confiscate the possessions of those convicted of an insider-trading charge . . . the seizing of property would discourage people calculating that their profit from insider trading might exceed the resulting fine and a jail sentence . . . Confiscation of property is allowed under the Racketeer Influenced and Corrupt Organization Act.

Robert Johnson
The Wall Street Journal
July 28, 1988

Part II deals with three of the major elements of the investment industry equation: the drive for efficiencies, the benefits/costs of markets, and the role of law. The first paper discusses the strengths and weaknesses of takeovers by presenting the contrasting views of a major player in today's Wall Street and of a professor of ethics. The second paper, on the advantages of the marketplace, is by the former chief economist of the Securities and Exchange Commission who is currently a senior executive of an investment firm. The final paper is on the role of law in the investment industry, and was prepared jointly by two long-time practitioners and professors of law, one with much experience in securities law and the other the principal drafter of the Racketeer Influenced and Corrupt Organization (RICO) Act.

Ethics and Takeovers: A Debate

The first paper is a debate between Paul Tierney, Jr., and Kirk O. Hanson. While some might call him a Wall Street raider, Paul Tierney describes his work in terms of looking for companies whose shares are significantly undervalued. It is a complicated process of analysis and valuation that he and his partners in Coniston use in finding truly undervalued shares; the expenses are substantial and the risks are considerable, involving tens of millions of dollars. Paul Tierney's liberal arts education at the University of Notre Dame and his experience as a Peace Corps volunteer give him a broad perspective:

> As a practitioner of investment management, I have to make decisions every day as to what is legal and ethical. Generally, we purchase very large blocks of company stock after exhaustive research of publicly available information. We do not trade on hearsay or rumors, nor do we generally have trouble understanding the SEC regulations as they pertain to our accumulations.

He opens his presentation by contrasting the ethos of Wall Street with that present in London, providing some insight into the "cultural, attitudinal and ethical principles which underpin U.S. investment activities." He compares the differences and similarities of the two markets in six functional areas: performance pressure, ownership versus trading, management support, social consciousness, regulation and insider trading.

Tierney outlines some fundamentals of the industry. "Investors invest to generate a return on capital. They need to be convinced that a company is maximizing shareholder values. They are neither management allies nor antagonists. They are limited players in the marketplace. Capitalism is allowed to run its course." To illustrate his perspective, Tierney discusses his firm's experience in the hostile takeover of Allegis

Corporation, a company which was then composed of United Airlines, Hilton International, Hertz Corporation, Westin Hotels and Covia (the Apollo Reservation System). His question is this: was the restructuring of this conglomerate harmful to the stakeholders of the Allegis Corporation, that is, shareholders, employees and customers? He examines the evidence and judges: "When the restructuring of Allegis is complete, each of its five main components looks as though it will emerge as a healthier entity with better capitalization, better prospects for growth, higher morale and greater economic value than was the case prior to our activities."

Offering another view is Kirk O. Hanson, professor at Stanford University and a management consultant in the field of ethics. He focuses on four areas where he feels Tierney may have overlooked significant data: "The first is the impact of this whole phenomenon on U.S. competitiveness; second, the impact on the various stakeholders; and third, the impact on the U.S. culture and the ethos of the broader American society by this Wall Street ethos." The fourth point that Hanson wants reviewed is Tierney's assumption that outlawing takeovers or mergers is the only alternative to allowing the present scene to continue.

Markets and Ethics

Gregg Jarrell is a former chief economist of the Securities and Exchange Commission (SEC) and a consultant on antitrust matters with the Federal Trade Commission (FTC). After examining the recent investment scandals and acknowledging that legitimate questions are raised, he offers the opinion that strong new regulation may well be counterproductive. He forecasts: "These proposals all originated with self-interested lobbying groups and were carefully designed, not to retard insider trading or illegal parking of stock, but to insulate top corporate management from the competitive discipline of the takeover market."

He justifies this fear by examining several case studies of scandals that have rocked the industry. To buttress his case, he presents statistics about mergers, acquisitions and leveraged buy-outs of the 1980s. Drawing on economic analysis and theory, he presents many explanations for the intensity of corporate takeovers and suggests that there is a desirable social consequence to all this activity: the greater efficiency and rationality of American business firms. From his vantage point in the SEC and FTC, he traces the roots of these developments during the Reagan Administration. For example, the pro-merger antitrust policy of the Reagan Administration stems from the Chicago school of economic analysis; he writes: "Horizontal mergers, completely taboo before 1980, have become common, even between huge public firms. Vertical mergers, involving firms in different industries, have rarely faced serious antitrust challenge, quite unlike the frequent challenges based on exotic economic theories during the 1960s and 1970s."

Consonant with the economic policy-making of the Reagan Administration, there have been profound changes in the financial markets such as the deregulation of the securities industry and the expanding institutionalization of stock ownership. Deregulation, he points out, has encouraged the development of various weapons in the merger war such as two-tier tender offers and poison pills. He examines the phenomenon of institutional investors and suggests that these investors have changed the market in two ways: shorter term patience by investors and greater willingness to divest companies in order to exploit break-up value. He judges that both of these factors make for a "more competitive market for corporate control."

November 14, 1986, was the date that the public learned of the insider trading scandal involving Ivan Boesky, once the most famous arbitrager in the U.S. financial market. Jarrell believes that this scandal altered public opinion to such a degree that we stand in danger of enacting federal and state laws that could be harmful to our economic well-being.

But this, in truth, is a rhetorical shell game. Many of the restrictions go to the heart of the economics of takeover bids, imposing significant effects on inside trading, except in a derivative sense. Restrictions that deter hostile takeovers will certainly eliminate many opportunities for illegal profiteering, but only by curtailing a largely beneficial economic activity.

It is Jarrell's judgment that there is already sufficient legislation to deter abuse, for example, "treble damage" clauses, which have powerful incentives to reduce incidents of inside trading. He also notes that technological improvements in monitoring stock trading patterns now enable regulators to spotlight market abuse.

The Law and Insider Trading

The final essay is a joint article by two Notre Dame professors of law, Patricia O'Hara, a scholar of securities law, and Robert Blakey, the principal draftsman of the RICO Act. Their focus is twofold; first, a detailed examination of insider trading laws presently on the books is offered and second, an analysis of the appropriateness of the RICO Act to deal with insider trading is made. In their view, the role of law in insider trading is to restore and insure confidence in the fairness and integrity of our capital markets. They cite the critical role of information in the financial market:

> If such information is material, insiders can earn substantial profits by engaging in securities transactions before that information becomes generally known in the market place. The abuse of informational advantages that other investors cannot hope to overcome through diligence or zeal is unfair and inconsistent with the investing public's legitimate expectation of honest and fair securities markets where all participants play by the same rules.

The principal weapon available to the SEC and private plaintiffs to attack fraud and insider trading is Rule 10B-5. Several cases, including the recent *Chiarella* (1980), *Dirks* (1983), and *Carpenter* (1987), are examined to provide a history of how the law may influence financial markets. Lastly, the essay explores the use of a "powerful new tool," the RICO Act of 1970. RICO, used for insider trading violations, provides new legal tools in the evidence-gathering process, sets forth new penal prohibitions and also requires stricter sanctions.

Six

Ethics and Takeovers: A Debate
(1) The Ethos of Wall Street

Paul E. Tierney, Jr.

Ethos: "The Distinguishing Character, Sentiment, Moral Nature, or Guiding Beliefs of a Person, Group, or Institution."

The contrast between the New York and London securities markets provides some insight into the cultural, attitudinal and ethical principles which underpin U.S. investment activities. Even in the autumn of 1987, despite the deregulation of the U.K. financial markets, the internationalization of trading, the existence of computerized information transfer and eight years of Margaret Thatcher's Conservative government, the British stock market operates in a manner consistent with the historical development of the City of London (the financial center of the United Kingdom). The most interesting differences between the City and Wall Street are not the obvious ones of size and liquidity nor the technical distinctions of execution and transaction settlement. The more interesting contrasts lie in the way in which investors, especially institutional owners of stock, approach their professional responsibilities. The idea that capitalism is to be practiced in the freest form of market activity on the national securities exchange is understood differently in the United States from the way it is in the United Kingdom.

Both countries have large groups of institutional equity investors: insurance companies, pension funds and money management firms that dominate to varying degrees the trading in publicly quoted stocks. To a lesser degree the retail investors also influence the market in stocks, but their impact is declining in both countries and their attitudes are not in such sharp juxtaposition as is the case with institutional investors. I would like to consider six ways in which U.S. institutional investors differ from their British counterparts in defining the environment surrounding the tough ethical questions of today's securities markets in the United States.

Institutional Investor Profile

While it is true that both the U.S. and the U.K markets are dominated by large institutional investors, the extent of the domination and the interrelationship between the institutions is quite different. In the U. S. the typical large capitalization stocks are owned 50 percent or more by institutions. For example, the industry average for airlines is 77 percent; oil companies, 45 percent; conglomerates, 52 percent; consumer product companies, 54 percent. In the U.K. the averages tend to be higher, often as much as 70-80 percent. Furthermore, certain institutional investors in the U.K., such as Prudential Assurance, Phoenix Mutual and the Postal Retirement Fund, are so big that they appear as major shareholders of nearly every company within the Alpha Group (the larger public companies). Not only is ownership more institutionalized and concentrated in the U.K., it is also more interrelated. Oftentimes one large institution will be part-owner of another financial group and both will own stakes in the same industrial company. Additionally, the investment trusts, the U.K. equivalent of the U.S. closed-end funds, are owned predominantly by institutions and are another huge collective owner of stocks in every sector. U.S. investment trusts are a relatively small source of equity capital and are almost entirely bought by retail investors.

In addition to the foregoing differences in ownership profile, it should be mentioned that more of an "old boy" network still exists in the City than on Wall Street. It is still apparent that the web of merchant bankers, brokers, money managers, directors and corporate managers in the U.K. is stronger, tighter and more mutually reinforcing than in the U.S. on both a personal level (school ties, social friendships, etc.) and on a professional/cultural level. Matters are less interrelated, less cooperative and more competitive and open in the U.S. equity markets.

Performance Pressure

Performance is the bane of the U.S. portfolio manager: What were the results last quarter, last month, last week? What have you done for me lately?

There is a great deal more attention to performance, especially short-term results, in the U.S. than in the U.K. Our country's money flows are shifted from one money manager to another, depending upon relative performance. Huge incentives exist for highly paid money managers to earn profit-sharing fees or to keep lucrative, large, fixed-fee accounts by "out-performing" the competition. A large service segment of pension fund consultants and actuaries has grown up to measure performance for clients and to direct funds away from underachievers.

The picture in the U.K. is certainly different. While not without competition, money management is not so performance- or short-term oriented and does not have so much incentive to act like their U.S. counterparts. For those money managers controlling huge pools of institutional funds and invested primarily in the U.K., there are also fewer opportunities to trade out of one stock and into an acceptable replacement.

Ownership Versus Trading

British financial institutions think of themselves as long-term owners of businesses. Americans have more of a sense of contingent ownership bordering on a trading outlook. The existence of the legal notion of rights offerings in the U.K. demonstrates this point. It is very difficult for a public company in the U.K. to raise equity other than through a rights offering, i.e., a sale of shares to their existing owners. This gives an institutional shareholder the right to maintain his or her percentage interest in the company, and it protects the shareholder against dilution. The owners, though diverse and passive, think of the industrial entities as *their* companies. They perceive a long-term ownership relationship in many core positions which go beyond short-term considerations of price and liquidity.

In the United States the underwritten rights issue is a rare event and the notion of ownership is more opportunistic. This is not to say that core positions are not built and kept for many years by large institutions. However, it is evident in the U.S. that money managers are more driven to invest and divest strictly on the basis of their opinion of relative valuation. If they deem a stock cheap, it is purchased; if it is expensive, it is sold. The marketplace is just that: a large, impersonal exchange of securities, a place to put down one's economic bets.

Management Support

Attitudes towards management fluctuate in accordance with historical economic cycles. It appears, for instance, that the British are more satisfied with the accomplishments of their industrial managers than are

U.S. investors. Americans seem down on their managers, no doubt a reflection on this country's trade deficit, weak dollar, loss of manufacturing competitiveness and massive restructuring requirements.

However, I believe there is a difference in attitude between the two
investment cultures that transcends present economic conditions. In general, the British are more tolerant and supportive of their managers.
They regard these people as rightful custodians of the corporate charter
and are loath to criticize them publicly or initiate unfriendly, unilateral
moves from the outside. Proxy contests and consent proceedings are prac-
tically unknown in the U.K. In the U.S. such contests are becoming more
common, and institutional investors are clearly increasing their propen-
sity to vote or sell in favor of whoever can offer the greatest "bang for the
buck." Loyalty to management is secondary to U.S. money managers' fiduciary responsibilities to maximize performance on their funds.

Social Consciousness

Decision-making in the U.S. seems more clearly a question of price
than in the U.K. The American system encourages intense review of economic data, with the deliberate exclusion of social, political and cultural
side effects. This is not to say that U.S. society as a whole does not concern
itself with those important issues, but the money manager operates in a
purer world of valuation and trading.

Her or his counterpart in the U.K. is more prone to consider the side
effects of any decision to buy or sell a block (i.e., a large accumulation of
shares) or to support or oppose a management slate. Such decisions are
also more likely to draw the attention and scrutiny of the press and public
than in the U.S. If a corporate restructuring is facilitated by a U.K. institutional investor, the resultant employment shifts, dislocations, etc.,
would be attributed, at least partially, to this investor. She or he is wary
of the deep-seated antipathy of Britain's general population towards the
City and the fast profits and fees that usually accompany radical shifts in
ownership and reorganizations.

In the U.S. the logical sale of such a block normally would not be
criticized if the seller were acting simply in his or her (or client's) best
short-term economic interests. More people own stocks in the U.S. (25
percent versus 20 percent) and stock accounts for a greater percentage of
personal wealth (20 percent versus 5 percent), so the average citizen is
more likely to have the same kind of financial incentive as the institutional investor to encourage short-term appreciation of market value.

Regulation

In addition to the attitudinal and historical differences in the two markets, there is a significant difference in the way the two markets are regulated. In the U.K. the dominant regulatory agency is the City Take-over Panel, an industry group with no statutory standing. In the U.S. it is the Securities and Exchange Commission (SEC), a governmental regula-tor with broad legal powers of enforcement.

The City's takeover code is administered by the panel, and its deci-sions are virtually irrefutable because of the power of the panel members. No violator of panel decisions would find it possible to continue to do business in the City. However, what constitutes a violation and what causes the panel to object to a takeover is often difficult to interpret. Some parts of the code are quite specific, but others give broad judge-mental powers to the panel on what constitutes "proper behavior" and "fair treatment" of shareholders and institutions.

The procedures of the SEC, on the other hand, entail the enforce-ment of a huge body of very technical rules and regulations. The specific body of regulations is so complex as to generate a labyrinth of behavioral alternatives for almost every hypothetical action involving the purchase and sale of securities. Partially in response to this form of regulation, the behavior of market participants has tended to probe the boundaries of the written rules rather than respecting the sense or goal of the statute. Vast groups of lawyers and advisors are now employed by investors to explain how far the investors can go in interpreting these regulations.

Insider Trading

The most publicized concern of the past year in the U.S. market has been the definition and application of a prohibition against insider trad-ing. The SEC prohibits the trading of securities when the seller or buyer is an "insider." Some types of "material nonpublic" information are clearly outside the intent and specific written rules, and such information, most obviously, includes that received from a company about its pending actions. A lawyer, investment banker or company employee cannot trade on the basis of confidential information gathered in the process of per-forming services to the issuer (company). Thus, we note the convictions of people like attorney Ilan Reich, investment banker Dennis Levine, and arbitrageur Ivan Boesky. Boesky apparently employed agents such as merger specialist Martin Siegel to deliver him information on which he could trade. Siegel, therefore, violated both the professional contract between his firm and its client *and* the prohibition against participating in a self-enriching conspiracy with Boesky where they used information to buy stock from disadvantaged sellers who did not have such access.

There are other types of actions based upon special (not herein defined to be "insider") information which clearly *are* perfectly legal. These actions include the purchase of an initial stake in a company up to 5 percent of the shares (the level at which a form 13-D must be filed with the SEC and made available to the investing public) prior to the launching of an offer to buy control. Even though the buyer may know that she or he will offer to pay a premium for the remaining shares, the initial purchases at lower prices are based on information which is solely and legally her or his own. No privileged information in this example is received from the target company.

Another form of special information can arise from the pursuit of traditional financial analysis and investigation. It is the job of an arbitrageur, analyst or investment manager to get as much information and do as thorough an analysis as possible about investment opportunities. Some people are simply better, more thorough and more insightful than others. When information is received from publicly available sources (e.g., SEC forms, court filings, public records, management speeches), it is possible to come up with unique inferences and conclusions which the analyst is free to use to his or her own best advantage.

Between the two extremes of obviously inside information and clearly legitimate—but special—information, there is a vast gray area which is being tested and debated by the SEC, the U.S. Attorney's office in New York, the Congress and a variety of courts. There is no time here to debate the endless permutations of this legal and ethical swamp. These kinds of dilemmas include the now famous Foster Winans case. Winans was a *Wall Street Journal* reporter who leaked information prior to publishing it in his employer's newspaper. Others experienced financial gain when the stock went up because of the column's influence; apparently he did not. His information was not from the company about which he wrote. The Supreme Court will now decide the extent of his transgression. The one thing he clearly seems to have done is to have violated a confidentiality policy of the *Wall Street Journal*, for which he was fired. The question is whether he did more than that and how severe a punishment the government can exact on Winans if his transgression was against his employer and not against the securities laws. Other tough decisions are those where the allegations are straightforward but the evidentiary proof is very scattered, undocumented and contradictory. This situation appears to cover a vast number of cases rumored to be under investigation by the SEC and the U.S. Attorney's office. Then there are cases where no one seems to know what information is inside and when it can be used. What, for instance, is the responsibility of a stockbroker who overhears a conversation where someone quotes another who, in turn, is said to have learned of an impending merger from his relative who alledgedly worked for a competitor?

Investment Management

As a practitioner of investment management, I have to make decisions every day as to what is legal and ethical. Generally, we purchase very large blocks of company stock after exhaustive research of publicly available information. We do not trade on hearsay or rumors, nor do we generally have trouble understanding the SEC regulations as they pertain to our accumulations. It is of greater concern to us that Congress may overreact to the spate of insider-trading violations and allegations and, coupled with pressure from corporate management which feels at risk in today's world of takeovers, pass legislation that will proverbially "throw the baby out with the bath water." I think there is a category of insider trading activity which clearly is wrong (i.e., illegal) and needs vigilant enforcement (e.g., Boesky delivering suitcases of money to Siegel). There is a category that needs definitional improvement and there are structural changes needed within Wall Street firms to ensure the separation of equity trading and arbitrage from corporate finance and mergers and acquisitions.

There is not, however, a need to limit what I believe to be an essentially healthy transitional period of mergers and restructurings in corporate America. In contrasting the U.S. market with that in the U.K., I have attempted to describe the environment surrounding today's investor in the U.S. It is not an entirely flattering picture. It is one of competition for investment performance, emphasis on short-term results, single-minded adherence to financial criteria for investment selection, and general behavior as a rational, economic player sometimes testing the regulatory limits. Thus, some disparage the existence of today's "casino society" with too much wealth accruing to Wall Street as the "house" and its brash young men and women as the "croupiers." On the other hand, there are many positive aspects of the investment climate in the U.S., at least in comparison to the U.K. or any capital market of which I am aware. To my mind, the overriding virtue in our investment decisions is clarity of purpose. Investors invest to generate a return on capital. They need to be convinced that a company is maximizing shareholder values. They are neither management allies nor antagonists. They are limited players in a marketplace. Capitalism is allowed to run its course. The marketplace supports the productive companies and forces a restructuring of the unproductive. Social policy is articulated and legislated by those who govern—not by those who invest.

Changing the trading rules or tax policy to discourage mergers misses the point. Not only would such discouragement come at precisely the wrong time in a very, very delicate stock market cycle, but it would cut short a healthy process of making corporate America more competitive. Not for a minute would I defend every merger as productive nor applaud every restructuring as having been accomplished without an overload of debt, nor would I argue that certain corporate spending cutbacks in reaction to a restructuring are not ill-timed. I *do* believe that today's atmosphere of increased management accountability is positive. While corporate boards of directors and chief executives (CEOs) complain of spending too much time looking over their shoulders for hostile predators, these complaints merit limited sympathy. For too long the CEOs of many companies considered themselves unaccountable to shareholders other than in a formal, public reporting sense. The increased accountability and attention to shareholder values brought about by recent merger, restructuring and proxy contest activities generally have brought healthy results. I would like to recount briefly our most recent experience with Allegis Corporation as illustrative of this point.

Our Allegis Experience

Allegis is the parent company of United Airlines, Hilton International, Hertz Corporation, Westin Hotels and Covia (the Apollo Reservation System). For many years, under the leadership of CEO Richard Ferris, Allegis had pursued a strategy which was described as building an integrated travel company. The basic idea was to acquire businesses deemed complementary to United Airlines, such as hotels and rental cars, and attempt to integrate the customer flow of the various units with one another.

We had been familiar with Allegis from previous transportation investment activities, and been somewhat skeptical of both the concept and execution of the espoused strategy. However, our primary starting point as investors is a value analysis to determine whether or not to own a stock. In March 1987, Allegis stock was selling in the mid 50s and our analysis showed that the after-tax value of its various components was comfortably in the range of $90 to $100. We believed the company's strategy was not working to maximize shareholder value. Repeated equity offerings to finance expansion were constantly diluting shareholder equity and ought to have enraged institutional holders. Our initial purchases of Allegis began in March 1987. On April 1, Allegis executed another dilutive stock offering, and we decided that the ensuing volume of trading would present a buying opportunity in an undervalued situation. By May 11 we had acquired approximately 2.75 million shares, representing 4.7 percent of those outstanding. The company noticed the trading volume, became alarmed by takeover rumors, and put in place a defensive, uneconomic convertible note agreement with the Boeing Company on May 12, 1987.

The Boeing note was concocted hurriedly as part of the financing for a large airplane order, and gave over to Boeing an extraordinary number of rights to restrict Allegis corporate action through a set of positive and negative covenants. The note also gave Boeing the right to convert into approximately 15 percent of the common shares of Allegis at a very generous formula price. Prior to the announcement of this dilutive and restrictive financing, the Allegis shares had traded above the conversion price. Most analysts' estimates of inherent value per share exceeded the conversion price by 40 percent. The financing appeared to be a direct assault on shareholder value for the sole purpose of entrenching existing management. On the face of it, if the Boeing deal were left in place, everyone's stock would be worth less.

We were faced with the dilemma of whether to abandon our investment in Allegis or buy more. As it turned out, we seem to have made the correct decision to accumulate a greater position in the tumultuous trading sessions that followed the Boeing announcement. By May 15, we had brought our position up to 7.7 million shares, currently representing over 13 percent of those outstanding.

Shortly after accumulating the 13 percent and filing our 13-D report with the SEC, we commenced a consent solicitation to unseat the board of directors. In many ways a consent solicitation is a process similar to a proxy contest, although not executed in conjunction with an annual or special shareholders meeting. Since the board of directors had not taken the action to "cashier" Ferris and his financial officer, John Cowan, we decided to cashier the board.

The costs of pursuing such a project are quite substantial. In addition to the seven-day-a-week effort by our entire office, we required the assistance of four law firms headed by Cleary, Gottlieb; a proxy solicitor, Don Carter; an investment bank, Bear Stearns; a dissident slate of outside directors; and a host of other able subcontractors. After filing and clearing proxy solicitation materials with the SEC, we were organized to reach and talk to every shareholder. However, the general reaction to our proposal to change the strategy away from captive integrated travel was so positive that the board of directors decided to reverse themselves and abandon both the basic operating strategy as well as a recapitalization plan which is now under way.

Many things have gone well; many remain to be done. Accomplishments to date include the sale of Hilton International for nearly $1.1 billion, Hertz for $1.3 billion and Westin for $1.5 billion. Bidding for Covia is active and well advanced. Allegis stock is an attractive value in a market that has been very hard on airline securities. AMR, the parent of American Airlines, sold at $52 on April 1, 1987, and currently is at $35. During a time when one of the best airline company's stock is down 33 percent, Allegis' market value has increased 32 percent and has great additional potential for appreciation in any normalized market.

Tasks still to be accomplished include a refinancing of the Boeing note and a conclusion to the litigation surrounding it. Secondly, permanent leadership for United Airlines needs to be selected as Frank Olson prepares to end his able stewardship of Allegis and to run Hertz for the Ford Motor Company. Thirdly, a series of labor issues needs to be negotiated. I have not discussed the United Airlines pilots' continuing interest in purchasing their airline. Their role, of course, was important in the consent proceeding because it helped define values and broaden options for shareholders. Their role in the continued performance of the airline is even more crucial. We are hopeful that the challenges of the future will be dealt with in a timely manner.

Now that we have successfully concluded the first step of the Allegis restructuring, a proper question is whether this whole exercise has been beneficial to shareholders in the short term but harmful to the underlying business or the other constituencies of Allegis, principally the employees and customers. Does the general threat of proxy contests, or other outside actions available to investors, cause management to give up on valid long-term plans? I do not think so. My belief is that it merely requires management to become accountable, to become more practical. There are numerous examples of companies with ambitious long-term goals which are accepted by the marketplace and highly valued. Scientific, organizational and service developments can and should be embraced in long-term plans, but they need to be justified. Most companies are *not* better split apart or taken over by financially-oriented managers. However, Allegis could not make its own case believable. It is a great example of a whole which submerged and diminished both the investment *and* the operating values of its parts. When the restructuring of Allegis is complete, all of its five main components look as though they will emerge as healthier entities with better capitalization, better prospects for growth, higher morale and greater economic value than was the case prior to our activities.

I agree also with the principle that owners of companies need to deal fairly with employees, and it does not relate to new owners—it relates to all owners, past, present and future, and to any investment situation. It is not that you start from scratch. You inherit the company and a whole series of obligations related to pension fund benefits, severance pay, etc. Now, if you invest in the steel industry, and if you have any ideas about foreclosing steel plants, you have to look very hard at your severance requirements. To begin with, there are regulations and laws you have to inspect. Beyond that, each situation is different. I believe you should be very sensitive to what labor groups demand, not just because it is an ethical consideration but it is an economic necessity.

In Allegis right now the single biggest challenge is renegotiating three gigantic labor agreements. We have 8,000 pilots, 19,000 machinists, and I do not know how many flight attendants because they change a lot, and then several thousand non-union workers. There is no plan to do anything. We are not talking about massive layoffs, we are just talking about renegotiating labor contracts.

I have never been in a situation where restructuring the company in which we have had investment has led to broad-scale firings, and I do not think this needs to occur. To the best of my knowledge, so far we have released only two employees. As people have talked about restructures and mergers at this conference, it sounds as though they have, in the back of their minds, scenarios where restructuring (through mergers, raiders or takeovers) means massive unemployment, towns destroyed, people let go. This has not been my experience. In the few instances where I have seen that happen, it has been because that particular part of the business was uncompetitive; it did not have much to do with who owned the company at that time.

Conclusion

I can make statements about two other board memberships won by Coniston in the recent past. At Storer Communications a top-heavy collection of cable systems and television stations was taken over privately through Kohlberg, Kravis and Roberts, and subsequently restructured. At Sooner Federal Savings and Loan, substantial internal restructuring took place after a change in top management and we went on the board. Both companies were reorganized and experienced a change in control. In neither case did short-term opportunism reign at the expense of long-term values and corporate strength.

Furthermore, my feeling is that these contests will still be relatively unusual events. They do not pose a generic threat to management stability. The process for a dissident corporate takeover is expensive, time-consuming, fraught with litigation and publicity, and unappealing as an activity for most investors. Moreover, there are relatively few investment situations where such an action is warranted. For us to pursue a proxy contest we must abide by very strict criteria. While I do not want to divulge any trade secrets, it is obvious we need to find a company that is substantially undervalued, own a significant portion of it, and have a program we believe will be highly likely to get us elected. The justification for a radical action to remove corporate governance from the outside is not to be taken lightly. As Edmund Burke said:

> The prospects of the future must be as bad as the experience of the past. When things are in that lamentable condition, the nature of the disease is to indicate to those whom nature has qualified to administer in extremities a critical, ambiguous, bitter potion to a distempered state.

We are living in a period of extreme volatility and convulsion for the stock market. Mergers, acquisitions and restructurings have become more and more an influence on stock market values. It is a time of discomfort and concern. There are some ugly events that are part of the process of change. These include the greedy, antisocial activity of insider trading, the disproportionate accumulation of wealth by Wall Street participants as they exact their toll charge on other companies' capital that passes through their monetary franchise, the dislocation of workers caused by the closure of uncompetitive plants, the tension within management groups to balance long-term strategy with stockholder pressure, and the diversion of top, young minds away from inventing and producing products in favor of shuffling paper securities. There is, however, no way to go through radical change in a comfortable way. Massive change has been forced upon us by the worldwide competitive environment in which we live. There is a tremendous need for our government to exert leadership. There is a need for our society to stop consuming so much and to start saving and investing more. Our nation is beginning an enormous adjustment to reduce our net debtor status and regain a degree of competitiveness. Wall Street is not the creator of the policy; it is an important facilitator. Restructurings and mergers should be allowed to run their course until prices reflect true values and managers win back the confidence of their multiple owners.

Ethics and Takeovers: A Debate (2) A Cautionary Assessment of Wall Street Ethics

Kirk O. Hanson

Most of our ethical obligations as well as our ethical perspectives are dictated by the various roles we play. I am a teacher at Stanford University of some of the top young minds being diverted to Wall Street and so the subject of the Wall Street ethos has a special interest. I chair Stanford's Investment Responsibility Committee, which means that I am supposed to help Stanford develop the policies it follows in its involvement in the investment industry. I have also had the opportunity to be an adviser to a large number of companies, under fire both from raiders and some Wall Street firms, that have been struggling themselves with the Wall Street ethos. So I come with those three roles but also perhaps, you will conclude, with biases for each.

Some years ago I wrote an essay for the volume *The Judeo-Christian Vision and the Modern Corporation*, and I think the statement of my fundamental belief about ethics will be helpful:

I believe the best definition of an ethical concern is simply concern for how a business decision will affect some segment of a firm's public. Those influenced by a company's decisions include stockholders, employees, customers, suppliers, neighborhood residents, potential employees, and others who would like to do business with the company, other businesses, and the public at large . . . . Ethics is concerned with how the firm treats its various constituencies; ethical norms are standards of fair treatment between the firm and its constituents. Does a firm owe its community certain types of charitable contributions, assistance in major civic initiatives, assistance in lobbying the state and federal government for needed aid? If a company opens a new plant in a rural area, does it owe that community some assistance in planning for local growth or financing new housing? If a company believes in equal employment, does that also mean the company should refrain from funding memberships for its executives in luncheon clubs and country clubs that have no black, Jewish, or female members? If it believes in equal employment, does that mean it owes women employees flexible work arrangements so that they can balance work and home responsibilities? These are all ethical questions which arise daily in executives' lives.[1]

I am particularly pleased with Paul Tierney's paper in which he describes the Wall Street ethos. However, I am surprised with the conclusions he draws after his recitation of what I think is a fairly hard-hitting analysis of some of the problems Wall Street faces at this time. I want to review quickly what that analysis is and suggest at least five areas where I think he vastly underestimates or undervalues some of the impacts of that Wall Street ethos on U.S. society, its corporations and their competitiveness.

You will notice that his observations are indeed that there are very strong short-term orientations on Wall Street, that the money managers are paid on an incentive fee basis, that institutional investors take a considerable distance from ownership and, under increasing pressure and evolving definition of fiduciary responsibility, these investors tend to seek short-term return as their primary performance measure.

Secondly, the institutional investors, as he says, operate in a world of pure trading, one that is characterized by economic rationality and no social consciousness. He applauds that as clarity of purpose, which is one of the things I wish to question. I want to suggest that he should not applaud this trading as clarity of purpose but should be worried about it as being destructive of a certain ethos we hope exists more broadly in U.S. society.

Thirdly, he concludes that the individual U.S. citizen is increasingly drawn into the world of investing, be it through pension funds or whatever. I think a corollary, if I understand Paul Tierney's observations and beliefs aright, is that the individual investor, through his or her pension fund and own individual investments, is drawn closer to the way institutional investors are functioning under the short-term focus and with little or no social consciousness.

His fourth observation which, again, I think is accurate is that sleepy managements do exist in so many U.S. companies and that fact is holding up the competitiveness of our economy. Those sleepy managements do indeed need to be shaken up. My questions will be directed towards whether we are sure the takeovers and restructurings that have been a characteristic of the Wall Street scene in recent years really have produced those particular outcomes of improving competitiveness.

Paul Tierney's fifth observation is that the U.S. brand of regulation is to write very technical rule books and that Wall Street's response is to hire a cadre of lawyers to try to find ways around these restraints and indentify the loopholes through which one can slip.

> Laws have their costs and their limitations; we have witnessed some of the costs of the recent regulatory expansion. If we try to write a rule or regulation for every type of public-interest action we want from business, we risk stifling innovation, slowing productivity, and burying businesspeople under more paperwork than they can handle. What is the alternative? I would argue that we must rely on the responsible behavior and self-policing of the business community, on good corporate decision-making that is sensitive to the public interest and to ethical considerations.[2]

One more observation I sense in the core of the paper is that he does not believe the cadre of raiders on Wall Street necessarily has a great mission to restructure U.S. business to make it more competitive, but instead is actually there *to make a pile of money* and that there is nothing *wrong* with that. I want to argue with that last proposition as well.

Four Areas of Concern

Let me discuss the four areas I think he undervalues. The first is the impact of this whole phenomenon on U.S. competitiveness; second, the impact on the various stakeholders; third, the impact on the U.S. culture and the ethos of the broader American society by this Wall Street ethos; and, fourth, the underestimating he gives to the possibility that we can indeed intervene in less intrusive ways than the draconian measures he suggests ought not to be embraced of *outlawing* takeovers or mergers.

The Impact on U.S. Competitiveness

Paul Tierney says he will not argue that all takeovers and restructures have aided competitiveness, but his presumption that almost all of them are good, I find to be a questionable proposition. Certainly, the impact we have watched on a number of industries validates the concern that companies could be made more competitive but I, for one, would contend that there are at least as many examples in which competitiveness, particularly in long-term investment, has been hurt by the short-term orientation and by the desire to keep earnings and cash flow on a quarterly basis to sustain stock prices.

The short-term orientation again impacts U.S. competitiveness—the short-term orientation of Wall Street seems to me to have a tremendous impact on the operating manager in most U.S. companies. But the discipline of those quarterly earnings or quarterly cash flow statements puts a great deal of pressure on the kinds of investments the managers make in R&D or in long-term capital investment. I think Paul Tierney believes that managers do not feel this pressure as much as I have experienced in my dealings with them.

I think pressures on competitiveness are also created by leveraged buy-outs and by the huge debt load taken on by many companies. This is not just by the raiders, this is also by those defensive managements that run off to engage in leveraged buy-outs to save their own positions. But, through whatever set of influences, the tremendous debt load incurred seems to me to be a barrier to increased competitiveness at least as often as it is an aid.

Finally, there is the point that all these problems arise whether they are engaged in by the raiders or by the managements themselves. I think the barriers in many of the practices in terms of poison pills, golden parachutes and so on, do as much damage to competitiveness as do many of the tactics of the restructurings by the raiders.

The Impact on Various Stakeholders

I said I believe Paul Tierney undervalues the impact on stakeholders. Whereas he may have caused only two people to be laid off, I think there is a pattern of the abrogation of contracts and implied contracts to employees that has resulted in many of the takeover instances: the abrogation of pension benefits and promises (whether or not they are legal promises is obviously something that is tried in the courts in individual cases); the great disruption of human lives which may or may not be necessary, depending upon whether the restructuring addresses a genuine competitive need or not; and the impact on communities, and, again, I do not think that is limited to just those cases where a company is so far gone that the community is going to be hurt anyway.

The point here is that the decision-makers, to the extent they become more remote figures, more financially oriented figures, become removed from the social structure and, if you like, the social strictures of mutual promises and obligations which have guided corporate decision making; at the same time the corporate decision-making has also been motivated by financial considerations.

The Impact of the Wall Street Ethos on U.S. Culture

My third criticism is that Paul Tierney underestimates the impact of this Wall Street ethos on U.S. culture, and that he seems willing to justify the impact as a necessary transitional period. I would argue that the simultaneous existence of pain being experienced by the stakeholders while huge gains are being enjoyed by the deal-makers is an occurrence which greatly hurts our sense of fairness and justice. That is why I was glad to hear John Phelan, chairman of the New York Stock Exchange, arguing that there is a set of values which needs to be pursued in terms of employment relationships as a base, at least, to soften or dampen that simultaneous inconsistency of the pain for some and the huge profits and gains made by the deal-makers.

The fact is that rampant greed and wealth accumulation is occurring within the country at the same time as a genuine economic crisis. The notion that Wall Street would indeed take a disproportionate share, a disproportionate toll of the deals that are made, of the restructurings that are done, seems to me to be an unfortunate juxtaposition of some people enjoying and benefiting from a time of crisis. That is something foreign to our American spirit of somehow sharing the pain.

Another concern is that the prominent model of Wall Street investing as being one without social consciousness, of being purely motivated by economic rationality, seems to me to be, in the long term, damaging to a kind of American spirit and mind set in which we have tried to combine economical, political and social values in decision making in all institutions. I find the notion of clarity of purpose to be a very objectionable one because it continually squeezes out any of those other aspects of decision making.

It is clear that every business decision today is made within a web of influences which represent or try to represent the public interest. The most important influence is obviously the workings of the competitive market system. Relying on the expression of personal or consumer preference in the marketplace, the enterprise system allocates resources according to competitive forces, and reins in those business executives who try to flaunt its discipline. We have also supplemented that market system with a network of laws which seek to constrain or encourage corporate behavior in ways deemed important: state chartering laws and Security and Exchange Commission requirements protect the integrity of equity markets and the interests of investors; tax law and its incentives encourage some corporate decisions and discourage others (capital investment and employment incentives, for example, are based on our belief that these are in the public interest); federal, state, and even local regulatory laws address dozens of other public-interest objectives— from affirmative action to environmental control to occupational health to consumer protection. The conscientious businessperson spends a considerable amount of time simply keeping up the public interest constraints already in place.[3]

The Undervaluing of the Possibility of Intervention

My final comments are on how I think Paul Tierney underestimates the possibilities of addressing these problems by something short of the draconian measures he has discussed. We have had policy proposals to restrict the incentives for short-term profits as a way, perhaps, of creating a longer-term focus. Whether that be 100 percent tax on short-term trading profits or not is obviously to be debated. From the standpoint of my and Stanford's investment responsibility, perhaps it is some kind of limitation on the incentive basis for money managers. Maybe we ought to have a policy where we do not hire money managers for that particular form of compensation which would reward them for very short-term orientation.

Strong ethical leadership about how stakeholders ought to be treated could be a measure short of draconian regulation, but could lay out in essence a standard to which Paul Tierney's counterparts and others might be held, at least by public opinion.

Another possibility would be a clear exposition and ethical leadership on what types of restructuring are functional and useful for the society. We need a statement about what kinds of restructurings are helpful and what kinds are not. I think there is a hesitancy amongst those on Wall Street to point to those particular restructurings which are dysfunctional from all the different perspectives we have been discussing.

Clearly, there is an opportunity for some regulation on both sides— on the management as well as the raider side. What troubles me right now, from the perspective of investment responsibility for a large institutional investor like Stanford, is that maybe we ought to refocus not just on the compensation plan for our investment managers but also voluntarily refocus on how to make our money; if you like, we must seek more *patient* money, and not look at the short term to the extent that we have in the past. It is a complex question in terms of fulfilling the fiduciary responsibilities of the instutition, but still one that needs some kind of consideration.

Finally, I want to address the potential for support for regulatory provisions which protect particular stakeholders. Maybe the time has come to have plant closing legislation. I recognize all the economic arguments against that in terms of restriction of the free flow of capital, but perhaps there is at least a minimum treatment of employees and community that ought to be stated in some type of legislation.

I think Allegis is too easy a case for Paul Tierney to discuss. Because of the way the Conistan partners handled that deal there was no huge debt incurred nor was there any breakup and shutdown of operations. There was the breaking up of various pieces of this travel empire, but each of those individual entities continues to exist more or less as it was before, although under new ownership. A much tougher example would be one in which there were substantial restructuring, substantial layoffs, and more substantial effects.

My conclusion is not Paul Tierney's: that we must not hinder this transitional period of restructuring. Instead, I say it is time to think very hard about how to direct it towards more productive social purposes.

NOTES

1. Kirk O. Hansen, "Corporate Decision-Making and the Public Interest," *The Judeo-Christian Vision and the Modern Corporation*, ed. Oliver F. Williams, C.S.C., and John W. Houck (Notre Dame, IN: University of Notre Dame Press, 1982), p. 334.

2. *Ibid.*, p. 332.

3. *Ibid.*, p. 331.

Seven

The Insider Trading Scandal: Understanding the Problem

Gregg A. Jarrell

I. Introduction

Not since the Pecora hearings following the Great Crash of 1929, which gave rise to the U.S. Securities and Exchange Commission, has there been such intense debate about the ethical and moral character of the business of Wall Street. This soul-searching appears to be the direct result of the insider trading scandals involving Ivan Boesky and other prominent investment bankers. Mixed in with this quite legitimate reexamination, however, is a large element of political opportunism which, if allowed to prevail, will have equally objectionable consequences. The current legislative proposals that are supposed to crack down on Wall Street crime will undoubtedly create large benefits for the very community of investment bankers and arbitrageurs from whose ranks the SEC has snared its impressive cast of convicted or accused criminals.

This ironic consequence will not be an unintended side-effect of otherwise well-meaning legislative proposals. Far from it! This "new wave" of state and federal legislation is actually drawn from a set of regulatory ideas collected over the last decade of debate regarding the proper regulation of hostile takeovers. These proposals all originated with self-interested lobbying groups and were carefully designed, not to retard inside trading or illegal parking of stock, but to insulate top corporate management from the competitive discipline of the takeover market. The calculus of politics is evident to the professional student of takeover regulation, and it means that the surviving proposals have impressive political coalitions to support them, including captains of corporate America, Wall Street bankers and lawyers, arbitrageurs and professional regulators. The losers from the new wave of regulation will almost certainly be the broad majority of shareholders, and ultimately, all those workers and consumers whose standard of living depends on the health and vitality of America's economic engine.

This cynical view of Congress' regulatory response to the Boesky scandals will strike many as unduly pessimistic. Coming from one who has consistently opposed most regulation of takeovers, as I have, this attitude might strike some as reflecting sour grapes about the ills of Wall Street and the obvious need for more drastic regulatory medicine. But my cynicism is born of a decade of experience following takeover battles and the related policy disputes, and it is supported by impressive empirical evidence in scholarly studies of the effects of existing regulations. I will attempt here to marshal the evidence and convey my experiences to convince the reader that Congress' current regulatory proposals will not eradicate inside trading and related scandals. Nor will they reduce what many regard as the capitalistic excesses of Wall Street's frantic deal-making.

In the course of making my case against the legislative proposals on takeovers, I will review briefly the SEC's major inside trading cases of the 1980s, from the disgrace of Paul Thayer, the former Deputy Secretary of Defense, to the Ivan Boesky scandal and the on-going investigations of Michael Milken of Drexel Burnham Lambert, the top issuer of so-called "junk bonds." I will provide also some statistics to describe the boom in mergers, takeovers and leveraged buyouts during the 1980s, and discuss the economic causes and consequences of this intense activity. This discussion will lay much of the groundwork necessary to support my thesis about the political calculus governing the plethora of state and federal anti-takeover proposals.

Accepting my argument that reform of takeover policy is the wrong response to inside trading scandals, however, does not force one to accept inside trading and unethical business conduct. I will discuss the problem of inside trading, how its incidence is related to the increased takeover activity, and what needs to be done to solve this serious problem. Included among my recommendations is that our business schools should play a leading role in providing tomorrow's business leaders with the abilities and convictions to exercise good judgment when they face conflicts between morality and business expediency.

Inside trading is motivated by foreknowledge of impending corporate events that, when revealed, have a large and predictable effect on the market price of identifiable publicly-traded firms. Corporate control transactions certainly satisfy this criterion. Target firms' stock prices appreciate very sharply and rapidly on news that they will receive a merger or takeover offer. The explosion in mergers and acquisition activity, therefore, has an important and direct effect on the opportunity for illegal inside trading. Indeed, it is this obvious connection between M&A activity and inside trading violations that provides the logic for deterring such takeover activity. Although I agree that this argument is a rhetorical smokescreen in the hands of those urging current reform, this direct connection is undeniable.

To understand the problem of inside trading and why curbing takeovers is an inappropriate "cure" requires a review of the economic causes and consequences of the 1980s merger boom. So I spend the next few pages discussing the regulatory and economic changes that experts point to in explaining the trend of restructuring corporate America.

II. The Rise in Mergers and Acquisition Activity Since 1980

Corporate takeovers and mergers have become very big business in the 1980s. A few figures are enough to make this point vivid. The Office of the Chief Economist (OCE) of the Securities and Exchange Commission (SEC) estimates that shareholders of target firms in successful tender offers from 1981 through 1986 received payments in excess of $54 billion over the value of their holdings before the tender offer. Including mergers and leveraged buy-outs, W. T. Grimm & Co. estimates total premiums over the same period to be $118.4 billion. If we assume that most corporate restructurings are motivated by the same factors driving mergers and tender offers, then we should add another roughly $100 billion in premiums to shareholders since 1980. It is no wonder that today's most popular subject among top managers of public firms is creating shareholder value.

A. Legal and Regulatory Changes in the Market for Control

There are several broad explanations for this record activity in mergers and acquisitions. The same trends explain why the bulk of this activity has been concentrated on large publicly-traded firms, and how this has shaped much of the political response to the modern merger boom. I begin by considering the major regulatory and judicial changes that have helped to spur mergers, takeovers and restructurings since 1980.

Pro-Merger Antitrust Policy

The "Chicago School" of antitrust regulators was ushered in as part of the Reagan administration's general plan to deregulate American businesses. By all appearances, antitrust policy has changed dramatically since its arrival in 1980. Horizontal mergers, completely taboo before

1980, have become common, even between huge public firms. Vertical mergers, involving firms in different industries, have rarely faced serious antitrust challenge, quite unlike the frequent challenges based on exotic economic theories during the 1960s and 1970s.

It is too early to tell whether this new mergers-for-efficiency doctrine will long rule, but one reason suggests that these changes are durable, if not permanent. That reason is the increasing reliance on international competition—a global marketplace viewpoint—to protect the consuming public from monopolistic behavior.

Whatever the true reasons for the policy shift, it is clear that the firms most affected are the large, publicly-traded ones whose sheer size made them takeover-proof under the old anti-merger antitrust policy. The data show a marked increase in the size of the target firms in the 1980s compared with the 1970s. The average market value for targets of tender offers made in the 1980s is $327.4, which is over four times the average size of targets from the 1970s. Moreover, in modern times the hostile targets are double the size, on average, of the friendly targets of tender offers, a disparity absent in the pre-1980 cases.

Under the old antitrust rules, the acquirers were principally large conglomerate firms. The 1980s bidder is more commonly the medium-sized competitor in the same or a related industry, or some partnership aiming to take the target private and sell the major pieces to the targets' competitors. Ironically, it is by this very process that the conglomerates of yesterday are being dismantled through "bust-up" restructurings, many to defend against takeover attempts.

Industrial Deregulation

Another goal of the Reagan revolution was industrial deregulation. This new competition heightened further the upward trend in merger activity, especially horizontal mergers that involve competing firms. For this reason, industrial deregulation's effects are greatly enhanced by the simultaneous relaxation of antitrust restrictions on horizontal combinations. Deregulation has been a significant shock in several major industries over the last decade, including oil and gas, airlines, broadcasting, trucking, railroads, inter-city bus lines, telecommunications, securities and banking industries.

Although seldom complete, deregulation has in all cases forced on market participants a sudden new reliance on market competition. This generally has brought many technological and managerial innovations needed to cope with the new skills and strategies made necessary by the competitive conditions. In view of the wrenching changes accompanying deregulation, it is no surprise that mergers and acquisitions activity usually increases significantly, at least for the first few years after the onset of deregulation. Some recent data show that industries deregulated since 1980 have accounted for a disproportionate fraction (over half) of the mergers and acquisitions activity over this period.

Supreme Court Disallows State Antitakeover Laws

The 1982 Supreme Court decision in *Edgar v. Mite* effectively struck down the dozens of state antitakeover laws that had been enacted since the mid-1970s. In striking down the Illinois act, the Court held that the law violated the commerce clause as well as the supremacy clause. The commerce clause is violated because state antitakeover laws regulate many nationwide transactions, thus seriously interfering with interstate commerce. The supremacy clause is violated because state laws effectively infringe on Federal prerogatives as set forth in the Williams Act. In their 1982 ruling, the majority embraced a sweeping free-market philosophy towards the market for corporate control. Justice White wrote that the Illinois law distorted the "reallocation of economic resources to the highest-valued use, a process which can improve efficiency and competition.

In a startling reversal, however, the Supreme Court on April 21, 1987, dealt a stunning blow to corporate "raiders" by upholding the new Indiana statute blocking hostile takeovers. This ruling has already incited a rush to copy Indiana's strictures and has given courage to those defending the even tougher New York and New Jersey laws from constitutional challenge.

Nonetheless, the impotence of state securities regulators during most of the 1980-87 period is an important reason why takeovers have been so active. State regulators apparently have powerful political incentives to protect hometown corporations from hostile takeover attempts, even if national economic welfare is best served by a passive policy. Probably, this is because the employees, managements and local economic interests that can benefit from protection have a visible and vocal presence in-state, whereas in most cases the great majority of shareholders of these large national firms reside out of state.

The Court's Growing Impatience with Takeover Defenses

Although the recent Wall Street scandal threatens the trend, the judiciary since 1980 has retreated from its activism in protecting the independence of hostile takeover targets. In previous decades, courts were quick to grant injunctions and restraining orders against hostile bids. Now, most courts rely on the federal regulation embodied in the Williams Act, with its emphasis on adequate disclosure and "cooling off" periods for target shareholders, and seldom impose further restrictions on the process.

This changed attitude has been brought about in part by the embarrassment caused when past court actions blocking premium bids imposed huge capital losses on shareholders. These experiences have made judges skeptical of the motives of the incumbent management who argued that target shareholders were being victimized by the "raid" on the firm. The prevailing judicial attitude now is to promote effective auctions for target firms that have been put "in play" by a premium bid, without undue favoritism towards any competing bidder. Incumbent target managers often have been forced to compete openly with the hostile raider, using recapitalizations and going-private transactions. This has increased the odds that the typical target will be restructured, while reducing the odds that the original hostile bidder will oversee the restructuring.

B. Financial Innovations Affecting Merger Activity

The last two decades have brought profound changes in the financial markets, ranging from the deregulation of the securities industry and the growing institutionalization of equity ownership to the inventions of various weapons of war such as poison pills and two-tier tender offers. This section catalogues the most important or often-mentioned of these innovations. The reader should be forewarned that I apply the term "innovation" quite liberally, lumping together trends with modified financial instruments under the same general heading. My rule is, if it's new and affects M&A activity, then it's eligible for at least passing mention on this list.

The Rise of Institutional Investors

The most fundamental change in the securities markets over the last two decades has been the growing fraction of equity ownership and trading that is accounted for by institutional investors. This proportion has increased from about five percent in the early 1960s to between two-thirds and three-quarters today. Many factors have coincided to cause this. The pension fund laws of the 1970s, deregulation of fixed commission rates in 1975, and the rising demand for portfolio investment opportunities by the growing numbers of small investors have all contributed to this trend. There appears to be nothing ahead that would reverse this increasing professionalism of the stockholder population.

Perhaps the most important consequence of this institutionalization is that it increases the mobility of capital, especially to the control-oriented investor seeking large accumulations over short time periods. But, it does more. It sharpens the capital market's pencil for valuations, increasing the monitoring of the productivity of managerial strategies while it provides predatory pools of capital to facilitate the arbitrage process of aligning current market value with maximum "break-up" value. Both forces help bring about a more competitive market for corporate control.

Increased Skill in Valuing Corporate Assets

As the market has increased for sophisticated analysis of hypothetical valuations of bundles of corporate assets, the degree of specialization and overall quality of valuation analysis have also increased. The development of mathematical approaches for valuing options and futures and the remarkable advances in computer technology used in the valuation business have had profound effects on the way professionals in this field conduct their work. Together with the increased disclosures for public corporations and the growth in the number of security analysts, these developments tend to improve the informational efficiency of the capital markets, making them more amenable to control-oriented security transactions where valuation accuracy is so important.

High-Yield Bonds

So-called "junk bonds," which are non-investment grade corporate bonds, have been among the most controversial recent innovations. The spotlight has been directed at several recent hostile takeover attempts of large targets that were financed by non-investment grade bonds. These bonds are mostly sold to wealthy investors and have recently been available to investors through mutual funds. In truth, junk bonds have had a far greater impact among the thousands of medium and small firms that issue junk bonds to raise capital for new business investments than they have had financing takeovers. These smaller issuers use junk bonds because they cannot at the time obtain investment-grade ratings, and because junk bonds can have advantages over bank borrowings, the other major source of non-equity capital to these firms.

The innovation behind the junk bond of the 1980s, as distinct from the "fallen angel" junk bonds that were investment grade when originally issued, is the improved technical analysis of the issuing firm's prospects for repaying the debt in the event of business problems. Also unlike investment grade bonds, junk bonds do not have many covenants, which are various restrictions designed to protect bondholders in times of financial distress. The junk bond is designed for use in highly-leveraged and risky circumstances, with more flexibility to facilitate recapitalizations and workouts, and without rigid covenants that would run too high a risk of bankruptcy if used in these situations.

The explosive growth in junk bond issues by scores of medium-size firms has undoubtedly created large savings in financing costs to issuers. During the 1980s junk bonds have become a major vehicle for raising corporate capital and they should continue to be so for some time. But, their notorious reputation was made beginning in 1985 when junk bonds first were used to finance hostile takeovers. Although junk bonds accounted for under 15 percent of total financings for successful tender offers in 1985, their visibility was enhanced because the targets were large and well-known. Junk bonds were associated also with failed takeover attempts early on, which did not help their image problems. However, in the last two years junk bond financing has become a major source of financing for all kinds of tender offers—hostile, friendly, management buy-outs and financial restructurings. They are used on both offense and defense, and by both raider and management bidders.

Equally important, substitute financing vehicles that compete with junk bonds, such as the merchant-bank type of arrangements by highly capitalized securities firms and more traditional bank financing, have also become more competitive in serving the bidder in search of the large target. It is the large availability of these excellent substitutes for junk bonds, speaking now only about their use in the takeover market, that implies that taxing the junk bond bidder will not have a large effect on the pace of takeover activity. Nor would such a tax necessarily tilt the scales towards the target in takeover contests.

Leveraged Buy-outs (LBOs)

Although leveraged buy-outs and other types of going-private transactions have been around for many years, their numbers have grown dramatically during the 1980s, and volume has increased disproportionally because of the unprecedented size of the targets. Like other control transactions, LBOs provide large premiums to shareholders. They also virtually guarantee a capital structure loaded with debt, and make interest servicing and debt reduction the focus of the business at least in the near term.

Unlike most takeovers or mergers, LBOs do not have directly observable measures of the post-transaction profitability of the target. This is because the bidder is not a public firm, so there is no stock-price response to the news of the bid. Also, because the target becomes a private firm upon execution of the LBO, there is generally no way to measure the change in the value of the target after it is taken private. An important exception (almost too important, indeed, to be useful!) is when the LBO target later goes public, providing a clear indication of how very well LBOs can work out, when they work out. Still, the main evidence that LBOs create large increases in value is the persistent willingness of managers and investors to invest so heavily in this form of reorganization.

Some excellent academic work on LBOs has shed some hazy light on the intriguing question: "Where do the gains come from?" Tax savings provide an important, but not dominant, part of the answer. There do not appear to be any mystical "financing" gains, as is implied by the theory that "debt is simply cheaper than equity." It is difficult to believe that the behavioral value of endowing managers with enormous, highly-leveraged equity positions can account for a significant part of the 30 percent average premium over market typically paid in LBOs.

Rather, the value created by LBOs has probably resulted from fundamental changes in the operating strategies of the firms. There are generally wholesale reallocations of corporate assets, changes that mainly result from managements viewing their firms as a takeover investor would. The financial innovations behind LBOs are the improved precision of the valuations that determine debt capacity and the new debt instruments that provide the financing. According to the free cash flow theory advanced by Jensen, the use of high leverage itself is a major innovation that could be the key to understanding the process of value creation.

Jensen's theory is that the high leverage is necessary to ensure that managers in these industries do not over-invest, and that burdensome interest payments accomplish this efficiently. Using a premium stock buy-back financed with debt, the firm essentially makes immediately available to shareholders the present capitalized value of creating this "guarantee."

This theory fits especially well the facts of the recent LBO and mergers activity in several mature industries that happen to generate vast amounts of cash because of past investments, such as the oil and gas, broadcasting, tobacco, forest products and food industries. The paring of under-performing business units that so often accompanies these leveraged restructurings can often be interpreted simply as admissions by top managers that past strategies for using the cash, such as mergers for diversification, have not been productive. As such, they lend further credence to management's pledge to pay out future free cash flow to shareholders.

Innovative Use of the Tax Code

Several important new financial techniques have been developed to facilitate the payment directly to shareholders of corporate income. They commonly benefit shareholders by partially avoiding the "double taxation" of corporate income, at the expense of largely making the cash flow unavailable for corporate reinvestment. The royalty trust has been widely used in the natural resources industry. The master limited partnership, pioneered by T. Boone Pickens, Jr., is another organizational innovation tailored for minimum tax burden on shareholders, and it operates to best advantage in the declining industries with little opportunities for reinvestment.

C. The Politics of Takeover Regulation

These regulatory and economic changes have exposed the top managers of the large, publicly-held corporations to the harsh discipline of the market for the corporate control. The response of business interests to these developments has been increasing pressure for "reform" of the takeover process. As America's target corporations have become vulnerable to takeover pressure and the threat of unwanted acquisition, their managers have clamored with increasing vigor for new restrictions on takeover activity. Their position has been that incumbent management should have the power to veto all unsolicited offers, while also retaining autonomy over their own decisions to mount acquisition bids for other corporations. Clearly, this is a self-serving position. Managers have tried to arrogate for themselves the power that current law vests with shareholders, namely, to decide whether the corporation should be sold. In support of this view, management lobbies have blamed takeovers for virtually every contemporary American economic problem except the size of the national debt. They have contended that takeovers prevent managers from focusing on the long term, destroy communities, force plant closings, and prevent America from being competitive.

Until 1987, management's claims fell on deaf ears, in part due to the prevailing political climate, and in part because of a spate of new economic research that rented most of the anti-takeover lobby's major criticisms of the takeover process. In January 1986, the Reagan SEC considered and voted down virtually every proposal for new takeover regulation that had been proposed by outside lobbyists over the past five years. The only regulations that were enacted dealt with abusive tactics by target managements defending against unwanted bids. Congress held major hearings on takeover activity in 1984, 1985 and 1986, during which time many new bills and proposals for takeover regulation were introduced by both Republican and Democratic representatives. None passed. By late 1986, the leaders of the investigation, notably Representative (now Senator) Timothy Wirth of Colorado, were arguing that the takeover phenomenon was complex, often economically constructive and not necessarily in need of new restrictions. Indeed, the only significant reversals suffered by pro-takeover partisans during this period were the Delaware Supreme Court's affirmation of the legality of so-called poison pill takeover defenses, which have the potential to impose significant additional costs on acquiring firms in hostile deals, and the Federal Reserve's restriction on "junk bond" financed acquisitions imposed late in 1985.

On November 14, 1986, however, the prevailing political winds shifted dramatically, sending a chill through the entire securities industry. On that date the public learned about the insider trading scandal involving Ivan Boesky. The most famous arbitrageur in the United States admitted to buying and trading securities of firms involved in upcoming takeover deals. The scandal fundamentally altered the balance of public opinion and political power on matters relating to Wall Street. The ensuing, wide-ranging revelations of abuse have shaken the fragile faith of many laymen in the integrity of the financial community and, by inference, in the economic merit of the business combinations that have been created in the takeover arena.

In 1987, due in large part to the Boesky revelations and despite the protestations of an increasingly scandal-ridden Reagan Administration, the clamor for new takeover regulation is being heard with new immediacy, both in Washington and in state capitals. A barrage of new bills has been introduced in the 100th Congress, and dozens of states have proposed or adopted new antitakeover statutes. In the wake of Boesky, virtually all the new proposals purport to restrict and penalize not takeovers, but insider trading and "abusive" takeover tactics. But this, in truth, is a rhetorical shell game. Many of the restrictions go to the heart of the economics of takeover bids, imposing significant, if not forbidding, new costs on hostile deals. Few of the proposals will actually have significant effects on inside trading, except in a derivative sense. Restrictions that deter hostile takeovers will certainly eliminate many opportunities for illegal profiteering, but only by curtailing a largely beneficial economic activity.

III. The Evolution of Insider-Trading Law

The 1933 Securities Act directly regulates the trading by company insiders in their companies' stock, outlawing short-swing profits and requiring disclosure of all trades. But, today's inside-trading scandal involves "constructive insiders"—advisors such as takeover lawyers and investment bankers and their tippees, not corporate officers and directors. The development of the law governing the trading behavior of this new class of constructive insiders has coincided with the 1980s boom in takeover activity and the huge growth in Wall Street's community of such outside advisors. These highly paid professionals are increasingly employed in today's litigious, auction-style takeover environment, and it is the large number of advisors who routinely come into possession of highly sensitive information that has created this huge regulatory problem.

The SEC has developed the "misappropriation theory" to handle inside trading violations by those individuals. Misappropriation is the principal doctrine that underlies much of the government's current crackdown on insider trading. It is designed to handle this new class of inside traders who do not fit the Supreme Court's narrow definition of "insider"—usually a corporate official with direct knowledge of market sensitive information.

The misappropriation theory became necessary because of the famous 1981 *Chiarella* opinion by the Supreme Court. Chiarella was a financial printer who traded in stocks, using confidential information he obtained from documents being printed. The SEC argued (unsuccessfully) that Chiarella defrauded unwitting investors who sold securities without the benefit of the inside information. This "damage" theory was unimpressive because, had the printer refrained, the same "defrauded" investors presumably would have made the same trades in the anonymous stock market. The Supreme Court in the *Chiarella* opinion said it would not "speculate" whether Mr. Chiarella might have been guilty under another theory, one which argued that he had stolen information from his employer.

The SEC at this time was bringing charges against James Newman, a stockbroker who conspired with Adrian Antoniu, a former investment banker, to trade in stocks using information he obtained while working at Lehman Brothers, Kuhn Loeb Inc. Antoniu pleaded guilty in 1981 and agreed to cooperate as the witness in the trial of Newman. The SEC designed the misappropriation theory in response to the *Chiarella* opinion, and was upheld by the Second Circuit Court of Appeals. The Supreme Court declined to review that case, effectively affirming the decision.

Since then, the misappropriation theory has been the legal theory behind several spectacular inside trading cases. Paul Thayer, the former Deputy Defense Secretary, was charged with tipping others while he was chairman of LTV Corp. He served time in jail for perjury resulting from the investigation. Dennis Levine was busted for engaging in a systematic scheme of illegal trading covering many takeover stocks. His cooperation put the SEC on to the trail of Ivan Boesky, Wall Street's king of arbitrage, and of Marty Siegel, one of the original models of success in Wall Street's M&A industry. The cooperation of Boesky and Siegel has been instrumental in pointing the SEC to Boyd Jeffries, the founder of the legendary third-market trading firm of Jeffries and Co. Mr. Jeffries' violations included illegal parking of stock, which is a scheme designed to help takeover entrepreneurs frustrate the SEC's disclosure requirements governing accumulations of stock.

Perhaps the most important legal developments will come from the government's case against R. Foster Winans, the former reporter convicted of insider trading in 1985 for misappropriating information about the *Wall Street Journal's* "Heard on the Street" column. This case was argued before the Supreme Court on October 7, 1987. (See pp. 111–112 and 168 for a discussion of the November 1987 decision.) Many experts had predicted that the Court would rule against the misappropriation theory. Partly in response to this possibility, the SEC has proposed the 1987 Insider Trading Act which, if Congress approves, would explicitly outlaw insider trading on misappropriated information and empower the SEC to enforce this law.

Meanwhile, the SEC is involved with a large investigation of Drexel Burnham Lambert (DBL). The government apparently suspects that DBL, with Michael Milken masterminding the scheme, worked with arbitrageurs and well-heeled clients together in an undisclosed, and therefore illegal, "group" to facilitate several takeovers and buyouts. The allegations speculated on by the press include inside trading, parking of stock and other reciprocal practices that would violate SEC disclosure rules. Also, the SEC is investigating three prominent Wall Street figures, Messrs. Freeman, Wigton, and Tabor, whom the government formerly charged with misappropriating and leaking inside information. The government dismissed those indictments in May 1986, because of the need for more time to pursue the cases and eventually to seek new indictments. The three have promised a spirited legal defense, which is a break from the pattern established by Levine, Boesky and Siegel of pleading guilty, paying up and pointing the finger.

There are also many considerable private legal actions as a result of this recent surge of inside trading convictions. Probably the most important are cases of acquiring firms suing inside traders, their employers and their associates for damages on the theory that their illegal trading increased the takeover price paid by the acquiring firm.

The upshot is that the explosion in mergers and acquisitions activity and managers' increasing reliance on outside Wall Street advisors has brought with it a significant increase in inside-trading cases and convictions. Several causal factors stand out. The development of the misappropriation theory provides the necessary legal theory to bring this new array of outside advisors under the purview of the law regarding use of confidential information about publicly-traded firms. The SEC's John Shad, the former investment banker who was chairman from 1980 to 1987, also made a heavy commitment at the SEC to stamp out inside trading, using "hobnail boots," as he put it. John Fedders, then Shad's head of enforcement, assembled a remarkably effective investigative team that continues to thrive under Gary Lynch, who now heads the SEC enforcement division. Incidentally, Mr. Shad recently underscored this commitment by donating $30 million to Harvard Business School (his alma mater) to support the development of courses in business ethics to MBA students. The other factors would be the technological improvements in monitoring stock trading patterns and the diplomatic breakthroughs necessary to conduct effective investigations in Switzerland and other secrecy-protecting places of doing business.

IV. The Question of Business Ethics

The surge of inside-trading scandals, each one a front-page headline story, is supporting the impression that the business of Wall Street is fundamentally unethical. The impact of the scandals is made more pronounced against the backdrop of the hostile takeover and leveraged buy-out wave of the 1980s. The unseemly debate surrounding hostile takeovers, with its colorful rhetorical strawman of raiders and entrenched managers, has put normal folks in the mood to blame all of Wall Street for these numerous big-money crimes. This proves to many that "the game was crooked all along" and makes the Wall Street scandals powerful political medicine. The political entrepreneur who convinces the public that a particular law will crack down on "all this nonsense" can achieve great popular support.

However, there are other reasons to be deeply concerned about the moral character of those engaged in Wall Street's business. Many of our country's brightest and most energetic college graduates are lured by the high salaries on Wall Street, making it very important to know something about the ultimate value and merit of the things they will be asked to do.

It is my view that there is nothing inherently unethical about the business conducted by the investment bankers, corporate lawyers and institutional traders. Mergers and acquisitions activity has the potential to create large economic benefits. The restructurings, takeovers and divesti-tures manifest a beneficial process of change that is absolutely vital to the efficient allocation of corporate assets among competing management teams. Although this process can visit harm on particular individuals, communities, or sectors, it is unavoidable and essential if America is to prosper in the face of growing global competition.

If they are not inherently unethical, however, the dramatic changes in the nature and pace of mergers and restructuring activity have caused severe growing pains. Professional traders, after all, live on market information that is produced through sophisticated research and picked up in the active rumor mill. This is a socially beneficial activity, too, because this activity is essential to setting efficient market prices of financial instruments. The prob-lem is that far too often confidential information from the M&A advisors in investment banking houses has leaked into the market for information by illegitimate means. The so-called "Chinese walls" that are supposed to pre-vent these abuses have not done the job.

Such abuses have damaged the reputations of the prestigious Wall Street firms that have been involved, and reputational goodwill is very precious in this business. It is, therefore, not surprising that the major investment banking houses are reviewing carefully all their procedures and practices regarding the handling of sensitive information received from clients. Several houses have already instituted sweeping reforms, with some eliminating entirely their arbitrage operations that specialize in investing in takeover stocks.

Moreover, the government's spectacular success in catching and prose-cuting inside traders has served to change the once-prevailing attitude that inside trading was extremely easy to get away with. The 1984 Insider Trad-ing Sanctions Act imposes treble damages on violators and people have been handcuffed in their offices, humiliated in the eyes of the public, and even sent to jail. The raw calculus facing the deliberate criminal in this area has definitely been changed to include the prospect of severe penalties and higher probabilities of detection. Therefore, the reforms of the Wall Street firms that have been burned by these scandals and the perception of higher expected penalties facing violators should provide powerful incentives to re-duce the incidence of inside trading violations in the future.

V. Conclusion

The SEC's campaign against inside trading has yielded a large number of cases involving prominent members of Wall Street's invest-ment banking and legal community. The catch is high because these blatantly criminal and highly profitable inside-trading schemes were surprisingly widespread. The success of the government's campaign is the result of new laws, highly effective investigations by dedicated government lawyers, and cooperation by foreign governments.

In the aftermath, we engage in self-evaluation to learn how these things could have happened, and how we can prevent their recurrence. I have complained here that certain political interests, aided by the press, are turning the public's justifiable frustration with the scandals into support for pure interest-group legislation. Increased minimum-offer periods and greater disclosure requirements are not the answer to inside trading. Erecting legal barriers to takeover activity is an inappropriate and costly response because it deters beneficial changes and insulates those charged with running the largest corporations from an otherwise competitive market for corporate control.

A serious attack on inside trading would build on the recent government success in nabbing violators and imposing stiff penalties. It also would reflect our learning that greater regulatory delay and disclosures, which require outside advisors to prepare, increase rather than decrease the opportunities for inside trading. Clear laws defining inside trading, well-funded and vigorous enforcement, and full-scale reform of the procedures for handling confidential M&A information can reduce the opportunity for and rewards to inside trading.

Business schools, too, should carefully reconsider whether or not their current policy of neglect still makes sense. Although I am not prepared to suggest specific reforms, it is clear that proposals to introduce full-fledged business ethics courses will meet significant opposition. The reason is the perception that business ethics, as conceived and taught in schools offering such courses, is fundamentally inconsistent with the value-maximization and profit-seeking principles underlying most business school courses.

Whether this perception is accurate or not, it is not really central to my concerns. I would simply argue that business schools should consider offering a course teaching the laws governing inside trading, as well as antitrust and trademark protection, and also teaching by case application proper business practices. This kind of course would inform students on these important legal rules and make them aware of society's value system regarding these practices. MBA students are mature adults and most come equipped with strong values, but they can lack the relevant experience. So, alerting them ahead of time about the laws and the unforgiving nature of the penalty system can help some avoid getting on the wrong path the first time they face these temptations.

Eight

Legal Aspects of Insider Trading

Patricia A. O'Hara and

G. Robert Blakey

I. INTRODUCTION

Civilization requires trust. Fraud undermines it. The recent insider trading scandals involving Dennis Levine, Ivan Boesky, Martin Siegel and others have rocked the securities industry. The very existence of such widespread fraud threatens the investor confidence so necessary to the vitality of our capital markets.

At the time of proposing legislation, which subsequently became the Insider Trading Sanctions Act of 1984,[1] the Securities and Exchange Commission (SEC) stated:

> Capital formation and our nation's economic growth and stability depend on investor confidence in the fairness and integrity of our capital markets.

> Insider trading threatens these markets. By abusing the trust and confidence reposed in them by shareholders, employers or clients, insider traders may reap huge profits in essentially risk-free transactions. Insiders—corporate officials, investment bankers, lawyers, accountants, financial printers, among others—often learn of profit or loss forecasts, imminent tender offers, mineral strikes, oil discoveries, lucrative contracts and product failures before such information is available to the investing public . . . .

> If such information is material, insiders can earn substantial profits by engaging in securities transactions before that information becomes generally known in the market place. The abuse of informational advantages that other investors cannot hope to overcome through diligence or zeal is unfair and inconsistent with the investing public's legitimate expectation of honest and fair securities markets where all participants play by the same rules.[2]

In a similar vein, Professor Victor Brudney of Harvard Law School has noted:

> The inability of a public investor with whom an insider transacts on inside information generates a sense of unfairness. . . . The unfairness is not a function merely of possessing more information—outsiders may possess more information than other outsiders by reason of their diligence or zeal—but of the fact that it is an advantage which cannot be competed away since it depends upon a lawful privilege to which [other investors] cannot acquire access.[3]

Although the basic inequity surrounding insider trading may be self-evident to all but total free-market economists, illegality is not always as clear. The current state of the law in this area is a product of a long line of judicial opinions. Lower federal courts initially favored a broad interpretation of remedial provisions under the federal securities laws for victims of insider trading. More recently, however, the Supreme Court has restricted the ability of private plaintiffs to recover. The resulting morass makes the legal consequences of insider trading turn on a number of technical considerations which, at least arguably, bear little relevance to the underlying wrong.

This essay briefly reviews those provisions of the Securities Exchange Act of 1934[4] and the Racketeer Influenced and Corrupt Organizations Act of 1970[5] which impact on insider trading. A review of the interpretative history of these provisions demonstrates the growing gap between legal obligations and ethical ideals in this area.

II. INSIDER TRADING UNDER THE SECURITIES EXCHANGE ACT OF 1934

A. An Overview of Rule 10b-5

Rule 10b-5, promulgated under Section 10(b)[6] of the Securities Exchange Act of 1934 ("1934 Act"), is the principal weapon available to the SEC and private plaintiffs to attack fraud under the federal securities laws.

Specifically, Rule 10b-5 makes it unlawful for any person:

(1) to employ any device, scheme or artifice to defraud,

(2) to make any untrue statement of a material fact or to omit to state a material fact necessary in order to make the statements made, in the light of the circumstances under which they were made, not misleading, or

(3) to engage in any act, practice, or course of business which operates or would operate as a fraud or deceit upon any person, in connection with the purchase or sale of any security.[7]

The 1934 Act gives the SEC the power to police violations of any of its provisions, including Rule 10b-5, in three major ways. First, the SEC may bring administrative proceedings against persons over whom it has disciplinary authority, such as broker-dealers.[8] Second, it may commence civil actions in federal district court seeking injunctions to halt prohibited activity.[9] Finally, the SEC may recommend cases to the Justice Department for criminal prosecution.[10]

Rule 10b-5 does not expressly grant a private right of action for damages to victims of violations of the rule. Early in the history of the rule, however, lower federal courts construed the rule as implicitly creating a private right of relief.[11] The United States Supreme Court has expressly affirmed the existence of a private cause of action under Rule 10b-5.[12]

Certain elements of a claim under Rule 10b-5 are common to both a government suit and a private action for damages. Anyone suing under Rule 10b-5 must establish:

(a) a violation of one of the three prohibitory subsections of the rule. This most typically takes the form of an allegation that the defendant misstated or omitted to state a material fact. Where the nature of the case involves an allegation of omission, a defendant will be held liable for his silence only if he was under a duty to disclose the information in question.[13] Materiality of the information is tested according to whether there is a substantial likelihood that a reasonable investor or shareholder would consider the information important in deciding to purchase or sell;[14]

(b) use of interstate commerce, the mails or a facility of a national securities exchange by the defendant in some part of the transaction;

(c) proof that the violation of the rule was in connection with the purchase or sale of a security. During the early era of expansive interpretation of Rule 10b-5 by federal courts, this requirement was broadly construed by the Supreme Court to be satisfied if the fraud "touch[es]" the purchase or sale of securities;[15]

(d) a state of mind on the part of the defendant amounting to "scienter." Alarmed by the burgeoning amount of litigation brought under the rule, the Supreme Court switched gears in the mid-1970's with respect to interpretation of Rule 10b-5 and began tightening the requirements for recovery. In *Ernst & Ernst v. Hochfelder* (1976)[16] the Court rejected contentions that mere negligence on the part of a defendant could result in liability. Focusing on the language of the statute, the Court ruled that a mental state embracing an intent to deceive, manipulate or defraud (i.e., "scienter") is necessary. The Supreme Court left open the question of whether reckless conduct may suffice.[17] Numerous circuit courts accept recklessness as sufficient.[18]

A private plaintiff must prove certain additional elements which are not required of the government. In the opinion which really began the Supreme Court's retrenchment with respect to Rule 10b-5, *Blue Chip Stamps v. Manor Drug Stores, Inc.* (1975),[19] the Court held that a private plaintiff must be an actual purchaser or seller of securities in the transaction in question. Characterizing implied private actions under the rule as "a judicial oak which has grown from little more than a legislative acorn," the Court refused to hold that a mere attempt to purchase or sell could confer standing.

As a general rule, a private plaintiff must also establish reliance on the misrepresented or omitted information about which he complains.[20] The reliance element of a plaintiff's 10b-5 case supplies the necessary causal connection between the substantive violation which the plaintiff alleges and the plaintiff's right to collect damages for the violation.[21] The requisite showing of reliance may vary depending upon whether the case involves a misrepresentation of fact or an omission of information and upon whether the transaction was effected privately or in a public market.

If the nature of the violation is a claim of omission of information, there are some obvious analytical difficulties in asking a plaintiff to prove reliance on information which was not disclosed. Thus, the requirement of reliance has been relaxed in cases involving omissions through creation of a presumption in favor of reliance if the plaintiff establishes both the materiality of the information in question and the existence of a duty on the part of the defendant to disclose the information.[22] The defendant may attempt to rebut the presumption.

If the nature of the violation is a misrepresentation, the plaintiff must generally prove that he actually relied on the information about which he complains. In a public market transaction, however, this requirement may be relaxed by resort to the "fraud-on-the-market" theory.[23] This theory rests on the "efficient market" hypothesis. In an open and developed securities market, the price of a company's stock should reflect all available material information about the company and its business. If a defendant deceives the market by disseminating materially misleading statements, an investor may be defrauded by relying on the integrity of a market price that is distorted. The investor's reliance on the integrity of the market price substitutes for proof of reliance on the actual misrepresentations involved. In *Basic Inc. v. Levinson* (1988),[24] the United States Supreme Court endorsed the propriety of applying a presumption of reliance based an the "fraud-on-the-market" theory in the context of a motion for class certification. The Court noted, however, that the presumption is rebuttable. The defendant may attempt to show that his misrepresentation did not distort the market price, or that the plaintiff did not trade in reliance on the integrity of the price.

Finally, a private plaintiff must show that he has suffered injury from violation of the rule. Although courts are split on the precise measure of damages, it is clear that a private plaintiff is limited to actual damages under the securities laws.[25] Punitive damages may be recoverable on a pendent state claim for common law fraud.[26] They are not recoverable, however, under Rule 10b.[27] Under the Insider Trading Sanctions Act of 1984,[28] the SEC may sue for civil penalties in an amount up to three times the profit gained or loss avoided on tips and trades made on the basis of material nonpublic information in violation of federal securities laws. Treble damages, however, are not available to private plaintiffs under Rule 10b-5.

In addition to primary wrongdoers, certain collateral parties to a fraud may be named as secondary defendants in a Rule 10b-5 action. These peripheral parties are typically sued under theories of civil conspiracy, aiding and abetting, *respondeat superior,* and the provision in Section 20 of the 1934 Act making persons who control primary wrongdoers liable themselves if they cannot establish a good faith defense.[29] In light of the express provision for control person liability in Section 20,[30] some courts question the propriety of applying the common law doctrine of *respondeat superior* in Rule 10b-5 actions.[31] This common law doctrine does not permit a good faith defense.[32] A majority of courts, however, permit the use of either or both theories.[33] The Insider Trading Sanctions Act of 1984 specifically excludes use of aiding and abetting, *respondeat superior* or control person theories in actions brought by the SEC for the treble damage penalties available under that statute.[34]

B. Rule 10b-5 and Insider Trading: The Interpretative History of a
Defendant's Duty to Disclose in Omission Cases

In simplest terms, insider trading refers to a situation in which
someone with access to material non-public information about a good or
bad corporate development trades on that information to his personal advantage or selectively tips the information to others who trade prior to
disclosure of the news to the market. As noted earlier, insider trading can
be triggered by any number of business situations which give rise to non-
public information. In the flurry of merger and acquisition activity
which has dominated the market in recent years, insider trading has been
especially prevalent in the context of hostile tender offers.

Announcement of a tender offer at a premium above the market
price typically causes a rise in the price of the target's stock. People privy
to information about the tender offer prior to the public announcement
are in a position to realize large gains if they purchase the target's stock
ahead of the public disclosure. In such circumstances, shareholders of the
target who sold stock during this period are likely to feel aggrieved. They
will contend that if they had known of the upcoming tender offer, they
would not have sold their shares.

Some legal commentators argue that the target shareholders have
not been injured in a causal sense by insider trading—i.e., that their decision to sell at that time was unaffected by the fact that others were buying
on the basis of secret information in the open market. Legal notions of
causality and economics aside, however, there is no doubt that target
shareholders who cash out ahead of the rise in price precipitated by a tender offer will feel gouged by those who purchased based on a confidential
informational advantage. In the final analysis, this perception of unfairness may be as important as the underlying realities.[35]

As illustrated by the above scenario, the private plaintiff's claim for
insider trading under Rule 10b-5 will normally rest on an allegation of
omission. The wrong is not that the defendant overtly lied. Indeed, given
the impersonal nature of market transactions, the plaintiff probably had
no contact with the defendant at all. At best, the plaintiff will usually
only be able to establish that he was in the market on the same day as the
defendant, but not that the shares which the plaintiff sold are necessarily
the same shares which the defendant bought. Rather, the plaintiff's
claim for fraud rests upon the defendant's silence—i.e., on the fact that
the defendant traded on the basis of secret information which he did not
disclose to the market at large. If the defendant was not at liberty to disclose the news to the market, then the plaintiff argues that the defendant

should not have used the information for his own personal advantage to the disadvantage of those on the other side of the market at the same time.

Although Rule 10b-5 on its face only expressly prohibits misrepresentations and half-truths, courts early acceded to the proposition that total silence could be actionable under the more elastic terms within the rule if the defendant was under a duty to speak.[36] During the early years of interpretation of Rule 10b-5, the SEC and lower federal courts broadly defined the parameters of this duty to speak.

At common law, the majority of courts did not require officers or directors of a corporation to disclose material nonpublic information to which they were privy when they engaged in open market transactions in their company's stock.[37] Early administrative decisions by the SEC, as well as lower federal court cases interpreting Rule 10b-5, reversed this position and broadened the prohibition against such trading.[38] Not only were officers and directors of a corporation held to a duty to either disclose such information to the market or abstain from using it until it could be disclosed, but *anyone* in possession of material non-public information, whether or not a company official, was prohibited under the rule from trading on such information. Possession of the information is what gave rise to the duty to speak.

These early interpretations of the duty to speak were based on the belief that Rule 10b-5 was designed to assure parity of information in the marketplace. As the United States Court of Appeals for the Second Circuit noted in the leading case of *SEC v. Texas Gulf Sulphur Co.* (1968):[39]

> The core of Rule 10b-5 is the implementation of the Congressional purpose that all investors should have equal access to the rewards of participation in securities transactions. It was the intent of Congress that all members of the investing public should be subject to identical market risks—which market risks include, of course, the risk that one's evaluative capacity or one's capital available to put at risk may exceed another's capacity or capital. The insiders here were not trading on equal footing with the outside investors. . . . Such inequities based upon unequal access to knowledge should not be shrugged off as inevitable in our way of life, or, in view of the Congressional concern in the area, remain uncorrected.[40]

More recently, however, as part of its retrenchment on judicial expansion of Rule 10b-5, the United States Supreme Court has rejected the parity of information approach of these early opinions. The Court has greatly restricted the circumstances which give rise to an affirmative duty of disclosure. In *Chiarella v. United States* (1980),[41] the Supreme

Court held that the only persons subject to a duty to disclose material non-public information prior to trading are those who stand in a preexisting relationship of trust and confidence with the other parties to the transaction in question.

Mr. Chiarella was an employee of a financial printing firm which had been retained by various bidders to prepare tender offer documents prior to the offer. Mr. Chiarella used information gleaned from drafts of the documents to purchase stock in the target companies prior to the offer. He then sold the stock at a profit following public announcement of the offer. At trial, the jury convicted Mr. Chiarella based on an instruction from the trial court fashioned in terms of the early broad interpretations of the duty to disclose. The Supreme Court reversed the conviction.

Holding that mere possession of non-public market information does *not* trigger a duty to speak, the Court ruled that silence is only actionable when the defendant has a duty to disclose arising from a relationship of trust and confidence with the other parties to the transaction. While Mr. Chiarella stood in a fiduciary relationship with his employer and his employer, in turn, stood in such a relationship with the bidder corporation, Mr. Chiarella lacked any such relationship with the selling shareholders of the target. Thus, he could not be convicted on a theory of non-disclosure to them.

On appeal, the government argued for the first time that Mr. Chiarella's conviction could be affirmed on the theory that he had breached a fiduciary duty to his employer by misappropriating confidential information during the course of his employment. The majority opinion of the Court refused to consider this argument since it had not been submitted to the jury at the trial level. This theory did find some support, however, in the concurring opinions and dissent.[42] Moreover, it has been endorsed by the Second Circuit in both civil injunctive and criminal actions brought by the government.[43]

Under the misappropriation theory, if a defendant purloins information from someone to whom he owes a duty of confidence and subsequently uses that information to trade, the government attempts to allege a violation of subsection (c) of Rule 10b-5. Subsection (c) of the rule prohibits any person from committing an act, practice or course of business which operates as a fraud on any other person in connection with the purchase or sale of a security. The government contends that the defendant's theft of the information is a fraud on his employer which arguably is in connection with his subsequent use of the information to trade.

The misappropriation theory, however, is only available to the government. The government has used it successfully in actions brought under both Rule 10b-5 and the federal mail fraud statute. The Second Circuit has specifically rejected its use in Rule 10b-5 actions by private plaintiffs who were on the other side of the defendant's trades.[44] The fact that the defendant breached a duty of trust to the person from whom he misappropriated the information does not necessarily supply the missing relationship of trust or confidence between the defendant and the parties on the other side of the market, which is required under *Chiarella* to make his silence actionable as to them.

In the wake of *Chiarella*, the SEC has relied heavily on the appropriation theory to bring actions against insider trading. Use of the misappropriation theory by the government in this context recently survived review by the Supreme Court in *Carpenter v. U.S.*[45]

Following *Chiarella*, the SEC also promulgated Rule 14e-3[46] pursuant to its general rulemaking authority under Section 14(e)[47] of the 1934 Act. Section 14(e) prohibits fraud in tender offers. Subject to certain exceptions, Rule 14e-3 precludes any person who possesses material information relating to a tender offer from trading in target company securities (i) if the bidder has commenced or taken substantial steps toward commencing a bid and (ii) if the person knows, or has reason to know, that the information is non-public and was acquired from the bidder, the target company or their representatives. The rule also prohibits representatives of the bidder or target from disclosing confidential information about a tender offer to persons who are likely to violate the rule by trading on such information.

Because Rule 14e-3 is based on different statutory authority than Rule 10b-5, the SEC contends that it obviates the fiduciary relationship requirement of *Chiarella*.[48] Some commentators, nonetheless, have questioned the validity of the rule. Assuming that it is valid, the SEC clearly has standing to enforce the rule. There has been little judicial construction, however, on whether the rule affords an implied right of relief for private plaintiffs. Moreover, although Rule 14e-3 does reach a *Chiarella*-type scenario, it is limited to inside trading in the context of a tender offer. The rule would not apply to more generic instances of insider trading.

The Supreme Court added judicial gloss to the fiduciary relationship requirement of *Chiarella* in *Dirks v. SEC* (1983).[50] The Court clarified application of *Chiarella* to a situation involving tipping, as opposed to trading. Raymond Dirks was an officer of a New York broker-dealer firm who specialized in providing investment analysis of insurance company securities to institutional investors. A former officer of a particular insurance company told Mr. Dirks that the company had been vastly overstating its assets. Mr. Dirks investigated the allegations. Although senior management denied any wrongdoing, certain other corporate employees corroborated the charges. Mr. Dirks disclosed his findings to a number of clients, five of whom liquidated $16,000,000 worth of the suspect company's securities. When the fraud within the insurance company was publicly disclosed, the company went into receivership.

The SEC censured Mr. Dirks for aiding and abetting violations of Rule 10b-5 by tipping material non-public information to his clients, who were able to sell their holdings to unwitting purchasers prior to the insurance company's demise. The Supreme Court reversed the SEC's disciplinary action. The Court reiterated the rule that an affirmative duty of disclosure arises only from a relationship of trust or confidence between the defendant and the shareholders of the corporation whose stock is traded. Unlike officers and directors of a corporation, outside tippees usually lack the necessary fiduciary relationship with the company's shareholders.

The Court reasoned that there are two ways in which a tippee might acquire the requisite relationship to the shareholders of the corporation whose stock is traded. In the first circumstance, an outsider might legitimately receive information from a corporate insider in the context of a special confidential relationship between the outsider and the company. If the company expects the outsider to keep the information confidential, the outsider becomes like an insider for this purpose and acquires the concomitant fiduciary *nexus* to the company's shareholders. Lawyers, accountants, investment bankers and consultants retained by the company whose stock is traded are classic examples of such "*quasi*-insiders."

The second way in which a tippee might acquire the necessary fiduciary relationship to shareholders of the company whose stock is traded is if the tippee receives non-public information from an insider of that company, who is breaching a fiduciary duty in revealing the information to the tippee. In this circumstance, if the tippee knows or should know of the insider's breach, he becomes a participant-after-the-fact in the insider's misconduct. As such, he inherits the fiduciary duty of the insider to the company's shareholders and in this derivative capacity acquires the duty to disclose.

Applying the above principles to Mr. Dirks, the Court concluded that he was not liable for his tipping. Mr. Dirks was not a corporate insider of the insurance company with any preexisting duty to its shareholders. Further, he did not receive the non-public information at issue in the context of *quasi*-insider relationship with the company. Additionally, it could not be said that Mr. Dirks was a participant-after-the-fact in any insider's breach. The Court held that an insider breaches a fiduciary duty only when he acts for personal benefit. The employees of the insurance company did not disclose the information at issue to Mr. Dirks for their personal benefit, but rather to expose a fraud. Thus, the employees of the company who spoke to Mr. Dirks were not breaching any fiduciary duty in talking to him. Finally, the Court noted in closing that Mr. Dirks did not misappropriate the information.

As mentioned earlier, the misappropriation theory recently survived a frontal attack in the Supreme Court in the case of *Carpenter v. U.S.* (1987).[51] R. Foster Winans was a reporter for the *Wall Street Journal* and co-author of an influential daily stock column entitled "Heard on the Street." Because of the column's perceived quality and integrity, it had the potential of affecting the price of the stocks which it examined even when it did not contain any corporate inside information. The newspaper's policy and practice was that the contents of the column were the paper's confidential information prior to publication. Although Winans was familiar with this rule, he entered into a scheme with two stockbrokers in which he tipped the brokers as to the timing and contents of the column. The brokers bought and sold stock based on the column's probable impact on the market and shared their profits with Winans. Winans was convicted of violations of Rule 10b-5[52] and of the federal mail and wire fraud statutes.[53]

The federal district court for the Southern District of New York[54] and the Second Circuit[55] held that Winans had knowingly breached a duty of confidentiality by misappropriating prepublication information regarding the timing and contents of the "Heard on the Street" columns. It was this misappropriation of confidential information that underlay the securities, mail and wire fraud counts.

With respect to the securities law claim, the lower courts held that the deliberate breach of Winans' duty of confidentiality and concealment of the scheme was a fraud and deceit on the *Wall Street Journal*. Although the victim of the fraud was not a buyer or seller of the stocks traded or otherwise a market participant, the fraud was nevertheless considered to be "in connection with" a purchase or sale of securities within the meaning of Rule 10b-5. The lower courts reasoned that the scheme's sole purpose was to buy and sell securities at a profit based on advance information of the column's contents.

In affirming the mail and wire fraud convictions, the Second Circuit ruled that Winans had fraudulently misappropriated "property" within the meaning of the mail and wire fraud statutes and that its revelation had harmed the newspaper. The appellate court further found that the use of the mail and wire services bore a sufficient *nexus* to the scheme to satisfy the mail and wire fraud statutes.

In November 1987, the Supreme Court rendered its decision in *Carpenter*. At that time the vacancy created by Justice Powell's retirement remained unfilled. The Court was evenly divided with respect to the validity of the conviction under Rule 10b-5. A tie vote results in affirmance of the lower court decision. The Court announced this result without discussion. Thus, at least at this juncture, use of the misappropriation theory by the government in civil injunctive actions and criminal prosecutions under Rule 10b-5 survives.

In contrast to the tenuous hold of the misappropriation theory under Rule 10b-5, the Supreme Court unanimously affirmed the mail and wire fraud convictions. The mail and wire fraud statutes are not limited to fraud in connection with the purchase or sale of securities. The mail and wire fraud statutes reach any scheme to deprive another person of property by means of fraud, provided that the requisite intent is present and that the mails or wires are used to execute the scheme. The Court found all these elements satisfied.

The Court affirmed the lower court holdings that the newspaper's right to the confidential and exclusive use of the timing and contents of the columns prior to publication constituted "property." The Court further held that the activities of Mr. Winans constituted a scheme to defraud the newspaper of that property. He deprived the paper of its important right to exclusive use of the information prior to publication. He violated his fiduciary obligation to protect his employer's confidential information and instead exploited the information for his personal benefit, all the while pretending to safeguard it. Moreover, the evidence strongly supported the conclusion that Winans acted with the required specific intent to defraud. Finally, the Court ruled that the use of the wires and mail to print and circulate the newspaper was sufficient to satisfy the requirement that the mails and wires be used to execute the scheme. Circulation of the column was an essential part of the scheme. In light of the holding in *Carpenter,* the government will no doubt buttress any 10b-5 case premised on the misappropriation theory with parallel counts under the mail and wire fraud statutes whenever possible.

Chiarella and *Dirks* make it significantly more difficult for either the government or a private plaintiff to prove a violation of the federal securities laws in insider trading situations. If the government proceeds under Rule 10b-5, it must either be able to establish the necessary fiduciary *nexus* between the defendant and the purchasers or sellers of the company whose stock is traded, or it must rely on the misappropriation theory. Alternatively, the government may use the misappropriation theory under the mail fraud statute, which, unlike Rule 10b-5, does not require that the fraud be "in connection with the purchase or sale of a security." Finally, if the insider trading occurs in the context of a tender offer, the government may use Rule 14e-3.

A private plaintiff is in an even worse position than the government. If a private plaintiff proceeds under Rule 10b-5, he must be able to establish the requisite fiduciary *nexus*. The misappropriation theory is unavailable to him. Absent the plaintiff's ability to show that the defendant had the necessary fiduciary ties, the plaintiff's only other recourse under federal securities law is if the inside trading occurs in the context of a tender offer. In this circumstance, the plaintiff may attempt to argue that there should be an implied right of recovery under Rule 14e-3.

Applying the above principles to insider trading in the context of tender offers, it becomes clear that the direction from which the non-public information emanates becomes critical. If the non-public information comes from the target corporation or its representatives, both the government and target company shareholders will have viable claims under federal securities laws against tippers and traders in the target company's stock even in the wake of *Chiarella* and *Dirks*. If the nonpublic information about the impending offer comes from the bidder or its representatives, however, the government and selling target shareholders face significant obstacles. The tipping and trading defendants will lack the necessary fiduciary nexus to target company shareholders who sell their stock prior to announcement of the tender offer.

In this latter instance, the government can bring a civil injunctive or criminal action based on the misappropriation theory under Rule 10b-5 or the mail fraud statute. Alternatively, it may pursue a violation of Rule 14e-3. Since the misappropriation theory is not available to private plaintiffs, the only argument open to target shareholders under federal securities law would be a claim that Rule 14e-3 should be interpreted to afford an implied private right of relief.[56]

III. INSIDER TRADING AND THE RACKETEER INFLUENCED AND CORRUPT ORGANIZATIONS ACT

In 1970, Congress enacted the Organized Crime Control Act, Title I of which is known as the "Racketeer Influenced and Corrupt Organizations Act" ("RICO").[57] Congress enacted the 1970 Act to strengthen the legal tools in the evidence-gathering process, to establish new penal prohibitions and to provide new remedies.[58] Among other things, Congress was concerned about fraud.[59] In addition to fraud, RICO covers violence, the provision of illegal goods and services, corruption in labor or management relations and corruption in government. Congress found that the sanctions and remedies available under then current law were unnecessarily limited in scope and impact.[60]

RICO allows private suits for treble damages by victims of a pattern of criminal conduct, including criminal securities fraud and mail fraud.[61] While the conduct that the plaintiff complains of must meet the elements of RICO's predicate criminal offenses, it is not necessary for the private plaintiff to show that the defendant has, in fact, been convicted of the offense.[62] As such, civil RICO embodies the concept of the "private attorney general" supplementing government enforcement, like the express and implied private causes of action granted to purchasers and sellers under federal securities laws.[63]

In order to establish a claim for civil relief under RICO, a plaintiff must prove that:

    (a) a defendant "person," including an "individual" or an "entity"
    (b) through at least two "acts"
    (c) constituting a "pattern"
    (d) of "racketeering"
    (e) "investor uses," "acquires or maintains," or "participates or conducts,"
    (f) an "enterprise"
    (g) with an "effect" on "commerce"
    (h) which "injures" the plaintiff "person" in his "business or property"
    (i) "by reason of"
    (j) the "violation."[64]

RICO contains a provision which expressly calls for liberal construction of its terms in order to effectuate its remedial purposes.[65] Moreover, the statute makes clear that it is not intended to supersede any existing legal provisions imposing criminal penalties or affording civil remedies in addition to RICO.[66] This concept that RICO supplements, rather than supplants, other available remedies is not novel. The federal securities statutes contain similar savings clauses.[67]

Although RICO was enacted in 1970, its use in civil cases in general, and federal securities cases in particular, has been relatively recent. While a detailed analysis of the elements of a civil RICO action is beyond the purview of this discussion, RICO's appeal to plaintiffs in insider trading cases is obvious. RICO affords the potential for treble damages, as opposed to actual damages, together with attorney's fees and costs. Moreover, it civilly enforces the criminal provisions of the federal securities laws and mail fraud statute. Thus, although courts are divided on the issue, it may allow private plaintiffs to recover civil relief under RICO in instances in which they may be unable to obtain civil relief under the securities laws.[68] For example, those private plaintiffs who are crippled in civil actions under Rule 10b-5 by the fiduciary relationship requirements of *Chiarella* and *Dirks* may be able to make indirect use through RICO of the misappropriation theory unavailable to them under federal securities laws.

IV. APPLICATION OF 1934 ACT AND CIVIL RICO TO RECENT SCANDALS

The interplay of RICO with federal securities laws may be illustrated by examining just one of the many transactions in the recent insider trading scandals.

The SEC alleged that Dennis Levine was involved in insider trading in the stock of 34 companies over a period of five and one-half years.[69] Levine worked at various times for Smith Barney, Harris Upham & Co., Shearson Lehman Bros. and Drexel Burnham Lambert Inc.[70] During the course of his employment with Shearson Lehman Bros., Shearson Lehman represented American Stores Co. in its bid for Jewel. The SEC alleged that Levine used knowledge of the forthcoming tender offer to purchase Jewel stock. When the tender offer materialized in June 1984, Levine sold his Jewel shares for an alleged profit of $1,200,000.[71]

Levine entered a guilty plea to criminal securities fraud with respect to this transaction.[72] In light of *Chiarella*, however, Levine may well have no civil liability under Rule 10b-5 to the shareholders of Jewel who sold their shares prior to the tender offer. Levine was employed by an agent of the bidder, American Stores. As such, he had no fiduciary relationship to the shareholders of Jewel. Unless the selling Jewel shareholders could convince a court to imply a private cause of action under Rule 14e-3, they may be without recourse under the federal securities laws. However, the selling Jewel shareholders may be able to use the misappropriation theory to establish the necessary pattern of predicate criminal offenses under Rule 10b-3 and the mail fraud statute for private civil relief under RICO.

V. CONCLUSION

In his book, *Trading Secrets*, R. Foster Winans, the defendant in the *Carpenter* case, writes: "I knew, as any journalist does, that it was unethical to have an undisclosed interest in the subjects I write about." He goes on to state, however, that "[a]s unethical as my behavior had been, I couldn't see what laws I had broken."[73]

In a somewhat similar vein, retired Justice Lewis Powell, author of the opinion in *Dirks*, wrote in a footnote to that decision:

We do not suggest that knowingly trading on inside information is ever "socially desirable or even that it is devoid of moral considerations." (Citation omitted.) Nor do we imply an absence of responsibility to disclose promptly indications of illegal actions by a corporation to the proper authorities—typically the SEC and exchange authorities in cases involving securities. Depending on the circumstances, and even where permitted by law, one's trading on material non-public information is behavior that may fall below ethical standards of conduct. But in a statutory area of the law such as securities regulation, where legal principles of general application must be applied, there may be "significant distinctions between actual legal obligations and ethical ideals." (Citation omitted.)[74]

As the discussion in this essay hopefully illustrates, the current construction of legal obligations with respect to insider trading is significantly out of line with most individuals' perceptions of the ethical implications of such conduct. Stripped to its barest essentials, use of material non-public information is conversion or theft. The trader uses information intended only for corporate purposes for his personal benefit. The problem with which the law struggles is that the party from whom the information is stolen—i.e., the corporation—may not be damaged by the wrong, while the parties who feel damaged by the wrong—i.e., the persons on the other side of the defendant's trades—may not always be able to establish a causal link between the defendant's conduct and their alleged injury.

If as a society we can agree on the evil of the conduct, however, we should be able to legislate better methods of governmental enforcement, supplemented by private relief for purposes of deterrence. Much of the existing legal morass in this area is attributable to the fact that the law is almost entirely a product of judicial construct, rather than a well-written statute addressed to the specific problem. Such a statute may well be necessary if the law is to reflect ethical norms in any significant manner.

NOTES

1. Pub. L. No. 98-376, 98 Stat. 1264 (1984), codified at 15 U.S.C. §78u(d)(2).

2. Letter from the Securities and Exchange Commission (SEC) to the Speaker of the House (Sept. 27, 1982), reprinted in H. P. Reb. 95-355, 98th Cong., 1st Sess. 22, 1984 *U.S. Code Cong. & Admin. News* 2294-2295.

3. Brudney, "Insiders, Outsiders and Informational Advantages under the Federal Securities Laws," 93 *Harv. L.* Rev. 322, 346 (1979).

4. 15 U.S.C. §§78a-kk.

5. 18 U.S.C. §1961-1968.

6. 15 U.S.C. §78j.

7. 17 C.F.R. §240.10b-5.

8. See, for example, §15(b) (4)-(6) of the 1934 Act, 15 U. S.C. §78o(4)-(6).

9. See §21(a) of the 1934 Act, 15 U. S.C. §78u(d).

10. See §32(a) of the 1934 Act, 15 U.S.C. §78ff(a), and §21(a) of the 1934 Act, 15 U.S.C. §78u(d).

11. A private right of action was first implied under §10(b) in *Hardon v. National Gypsum* Co., 69 F. Supp. 512, 514 (E.D. Pa. 1946). By 1969, 10 of the 11 federal circuit courts recognized the existence of an implied remedy under §10(b) and Rule 10b-5. See 6 L. Loss, *Securities Regulation* 3871-73 (2d ed. Supp. 1969) (collecting cases).

12. The United States Supreme Court confirmed the existence of an implied remedy under §10(b) and Rule 10b-5 in *Superintendent of Ins. v. Bankers Life & Casualty Co.*, 404 U.S. 6, 13 & n. 9 (1971). The Supreme Court reaffirmed its recognition of this private right of action in *Herman MacLean v. Huddleston*, 459 U.S. 375, 380 (1983), and in *Basic Inc. v. Levinson*, 108 S. Ct. 978, 983 (1988).

13. See *Dirks v. SEC*, 463 U.S. 646, 653-59 (1983); *Chiarella* v. *United States*, 445 U.S. 222, 225-30 (1980).

14. See *Basic Inc. v. Levinson*, 108 S. Ct. 978, 983 (1988); *TSC Indus., Inc. v. Northway, Inc.*, 426 U.S. 438, 449 (1976).

15. See *Superintendent of Ins. v. Bankers Life & Casualty Co.*, 404 U.S. 6, 11-13 (1971).

16. 425 U.S. 185 (1976).

17. *Id.* at 193 n. 12.

18. See 3A H. S. Bloomenthal, *Securities and Federal Corporate Law* §9.22 [4] [f], at 9-154 (1988).

19. 421 U.S. 723 (1975).

20. See Hazen, *The Law of Securities Regulation* §13.5, 461 (1985).

21. See *Basic Inc. v. Levinson*, 108 S. Ct. 978, 989 (1988).

22. See *Affiliated Ute Citizens v. United* States, 406 U.S. 128, 153-54 (1972).

23. See *Shores v. Sklar*, 610 F.2d 235 (5th Cir. 1980), vacated and remanded, 647 F.2d 462, 468-70 (5th Cir. May 1981) (*en banc*), cert. denied, 459 U.S. 1102 (1983); *Panzirer v. Wolf*, 663 F. 2d 365 (2d Cir. 1981); *cert.* denied, 458 U.S. 1107 (1982); *Blackie v. Barrack*, 524 F.2d 891 (9th Cir. 1975). See generally Rapp, "Rule 10b-5 and Fraud-on-the-Market—Heavy Seas Meet Tranquil Shores," 39 *Wash. & Lee L.* Rev. 861 (1982); Note, "The Fraud-on-the-Market Theory," 95 *Harv. L. Rev.* 1143 (1982).

24. 108 S. Ct. 978 (1988).

25. See §28(a) of the 1934 Act, 15 U.S.C. §78bb(a). See generally S.C .Jacobs, *Litigation and Practice under Rule 10b-5* §260.03[a] (2d ed. 1987).

26. See S.C. Jacobs, *Litigation and Practice under Rule 10b-5* §260.03[e], at 11-138 (2d ed. 1987).

27. *Id.* at 11-144.

28. Pub. L. No. 98-376, 98 Stat. 1264 (1984), codified at 15 U.S.C. §78u(d)(2).

29. See Hazen, *The Law of Securities Regulation* §7.8 (1985).

30. 15 U. S.C. §78t(a).

31. See Hazen, *The Law of Securities Regulation* §7.7 (1985 & Supp. 1988).

32. *Id.*

33. *Id.*

34. See §21(d)(2)(B) of the 1934 Act, 15 U.S.C. 78u(d)(2)(B).

35. For a good summary of the various schools of legal thought in favor of and against the regulation of insider trading, see Langevoort, *Insider Trading Regulation* §1.02 (1988 ed.) and the authorities cited therein.

36. See R. Jennings & H. Marsh, *Securities Regulation* 1043-44 (6th ed. 1987).

37. See *Goodwin v. Agassiz*, 238 Mass. 358, 186 N.E. 659 (1933). See generally H. Henn & J. Alexander, *Laws of Corporations* 646-648 (3d ed. 1983).

38. See *Shapiro v. Merrill Lynch, Pierce, Fenner & Smith*, 495 F.2d 228 (2d Cir. 1974); *SEC v. Texas Gulf Sulphur*, 401 F.2d 833 (2d Cir. 1968) *(en banc)*, *cert.* denied, 394 U.S. 976 (1969); *In re Cady, Roberts & Co.*, 40 S.E.C. 907 (1961).

39. 401 F.2d 833 (2d Cir. 1968) (en banc), *cert.* denied, 394 U.S. 976 (1969).

41. 445 U.S. 222 (1980).

42. See the concurring opinions of Justice Stevens and Justice Brennan, the dissenting opinion of then Chief Justice Burger and the dissenting opinion of Justice Blackmun in which Justice Marshall joined in *Chiarella v. U.S.*, 445 U.S. 222, 237-52 (1980).

43. See *SEC v. Materia*, 745 F.2d 197 (2d Cir. 1984), *cert.* denied, 471 U.S. 1053 (1985); *U.S. v. Newman*,664 F.2d 12 (2d Cir. 1981), aff'd. after remand, 722 F.2d 729 (2d Cir. 1983), *cert.* denied, 464 U.S. 863 (1985).

44. See *Moss v. Morgan Stanley, Inc.*, 719 F.2d 5 (2d Cir. 1983).

45. 108 S. Ct. 316 (1987).

46. 17 C.F.R. §240. 14e-3.

47. 15 U.S.C. 78n(e).

48. For a discussion regarding the validity of Rule 14e-3, see Langevoort, *Insider Trading Regulation* §7.05 (1988 ed.)

49. *Id.* at §9.04.

50. 463 U.S. 646 (1983).

51. 108 S. Ct. 316 (1987).

52. 17 C.F.R. §240.10b-5.

53. 18 U.S.C. §§1341, 1343.

54. *United States v. Winans*, 612 F. Supp. 827 (S.D.N.Y. 1985).

55. *United States v. Carpenter*, 791 F.2d 1024 (2d Cir. 1986).

56. In recent years with some exceptions, the Supreme Court has taken a restrictive approach towards recognizing new implied remedies under federal statutes, including the securities laws. See generally Hazen, *The Law of Securities Regulation* §13.1 (1985 & Supp. 1988).

57. Pub. L. No. 91-452, 84 Stat. 941 (1970), codified at 18 U.S.C. §§1961-1968. See generally Blakey and Cessar, "Equitable Relief under Civil RICO: Reflections on Religious Technology Center v. Wollershein—Will Civil RICO Be Effective Only against White-Collar Crime?," 62 *Notre Dame L. Rev.* 526 (1987); U.S. Department of Justice, *Racketeer Influenced and Corrupt Organizations (RICO): A Manual for Federal Prosecutors* (1985); Blakey, "The RICO Civil Fraud Action in Context: Reflections on Bennett v. Berg," 58 *Notre Dame L. Rev.* 237 (1983); Blakey and Coldstock, "On the Waterfront: RICO and Labor Racketeering," 17 *Am. Crim. L. Rev.* 341 (1980); Blakey and Gettings, "Racketeer Influenced and Corrupt Organizations (RICO): Basic Concepts—Criminal and Civil Remedies," 53 *Temp. L. Q.* 1009 (1980).

58. 84 Stat. 923.

59. *Id.* at 922.

60. *Id.* at 923.

61. See §1964(c) of RICO, 18 U.S.C. §1964(c), which provides the private cause of action; §1962 of RICO, 18 U.S.C. §1962(c), which describes the prohibited conduct; §1961(5) of RICO, 18 U. S.C. §1961(5), which defines "pattern"; and §1961(1), 18 U. S.C. §1961(1), which defines "racketeering activity" to include criminal securities fraud, mail fraud and wire fraud.

62. See *Sedima S.P.R.L. v. Imrex Co., Inc.*, 473 U.S. 479, 493 (1985).

63. See generally *Agency Holding Corp. v. Malley, Duff & Associates, Inc.*, 107 S. Ct. 2759 (1987) ("private attorneys general [for] a serious national problem for which public prosecutorial resources are deemed inadequate"); *Shearson/American Express v. McMahon*, 107 S. Ct. 2332, 2345 (1987) ("vigorous incentives for plaintiff") ; *Sedima S.P.R.L. v. Imrex Co., Inc.*, 473 U.S. 479, 493 (1985) (private attorney general).

64. See *Moss v. Morgan Stanley*, 719 F. 2d 5, 17 (2d Cir. 1983), *cert.* denied, 465 U.S. 1025 (1984).

65. See Pub. L. No. 91-452, §904(a) , 84 Stat. 947 ("The provisions of [RICO] shall be liberally construed to effectuate its remedial purposes."). See generally Note, "RICO and the Liberal Construction Clause," 66 *Cornell L. Rev.* 167 (1980).

66. See Pub. L. No. 91-452, §904(b), 84 Stat. 947 ("Nothing in [RICO] shall supersede any provision of Federal, State or other law imposing criminal penalties or affording civil remedies in addition to those provided for" in RICO.); see also *Haroco v. Am. Nat'l. Bk. & Trust Co. of Chicago*, 747 F.2d 384, 392 (7th Cir. 1984) ("Congress enacted RICO in order to supplement, not sup-

plant, the available remedies since it thought those remedies offered too little protection for the victims."), aff'd, 473 U.S. 606 (1985).

67. See, e.g., Section 28(a) of the 1934 Act, 15 U.S.C. 78bb(a) ; see also *Herman & MacLean v. Huddleston*, 459 U.S. 375, 386 (1983) (cumulative construction of securities laws furthers their remedial purposes).

68. Compare *Int'l. Data Bank Ltd. v. Zepkin*, 812 F.2d 149, 152-54 (4th Cir. 1987) (purchaser-seller rules enforced under civil RICO) with *Warner v. Alexander Crant & Co.*,828 F.2d 1528, 1530-31 (11th Cir. 1987) (RICO has no purchaser-seller limitations); see generally Blakey & Cessar, "Equitable Relief under Civil RICO," 62 *Notre Dane L. Rev.* 526, 562 n. 183 (1987) (Int'I. Data Bank Ltd. wrongly decided).

69. See SEC Litigation Rel. No. 11095, May 12, 1986, describing complaint for civil injunctive relief in *SEC v. Dennis Levine* (S.D.N.Y. Civil Action No. 86 Civ. 3726), reprinted in 2 *New Developments and Perspectives on Corporate Crime Law Enforcement in America* (L. Orland & H. Tyler, Jr., ed., Practicing Law Institute 1987), at 23.

70. "Greed on Wall Street," *Newsweek* Magazine, May 26, 1986, at 44-46.

71. See count one of the criminal information filed in *U.S. v. Dennis Levine* (S.D.N.Y. 86 Cr. 519), reprinted in 2 *New Developments and Perspectives on Corporate Crime Law Enforcement in America* (L. Orland & H. Tyler, Jr., ed., Practicing Law Institute 1987), at 17.

72. "Levine Pleads Guilty, Agrees to Cooperate," *Wall Street Journal*, June 6, 1986, at 3.

73. Quoted in Murdock, "The Future of Insider-Trading Laws," *ABA Journal*, Oct. 1, 1987, at 101.

74. *Dirks v. SEC*, 463 U.S. 646, 661 n.21 (1983).

Part III

Resources Available for an Ethical Perspective

Business people, managers, investors and financiers follow a vital Christian vocation when they act responsibly and seek the common good. We encourage and support a renewed sense of vocation in the business community.

U.S. Catholic Bishops' Pastoral Letter
Justice for All: Catholic Social
Teaching and the U.S. Economy

If you buy or sell with your neighbor, let no one wrong his brother.
Leviticus 25:15
The Jerusalem Bible

The ultimate consequences of the individualist spirit in economic life are those which you yourselves . . . see and deplore; free competition has destroyed itself; economic dictatorship has supplanted the free market; unbridled ambition for power has likewise succeeded greed for gain; all economic life has become tragically hard, inexorable, and cruel . . . as to international relations, two different streams have issued from one fountainhead: on the one hand, economic nationalism . . . on the other, a no less deadly and accursed internationalism of finance . . . whose country is where profit is.

Pope Pius XI
Quadragesimo Anno:109

Wall Street and financial markets are, to the average person, quite mysterious; most people' s knowledge consists of following the daily ups and downs of the Dow Jones Industrial Average. Given the general ignorance of the complexity of the financial markets, it may seem quite ambitious, if not impossible, to speak to educated lay people about the ethics of the investment industry. Part III attempts to accomplish this through three essays. The first essay, authored by an expert on Catholic social

121

teaching, bears the provocative title " 'Accursed Internationalism' of Finance." It expresses some significant reservations about the value of Catholic social teaching in this area. The second essay is by a knowledgeable scholar of Jewish social thought who analyzes several contemporary and well-known cases of insider trading. The final essay is by a business executive well-schooled in ethical and social philosophy as well as economics.

The Catholic Teaching

Dennis McCann, in the first article, explores the possible relevance of Catholic social teaching to the financial world. This tradition of Catholic social teaching can be traced back to medieval theologians, notably Thomas Aquinas and his use of Aristotle and Augustine. The Catholic tradition holds that the created order is fundamentally good; there is a belief that through the use of our intellects we can uncover God's intentions and, by responding to God's call, live out these intentions. Contemporary Catholic social teaching dates from Pope Leo XIII in his encyclical, *Rerum Novarum* (1891). Forty years later Pope Leo's successor, Pope Pius XI, published an encyclical titled *Quadragesimo Anno*. *Quadragesimo Anno* is much celebrated because of its three principles which have been dominant in Catholic social thought: the protection of the dignity of the person; the principle of subsidiarity stating that organizational authority ought to be exercised at the lowest possible level; and the concern to protect mediating structures (family, church, etc.) that exist between the person and the state. It is important to note that these three principles have gained acceptance across the political and philosophical spectrums.

Dennis McCann, however, is skeptical about the practical value of Catholic social teaching, especially in anything as complex as the world of investments. He is especially critical of Pope Pius' condemnation of "the accursed internationalization of finance," although he indicates that Pope Pius, while capable of rhetorical excess, was also capable of ethical subtlety. For instance, he quotes favorably the following passage:

> Those who are engaged in producing goods, therefore, are not forbidden to increase their fortune in a just and lawful manner; for it is only fair that he who renders service to the community and makes it richer should also, through the increased wealth of the community, be made richer himself according to his position, provided that all these things be sought with due respect for the laws of God in accordance with right reason. (QA:136)

For Dennis McCann, this passage serves as a basis for a more sophisticated and constructive approach to the ethics of investments and financial markets. On the other hand, the Catholic Church is deeply wedded to the maintenance of the status quo, especially in dioceses and communities. Anything that would unsettle this status quo, according to McCann, is questionable. Industrial mobility, liquidity of wealth and the worldwide pursuit of profit are, in Dennis McCann's words, "routinely viewed with deep suspicion." McCann writes ". . . this uncomprehending hostility to the institutions of capital formation was not an aberration, the result of a tragic failure of economic insight; rather, I see it as a systemic imperative in a Christendom most fundamentally committed to a geographically based pattern of social stability, namely, the Roman Catholic diocese."

On the other hand, McCann finds the U.S. Catholic bishops' most recent pastoral letter, *Justice for All: Catholic Social Teaching and the U.S. Economy* (1986), more acceptable. He supports it as reflecting "a renewed sense of engagement with the American experiment in cultural pluralism and representative government." He commends the U.S. bishops for their sensitivity to the challenges and difficulties facing the financial communities. He understands the U.S. bishops to be encouraging an adult moral dialogue between the church and the investment industry. For the bishops, the terms of the dialogue are the "common good and the norms of justice" and they see it as a "vocation" to achieve the proper balance between economic freedom and justice.

The Jewish Teaching

In the second essay, Burton Leiser outlines the Jewish approach to ethical matters. Jewish ethical reflection is based on the biblical text and authoritative interpretations by respected rabbis. The source book of these interpretations is the Talmud, written in 400-500 A.D., which serves as a guide for new situations encountered in Jewish communities. Down through the centuries there have been additions to this enormous body of literature. It is from these sources that Burton Leiser draws in discussing several contemporary cases of insider trading. He states:

Neither legislation nor education will eradicate the tragedies that befall the victims of such scandals as Equity Funding and the Affiliated Ute Citizens, or, for that matter, the tragedies that befall the perpetrators of such schemes. We can do no more than reiterate the ancient principles that have been handed down to us—principles that have not lost their vitality over the centuries, and that continue to inspire our legislators and, we hope, our citizens. It is still true that "the world rests upon three foundations: justice, truth and peace," for "where there is peace, there is no need for courts of law; and there is peace wherever truthfulness reigns. And therefore, all three of these foundations rest ultimately upon truthfulness."

Leiser, in discussing his paper, tells a story that is very illuminating about the role of Jewish tradition in contemporary problems:

> I would like to recall an interesting thing that happens in the Passover seder, the ceremony that almost every Jewish family celebrates on the first and second nights of that wonderful holiday marking the exodus from Egypt. A series of songs which begin and end with the words halleluia, praise the Lord, are recited. In the midst of the recitation of these magnificent biblical chapters, we stop and have dinner. After dinner and fine wine, those that are still awake finish the series of songs. During one particular celebration of the seder one rabbi said: "Is not this ceremony strange? It really is a very peculiar way to have a religious service. You break in the midst because you are getting hungry and then, to the extent that you are able, you finish the religious service." Another rabbi thereupon replied: "You have not understood what the meal was about. There is nothing secular about it; on the contrary, it is part of the holy work we are doing." If I may I would draw an analogy between that and what I think both of our faiths believe about business; it is that what they are doing is not only their work, designed to produce some advantages to themselves and their families, but what they are doing is also the Lord's work.

Leiser believes that this perspective is crucial for the financial actor in judging the rightness or wrongness of actions. In addition, he believes that ethical convictions need to be reinforced by appropriate laws.

Ethics and Economic Theory

The final essay is by George Brockway, the former chairman of the board of W. W. Norton and Company and currently the president of the Yale University Press. The essay reflects both extensive practical experience and a serious interest in ethical reflection. The author rejects the widening gap between economic thought and ethical reflection and argues that economics is an ethical, normative, humanist and historical discipline. For Brockway, the bedrock of all economic thought must be an ethical perspective and analysis. As to the cause of the split between economics and ethics, he is ambivalent, believing that a revolution is needed in ethical thinking as well as in economics. He observes:

> . . . I will say again that conventional economics is a historical idea. It is not trivial. It did not spring up casually. Economics was not split off from ethics by accident. The split would not have occurred if it had not satisfied an urgent need strongly felt by intelligent, vital and sincerely troubled men and women. The need, then as now, was for a revolution in ethics. Dogmatic moralism was no longer tolerable, but it was so domineering that the only escape from it seemed to be the denial of ethics altogether. This is where we are now.

He believes that four principles must serve as the basis for truly "ethical" economics: the worth of people rather than things, self-respect, the "absolute" equality of human beings and a more even distribution of economic opportunity.

Nine

"Accursed Internationalism" of Finance: Coping with the Resource of Catholic Social Teaching

Dennis P. McCann

If you ask a theologian about the resources that religion may contribute to an ethic for the investment industry, you are likely to get an unsatisfactory answer for theologians are trained to resist anything straightforward on this or any other topic. Were someone to suggest that the recent scandals on Wall Street and the general climate of uncertainty in the financial markets worldwide are due, in part, to accumulated defects in personal character, and that religion can help restore ethics to investment banking by helping to overcome these defects, that is, by sticking to basics, say, the Ten Commandments or the so-called Protestant work ethic, and teaching sound personal values to the next generation of investors and brokers, theologians would remain skeptical. They will tend to view such answers as a "quick fix" that can work only on the erroneous assumption that faith, too, is a commodity or perhaps some sort of hedging device, that can be purchased as necessary when things seem to be going wrong. Indeed, modern theologians—among whom I count myself—will tend to be skeptical about religion functioning as a "resource" for any human project. And so you can expect them to begin even a discussion on ethics in the investment industry with at least a brief attempt to clarify the meaning of religion.

Though I cannot do otherwise than meet this expection, I will try to confine my remarks in a way that will contribute to this discussion of the investment industry. There is, of course, no single, universally accepted definition of religion. Those who try for a generic approach usually end up in lofty abstraction. Paul Tillich, for example, defined religion as our "ultimate concern." Religion is whatever concerns us ultimately, and whatever concerns us ultimately is religious. Under this definition it could be true, quite literally, that money is our God. Frederick Streng, on the other hand, defines religion as a "means of ultimate transformation." This definition has the advantage of seeing religion as a process: what is secular may become sacred, and vice-versa; we may all be seeking transcendence, but in appropriately diverse ways. Let me add a third generic definition of religion, that of the anthropologist Clifford Geertz. Religion, for him, is a "cultural system"; it is distinguished from other elements in society in that it contains a worldview and establishes an ethos on the basis of some unique approach to transcendence or the Sacred.

There are still other definitions that could be considered, but these do point our discussion in a useful direction. The role of religion in society cannot be confined to questions of personal salvation, but must be understood as having a systemic character. The cultural system as a whole necessarily has a religious core to it, in terms of which the other institutional sectors of society receive their general sense of purpose and basic ethical orientation. The very word, religion, supports this conjecture, for at its root is a Latin verb meaning "to bind up." Religion in general binds up the basic institutions of a society and, in so doing, is bound to these institutions. Although there is some controversy on this point, students of religion insist that this is no less true of modern industrial societies, so-called "secular" societies, than it is of traditional agrarian societies, which normally strike us as far more religious than our own. The forms of religion that successfully perform this role may change—indeed, they must change as society changes, but the basic function itself does not. Religion is the glue that keeps a society from falling apart.

In a pluralistic society such as ours, however, there is not one established religion designated to fulfill this function. Though the nation be one, its religions are many. This arrangement, which Americans cherish as the constitutionally guaranteed "separation of church and state," does not mean that religion no longer binds us, but that whatever binding goes on, must go on within a set of interrelated religious denominations. Each of these denominations has its own traditions that constitute it as a distinctive community, all more or less loosely united under the rubric of what some sociologists call "civil religion." In a religiously pluralistic society, the religions themselves must somehow be bound together, if together they are to help keep society from falling apart. Our own civil religion—the sort of common faith symbolized by the motto that adorns our currency, "In God We Trust," and the Latinisms found on the Great Seal of the United States of America, *"Annuit Coeptis"* ("He hath favored our beginnings") and *"Novus Ordo Seclorum"* ("A New Order of the Ages")—does this binding by continually appealing to and yet also transcending the richer and more distinctive, but also more limited, perspectives of the various denominations.

Should theologians ask about the resources of religion for ethics in the investment industry, this is the context in which they will make their speculations. Though even modern theology can still be defined in traditional terms as "faith seeking understanding," in this context the faith that is understood will reflect the ongoing tension between denominationalism and the American civil religion, as both of these tendencies within the "cultural system" struggle to renew and maintain our general sense of purpose as a nation. Asked to comment on the general relationship between capitalism and the religions of the Bible, or even more broadly on the question of ethics and economics, or yet more narrowly focused on the topic at hand, I will inevitably situate myself at the center of this tension and try to interpret its meaning for our economic institutions. Theologians, of course, are also bound by the questions they must ask. Though I am seeking to understand how religion might continue to bind our society together, especially by providing guidance to the investment industry, I cannot make any progress unless I first confront the traditions of my own denomination, which happens to be Roman Catholicism. If I am going to speculate about religious resources, I am bound to consider the legacy of Catholic social teaching and place it in a mutually critical relationship with the ongoing development of American civil religion, in a way that speaks to our society's current hopes and fears concerning the investment industry.

This, then, provides the plan of my argument. After reviewing the relevant traditions, I will argue that in its classical formulations, Catholic social teaching is uncomprehendingly hostile to financial markets and, therefore, of only limited usefulness as a resource for ethical reflection upon them. The recent pastoral letter of the U.S. Catholic bishops, on the other hand, is more discerning in its view of financial markets, and therefore does provide a resource for helping the investment industry to understand its social responsibilities. Faithful to our situation of religious pluralism, I do not claim that Catholic social teaching either has or should have the last word on this matter; but it does provide a perspective that deserves to be taken seriously, if we prefer binding ourselves together to tearing each other apart.

Catholic Social Teaching: The View from Rome

As traditions go, Catholic social teaching is of recent vintage, perhaps less than a hundred years old. Though its roots go deep into the legacy of Medieval Christendom, Catholic social teaching officially begins with the encyclical letter of Pope Leo XIII, *Rerum Novarum*, published in 1891. Subsequent developments to this tradition have come usually in the form of still further Papal encyclicals commemorating the anniversaries of *Rerum Novarum*. In addition to the encyclicals and other Papal statements, the "Pastoral Constitution on the Church in the Modern World" (*Gaudium et Spes*) ratified at Vatican Council II (1962–1965), as well as statements from the Pontifical Commission on Justice and Peace, and in this country, the National Conference of Catholic Bishops contribute to the development of Catholic social teaching. The most recent of these contributions, of course, is the U.S. Catholic bishops' pastoral letter, *Justice for All: Catholic Social Teaching and the U.S. Economy* (1986). I will reserve my comments on the pastoral letter for separate treatment, for I wish to emphasize the contrast between the view from Rome evident in the Papal encyclicals and the perspective of the U.S. bishops.

There exists no systematic treatment of savings and investment, money, banking and financial markets in the whole of Catholic social teaching. These topics are touched upon only in passing, in an approach to economic and social justice that has been shaped primarily by the Roman church's concern for the working poor of the industrialized nations, and more recently, the destitute majorities of the so-called Third World. Catholic social teaching's perspective, however, consists for the most part in prophetic protest. The tradition typically directs its criticisms equally against both Marxist socialism and *laissez-faire* capitalism. Since the core of the protest concerns the godless "materialism" that is explicit in the one and allegedly implicit in the other, it is difficult to determine what the constructive alternative might be. The encyclical of Pope Pius XI, *Quadragesimo Anno* (1931), comes closest to defining it, but the modified "corporativism" that would organize society along the lines of some sort of vocational guild system seems so uncomfortably close to the aspirations of Italian Fascism that this alternative has usually been referred to ever so vaguely as "Tercerismo," an empty term signifying the longing for something beyond both capitalism and socialism. The spirit animating this tradition is that of a humane aristocrat profoundly uneasy with modernity in all its forms.

What Catholic social teaching has to say on topics related to the investment industry is not very promising. The low point comes fairly early on in the tradition, with *Quadragesimo Anno*'s condemnation of the "accursed internationalism of finance." (QA, par. 109) Yet this encyclical, written at the height of the Great Depression, at least is aware of the role of financial markets in modern industrial economies. After having defended in classical terms the right to private property, *Rerum Novarum* warns the "wealthy" that "the just ownership of money is distinct from the just use of money." (RN, par. 35) The point is made by way of introducing an exhortation to almsgiving:

> No one, certainly, is obliged to assist others out of what is required for his own necessary use or for that of his family, or even to give to others what he himself needs to maintain his station in life becomingly and decently: "No one is obliged to live unbecomingly." But when the demands of necessity and propriety have been sufficiently met, it is a duty to give to the poor out of that which remains. "Give that which remains as alms." (RN, par. 36)

It is striking that this passage could still have been written in 1891. Wealth is conceived in essentially static terms as is the social order as a whole. One's station in life seems fixed for all eternity. It simply does not occur to the Pope that one might actually help the poor more by saving and investing one's surplus in some form of productive enterprise.

Quadragesimo Anno, on the other hand, does mean to take into account "the changes which the capitalist economic system has undergone since [Pope] Leo's time." (QA, par. 104) But at the core of Pope Pius XI's condemnation of "the accursed internationalism of finance" lies the conviction that an economic "dictatorship has succeeded free competition." The investment industry serves as the high command in this economic dictatorship:

> In the first place, it is obvious that not only is wealth concentrated in our times but an immense power and despotic economic dictatorship is consolidated in the hands of a few, who often are not owners but only the trustees and managing directors of invested funds which they administer according to their own arbitrary will and pleasure.
>
> This dictatorship is being most forcibly exercised by those who, since they hold the money and completely control it, control credit also and rule the lending of money. Hence they regulate the flow, so to speak, of the lifeblood whereby the entire economic system lives, and have so firmly in their grasp the soul, as it were, of economic life that no one can breathe against their will. (QA, pars. 105-106)

I have quoted passages in full because I want you to feel the full force of the Papal rhetoric. Such statements later were to provide the pretext for the paranoid fantasies of the Catholic "Radio Priest," the Rev. Charles Coughlin who enthralled and harangued American listeners during the early years of the New Deal era. Fr. Coughlin, in my view, merely added color and even cruder invective to a Papal perspective that in the climate of the 1930s all too easily lent itself to anti-Semitic exploitation.

Nevertheless, there are subtleties in *Quadragesimo Anno's* teaching that should not elude us, even if they did escape the likes of Fr. Coughlin. The discerning, if not forgiving, reader can find in this encyclical the basis for a more constructive approach to savings, investment and financial markets. In a brief section devoted to "Obligations with Respect to Superfluous Income," the letter expands upon *Rerum Novarum's* exhortation to almsgiving. Now the list of Medieval virtues commended to the wealthy is expanded to include "beneficence and munificence." The latter, in particular, suggests that the reservation of savings for investment sometimes can promote the common good: "Expending larger incomes so that opportunity for gainful work may be abundant, provided, however, that this work is applied to producing really useful goods, ought to be considered." (QA, par. 50) Further on in the encyclical, the point is restated as a general principle:

> Those who are engaged in producing goods, therefore, are not forbidden to increase their fortune in a just and lawful manner; for it is only fair that he who renders service to the community and makes it richer should also, through the increased wealth of the community, be made richer himself according to his position, provided that all these things be sought with due respect for the laws of God in accordance with faith and right reason. If these principles are observed by everyone, everywhere, and always, not only the production and acquisition of goods but also the use of wealth, which now is seen to be so often contrary to right order, will be brought back soon within the bounds of equity and just distribution. (QA, par. 136)

Taken out of context, this principle might seem to require an endorsement of capitalism as such; but, in the Pope's view, capitalism must be severely criticized precisely for failing to demonstrate "due respect for the laws of God in accordance with faith and right reason."

When we turn from these Depression Era statements to those of the 1960s and beyond, the tone of condemnation is less evident but the lack of understanding for the positive role of money, banking and financial markets remains. The encyclical of Pope John XXIII, *Mater et Magistra* (1961), for example, echoes its predecessors' distinction between just use of property and its just ownership, but now the point is expressed as the familiar concern for the consequences of separating the ownership of "capital in very large productive enterprises . . . from the role of management." (MM, par. 104) *Mater et Magistra*'s response is not to abolish private ownership, but to distribute it more widely through "all the ranks of the citizenry." (MM, par. 113) What role financial markets might play in such a redistributive process is never clarified. Indeed, Good Pope John mentions the investment industry only in discussing the plight of farmers: "Wherefore, the general welfare requires that public authorities make special provision for agricultural financing, but also for establishment of banks that provide capital to farmers at reasonable rates of interest." (MM, par. 134) Presumably, financial markets cannot be relied upon to deliver capital to this sector of the economy at a fair return to investors.

So far, then, the Papal perspective addresses the investment industry, if at all, mostly to protest the sufferings endured by industrial laborers and farmers, whose lives too often must bear the brunt of the dynamisms—what economist Joseph Schumpeter called the "creative destruction"—generated by free market activity. Among its other achievements, Vatican II endowed Roman Catholicism with a self-consciously global sense of mission. Since the Council, the church has become a strong advocate for the poor of the so-called Third World. *Gaudium et Spes,* one of the most impressive documents to emerge from the Council, made these comments on the role of financial markets in Third World development:

> Investments for their part must be directed toward providing employment and sufficient income for the people both now and in the future. . . . They should also bear in mind the urgent needs of underdeveloped countries or regions. In monetary matters they should beware of hurting the welfare of their own country or of other countries. Care should also be taken lest the economically weak countries unjustly suffer any loss from a change in the value of money. (GS, par. 70)

Ever faithful to the traditional pattern of Catholic social teaching, *Gaudium et Spes* thus addresses the investment industry out of a sense of solidarity with the apparent victims of modern capitalist development. Neither here, nor anywhere else in the tradition, is there an attempt to understand money, banking and financial markets on a systematic basis.

Pope Paul VI's encyclical, *Populorum Progessio* (1967), which was published shortly after the closing of Vatican II, dramatizes the church's new concern for "underdeveloped" nations, and in this context further qualifies the church's traditional defense of the natural right to private property. This right, for example, cannot be used to justify the rapacious conduct of Third World elites:

> [The Second Vatican Council] teaches no less clearly that . . . plans for excessive profit made only for one's own advantage should be prohibited. It is by no means lawful therefore that citizens with abundant income derived from the resources and work of their native land transfer a large part of their income to foreign countries looking solely to their own private advantage, giving no consideration to their own country on which they inflict obvious harm by this conduct. (PP, par. 24)

Of course, although the encyclical does not make the point explicitly, the investment industry would have to be considered an accomplice to this "unlawful" activity, to the extent that it provides the means by which such transfers can be made quickly and at relatively low cost.

The Papal passion for social justice, however, is not matched by any clarity in economic analysis. Rather than breaking new ground in understanding the emerging global economy, *Populorum Progressio* falls back on the condemnations of *Quadragesimo Anno* and unconvincingly argues that "pernicious opinions about economics" are at the heart of the problem:

> But out of these new conditions opinions have somehow crept into human society according to which profit was considered the chief incentive to foster economic development, competition the supreme law of economics, private ownership of the means of production an absolute right which recognizes neither limits nor concomitant social duty. This type of unbridled *liberalism* paved the way for a type of tyranny rightly condemned by our predecessor Pius XI as the source of the *internationalism of finance* or *international imperialism*. Such economic abuses will never be rejected as completely as they ought to be because the economy must only serve man, a point about which it is fitting once more to give a serious admonition. But if it must be admitted that so many hardships, so many injustices and fratricidal conflicts whose effects we feel even now, trace their origins to a form of *capitalism*, one would falsely attribute those evils to industrial growth which more correctly are to be blamed on the pernicious opinions about economics which accompanied that growth. On the contrary, justice demands that we admit that not only the organization of labor but also industrial progress made a necessary contribution to promote development. (PP, par. 26)

Alas, it is difficult to make coherent sense out of this Papal pronouncement. The point seems to be that though capitalism is evil, industrial growth is a positive moral good. Furthermore, ideology, or avoiding "pernicious opinions" regarding the economy, seems to be a surer path to development than understanding the structural constraints—political and cultural, as well as economic—upon it. On the other hand, the statement makes what appears to be a bitter concession to realism, namely, that the abusive structures symbolized as the "internationalism of finance" will never be extirpated, so long as the economy serves only "man." What we have here is truly reactionary. Instead of making a set of recommendations that might enlist the investment industry more effectively for the task of Third World development, the Vatican is arming itself for ideological combat. Yet one must ask against whom or what is the Vatical protesting? Have conditions in the Third World given new life to the obsolete ideology of *laissez faire* liberalism? Or have they merely unmasked once more the essentially inhumane reality of capitalism? If so, why not say so, and get on with the business of developing an alternative? Instead, *Populorum Progessio* leads us backward once more to a Tercerismo, rendered all the more implausible for its self-righteous otherworldliness. What is the economy for, if not to serve the needs of "man"? Is it impossible that the laws of God somehow are already operative in the ambiguous workings of international finance? For any number of reasons, even after the Council the Vatican was simply unprepared to consider that possibility.

The encyclicals of the current Bishop of Rome, Pope John Paul II, indicate at least the intention of a more systematic approach to economics. His most significant letter, *Laborem Exercens* (1981), in this context provides an opening for further reflection. Between the lines one can discern this Polish intellectual locked in struggle with Marxist and neo-Marxist anthropology, even as he attempts to put Catholic social teaching on a firmer philosophical foundation. The dialogue with Marxism is at once the great strength and the great weakness of the encyclical, for it heavily colors the Pope's formulation of the encyclical's central principle, namely, "the priority of labor over capital." Rightly, the Pope wants to shift attention toward the process of production; and, in terms reminiscent of both Marx and Aquinas, he insists that "in this process labor is always a primary efficient cause, while capital, the whole collection of means of production, remains a mere instrument or instrumental cause." (LE, section 12) But inasmuch as labor includes the activities of all who participate in a production process, including its managers, the "priority of labor" principle amounts to a reassertion of the priority of persons over things.

Most interesting in this context, however, is *Laborem Exercens's* corresponding redefinition of "capital." Capital, being "the whole collection of means of production and the technology connected with these means," is nothing other than "the historical heritage of human labor." To consider capital independently of the historic relationship to human labor is to be guilty of the error of "economism." (LE, section 13) Economism is a fundamental mistake, for the failure to grasp the necessary interdependence of labor and capital is at the root of the ideological conflict between "liberalism" and Marxism, and the "socioeconomic class conflict" which has marred the industrial era. (LE, section 11) But what is economism, if not the tendency to treat both labor and capital as commodities for sale on the open market? Consider the Pope's assertions:

> Opposition between labor and capital does not spring from the structure of the production process or from the structure of the economic process. In general the latter process demonstrates that labor and what we are accustomed to call capital are intermingled; it shows that they are inseparably linked. . . . Guided both by our intelligence and by faith that draws light from the word of God, we have no difficulty in accepting this image of the sphere and process of man's labor. It is a consistent image, one that is humanistic as well as theological. In it man is the master of the creatures placed at his disposal in the visible world. If some dependence is discovered in the work process, it is dependence on the giver of all the resources of creation and also on other human beings, those to whose work and initiative we owe the perfected and increased possibilities of our own work. All that we can say of everything in the production process which constitutes a whole collection of things, the instruments, the capital, is that it conditions man's work; we cannot assert that it constitutes, as it were, an impersonal subject putting man and man's work into a position of dependence. (LE, section 13)

Laborem Exercens is to be welcomed for insisting upon the religious significance of human labor, and for pointing out how utterly counterproductive and needless, both in theory and in practice, is an adversarial relationship between labor and capital. But this good news rings rather hollow so long as Catholic social teaching is unable or unwilling to spell out in equally promising terms the relationship between this kind of "capital" and the ordinary workings of finance capital.

The point is that none of the "means of production" described by the Pope would exist, had not some agent, either an individual, or a private corporation, or a parastatal organization invested in them. Investment, as anyone who has ever attempted to start up a small business or purchase a home must know, comes from one of two sources, either savings or loans, or some combination of both. Investment funds, *Laborem Exercens* might say, are "capital" in the sense that they represent a surplus created in the course of the production process, but what the encyclical appears unable to deal with is the actual liquidity of such surpluses. They exist not in the form of a "means of production," such as a factory or a machine tool, but as a certain quantity of the recognized means of exchange. Investment "capital" thus exists as money, but the encyclical leaves us guessing whether it is possible to think about money or to manipulate it in any rationally self-interested way without being guilty of the error of "economism."

Such, in my view, is the legacy of Catholic social teaching as it has developed under Papal auspices. On the whole, the Vatican's position strikes me as reactionary, but unless we are simply to dismiss it from our deliberations, it can and ought to be understood sympathetically as an important protest against the social costs of modern industrial development, whether capitalist or socialist in its origins. By the time Pope Leo XIII initiated the modern tradition of Catholic social teaching, the ancient Papal condemnations of usury had already been allowed to slip into oblivion; nevertheless, the overall impression created by these modern encyclicals is medieval. They continue to exhibit an inordinate fear of the mobility of capital, and the separation of capital ownership and its management, made possible by new communications technologies and the new social and legal institutions characteristic of modern industrial capitalism. As we have seen, obligations and virtues that once made sense in a relatively static and immobile society, for example, the "almsgiving, beneficence, and munificence" praised in *Quadragesimo Anno*, are still preached without regard to the macroeconomic function of savings and investment in a capitalist economy. The pursuit of profit is routinely viewed with deep suspicion, as is the very liquidity of wealth.

However tempting this suspicion may be when considering specific abuses such as the flight of investment capital from the so-called Third World, it must be understood in light of Papal social teaching's traditional bias against international finance. The Vatican's essentially Platonic understanding of the problem, i.e., the unstated presupposition that the common good is "substantive, objectively knowable, and indivisible" (cf. Dennis P. McCann, *New Experiment in Democracy*, Sheed and Ward, 1987, p.162), and only in need of a properly instructed "philosopher-king" to implement it, begs all the questions that led to the relatively untrammeled development of international financial markets in the first place. The point is relatively easy to make in abstract theological terms: Papal social teaching has yet to come to terms fully with modernity. But what is at stake concretely in this observation is the tradition's inability or unwillingness to transcend a bias inherent in the feudal, agrarian society of Medieval Europe. This bias identifies morality with stability, fixed social classes and generalized cultural immobility.

I have often wondered about the source of this bias, for I do not find it prominently featured in the Bible. Ultimately, this bias may be inherent in the church's "decision" to organize itself along the Roman pattern of diocesan administration, for this pattern reinforced and nurtured tendencies toward the centralization of resources and their administration, fixed residence, and all forms of social and economic stability. Under these circumstances the Roman Catholic church became less a community of eucharistic memory and more and more a community based on permanent land tenure and hierarchical forms of religious and social authority. While it is true that under these same circumstances the Medieval Christian ethic of social charity may have emerged and flourished, by the same token they also produced an ethos that could hardly be conducive to economic growth. Savings was typically confused with miserliness, and the investment function, to a great extent, was both condemned and relegated to a mostly tolerated pariah caste. My point is that this uncomprehending hostility to the institutions of capital formation was not an aberration, the result of a tragic failure of economic insight; rather, I see it as a systemic imperative in a Christendom most fundamentally committed to a geographically based pattern of social stability, namely, the Roman Catholic diocese.

I conclude that the hostility directed against the "accursed internationalism of finance" still evident in the modern Papal social encyclicals is an important index of just how deeply ingrained this bias is. It also suggests that any attempt to discover resources for an "ethic for the investment industry" in Catholic social teaching will have to find a way to overcome this bias. The Papal condemnations and warnings, in short, cannot be taken at face value. As they stand, they simply are not a reliable guide to public morality in this area.

Catholic Social Teaching: The American Contribution

Until most recently, the reflections of the U.S. Catholic bishops have done little but echo the biases of Papal social teaching. This is particularly true of the Depression Era statements issued by the National Catholic Welfare Conference on behalf of the bishops. These statements go out of their way to dramatize Pope Pius XI's opinions regarding the

"accursed internationalism of finance." Nevertheless, even these statements prudently call for further study of "the whole intricate problem of
money and credit," a task that apparently was never carried out under
the formal sponsorship of the bishops. Here is one of their better statements:

> Pius XI calls attention to the tremendous economic power exercised
> by those who hold and control money and are able therefore to gov-
> ern credit and determine its allotment. This control moreover is ex-
> ercised by those who are not the real owners of wealth but merely
> the trustees and administrators of invested funds. Responsibility is
> thus divorced from ownership. Nevertheless, they hold in their
> hands the very soul of production since they supply its lifeblood and
> no one can breathe against their will.
>
> The increasing ratio of debt to total wealth has also had its influence
> on lessening the responsibility and advantage which should attach
> to the ownership of property. It makes for insecurity. Its relation-
> ship moreover to the cost of living or a reasonable price level needs
> careful inquiry. Further study should be given, likewise, to the
> whole intricate problem of money and credit so that such evils as
> exist in the present system may be brought to light and suitable rem-
> edies introduced. (*Statement on Social Problems*, pars. 13 and 14)

This statement was issued in 1937. Its moderate tone, compared to the
Papal rhetoric on which it depends, suggests that, perhaps, the bishops
were already quietly trying to distance themselves from the "prophetic"
utterances of Fr. Coughlin.

But in light of the National Conference of Catholic Bishops' recent
pastoral letter, *Justice for All: Catholic Social Teaching and the U.S.
Economy* (1986), such statements must be regarded as prehistoric. As I
have argued in *New Experiment in Democracy*, the pastoral letter is significant not so much for its insights into the workings of the economy, but
for what it implies about the coming of age of the American Catholic
community. Like its constituency, the letter reflects a renewed sense of
engagement with the American experiment in cultural pluralism and
representative government. It attempts to address both Catholics and
concerned citizens in a way that is consistent with the pattern of denominationalism that I mentioned in the introduction to this paper. Its reflections on the need for "a new cultural consensus . . . in order to meet the
demands of justice and solidarity" (JA, par. 83), its insistence that the
"preferential option for the poor" is not just a spiritual challenge to Cath-

olics, but the litmus test for defining "moral priorities for the nation as a whole" (JA, pars. 87-8), and finally, its call for a "new American experiment" in democracy in order to implement these priorities (JA, pars. 95, 295-325), all suggest that the Roman Catholic community may now be willing and able to play a critical role in the continual testing of the social covenant that we all honor in the American civil religion. Moreover, the pastoral letter embodies a process of adult moral dialogue that is open to all perspectives—including those dissenting from the mainstream of Catholic social teaching. Because it is so open ended, the process may be the single most important contribution the pastoral letter may make to the discussion of ethics in the investment industry.

But if the process is that promising, it is reasonable to expect that the pastoral letter already will have yielded some fresh thinking on money, banking and financial markets. And so it does, at least as compared with Papal social teaching. In a section of the letter that outlines what various sectors of the economy can contribute to the work for social justice, the bishops address the concerns of those who own and manage productive capital. Though much of what is said here echoes recent statements of Pope John Paul II, it does place them in a more realistic and appreciative estimate of the challenges facing the business community as a whole. The bishops begin by stating an important principle: "The freedom of entrepreneurship, business and finance should be protected, but the accountability of this freedom to the common good and the norms of justice must be assured." (JA, par. 110) Recognizing the crucial contribution of "owners [= investors] and managers" to economic development, the pastoral letter thus establishes the baseline for an ethic of responsibility: all work, including at least by implication work in the investment industry, must be seen in ultimately religious terms as a "vocation, and not simply a career or a job." (JA, par. 111) All those who are involved in the ownership and management of productive capital should collaborate in order to see that a proper balance of freedom and accountability is achieved.

The pastoral letter, however, tries to go beyond Pope John Paul II's call for an end to the essentially adversarial relationship between labor and capital. In ways not evident in *Laborem Exercens*, the American bishops begin to grasp the unique challenges involved in the ownership and management of finance capital:

> Resources created by human industry are also held in trust. Owners and managers have not created this capital on their own. They have benefited from the work of many others and from the local communities that support their endeavors. They are accountable to these

workers and communities when making decisions. For example, re-investment in technological innovation is often crucial to the long term viability of a firm. The use of financial resources solely in pursuit of short-term profits can stunt the production of needed goods and services; a broader vision of managerial responsibility is needed. (JA, par. 113)

Yet the vision that the bishops hope to inspire within the business community is neither utopian nor reactionary. It is not simply based on a sense of moral outrage mingled with nostalgia for the preindustrial world now irretrievably lost. Consider the following observation:

> Business people, managers, investors and financiers follow a vital Christian vocation when they act responsibly and seek the common good. We encourage and support a renewed sense of vocation in the business community. We also recognize the way business people serve a society is governed and limited by the incentives which flow from tax policies, the availability of credit and other public policies. These should be reshaped to encourage the goals outlined here. (JA, par. 117)

Now that strikes me as an extraordinary concession. Instead of blindly denouncing "greed," as Papal social teaching typically did, the bishops here speak favorably about "incentives." This implies that financial markets, along with government macroeconomic policy, may provide significant opportunities as well as constraints upon what any business may do in serving society. Hence the exhortation that follows upon this observation:

> Businesses have a right to an institutional framework that does not penalize enterprises that act responsibly. Governments must provide regulations and a system of taxation which encourage firms to preserve the environment, employ disadvantaged workers and create jobs in depressed areas. Managers and stockholders should not be torn between their responsibilities to their organizations and their responsibilities to society as a whole. (JA, par. 118)

This, too, is extraordinary. In a statement already studded with claims regarding economic rights, the bishops are claiming that businesses have a right to an appropriate regulatory environment, one that will seek to insure that the organizational imperatives and social responsibilities of businesses will not be made to appear at cross purposes with one another.

In short, create a regulatory framework in which both investors and managers can do well while doing good.

This more constructive approach to the situation of moral responsibility facing investors and managers should not be dismissed as a sell-out to business interests. The religious moral vision that the bishops preach still contains a "preferential option for the poor" at its core. But the option for the poor, as I understand it, is not just another "prophetic" call for the redistribution of existing wealth. Consistent with their overall theological interpretation of the human condition, the emphasis is upon empowerment and overcoming societal "marginalization." In short, the emphasis is upon enabling people, especially poor people, to make a productive contribution to society as a whole. Among the "moral priorities for the nation" that the bishops discern in this option is the following:

> *The investment of wealth, talent and human energy should be specially directed to benefit those who are poor or economically insecure.* Achieving a more just economy in the United States and the world depends in part on increasing economic resources and productivity. In addition, the ways these resources are invested and managed must be scrutinized in light of their effects on nonmonetary values. Investment and management decisions have crucial moral dimensions: They create jobs or eliminate them; they can push vulnerable families over the edge of poverty or give them new hope for the future; they help or hinder the building of a more just society. Indeed they can have either positive or negative influence on the fairness of the global economy. Therefore, this priority presents a strong moral challenge to policies that put large amounts of talent and capital into the production of luxury consumer goods and military technology while failing to invest sufficiently in education, health, the basic infrastructure of our society and economic sectors that produce urgently needed jobs, goods, and services. (JA, par. 92)

Not surprisingly, given their very broad focus, the bishops do not work out precisely how the investment industry should contribute to implementing this national priority. But it should be clear that just as the investment industry, like all forms of private enterprise, has a right to an adequate regulatory environment to allow it to do well while doing good, it also has inescapable social responsibilities.

What some of those responsibilities might be can be inferred from various policy recommendations that the bishops make in Chapter Three of the pastoral letter. Particularly significant, given the fact that the letter as a whole does not pretend to offer a systemic "social analysis" of our nation's economic problems, are the bishops' remarks on "The U.S. Economy and the Developing Nations: Complexity, Challenge and Choices." The title alone suggests the tone of the discussion: there are no villains here, only an enormously complicated set of problems that will require the goodwill and creativity of all concerned in order to achieve a just solution. Under the heading of "Finance," the pastoral letter discusses the Third World debt crisis. As one might expect, the option for the poor is invoked to plead on behalf of the debtor nations for a more flexible approach to debt management. (JA, par. 274) But the bishops also try to draw some long-term lessons from the crisis so that it may not be repeated. Here, noting the inadequacy of the Bretton Woods institutions, the pastoral letter insists that whatever reforms might be contemplated in the system of international finance, they must include a concern for the social impact of the system on all parties affected, including the poor:

> The United States should promote, support, and participate fully in such reforms and reviews. Such a role is not only morally right, but is in the economic interest of the United States: more than a third of this debt is owed to U.S. banks. The viability of the international banking system (and of those U.S. banks) depends in part on the ability of debtor countries to manage those debts. Stubborn insistence on full repayment could force them to default—which would lead to economic losses in the United States. In this connection we should not overlook the impact of the U.S. budget and trade deficits on interest rates. These high rates exacerbate the already difficult debt situation. They also attract capital away from investment in economic development in Third World countries. (JA, par. 277)

In the absence of a new Bretton Woods, of course, it is impossible to demand that the investment industry alone compensate for the lack of a competent international authority capable of coordinating macroeconomic policies worldwide for equitable development. But the social responsibilities of the investment industry would at least include active collaboration with the United States government and other international authorities in seeking a solution. Minimally, this would mean not blocking efforts to reconstruct an appropriate regulatory framework for international financial markets, even though such efforts might have a significant short term impact on the profit margins of various investment banking firms.

Chapter Four of the pastoral letter, "A New American Experiment: Partnership for the Public Good," (JA, pars. 295-325) is also suggestive of a new agenda for social responsibility in the investment industry. What this chapter does is present not just another policy proposal, but a complex strategy for implementing any or all of them. It contains the bishops' thinking at this point on the new experiment in democracy heralded in Chapter Two of the pastoral letter. For our purposes the experiment is most interesting, for it begins with an analysis of prospects for "cooperation within firms and industries." (JA, pars. 298-305) Here, among other things, the bishops encourage socially innovative forms of entrepreneurship that promise to bridge the chasm between the ownership and management of productive capital. Their theological understanding of justice as empowering people for greater social participation leads them to consider seriously the prospects for profit sharing plans, for employees' buying out the previous stockholders and managing the firm themselves, and other strategies for cooperative ownership. (JA, par. 300) Furthermore, the experiment in democracy would include some attempt to increase shareholder rights and recognize shareholder responsibilities for the overall management of the firm. (JA, par. 306) Here the breadth of the pastoral letter's moral vision is evident, as well as some of its implications for the investment industry:

> The parts played by managers and shareholders in U.S. corporations also need careful examination. In U.S. law, the primary responsibility of managers is to exercise prudent business judgment in the interest of a profitable return to investors. But morally this legal responsibility may be exercised only within the bounds of justice to employees, customers, suppliers and the local community. Corporate mergers and hostile takeovers may bring greater benefits to shareholders, but they often lead to decreased concern for the well being of local communities and make towns and cities more vulnerable to decisions made from afar. (JA, par. 305)

If a business corporation is to respond to the pastoral letter's moral vision, it will have to consider redefining the manager's fiduciary responsibility in terms that include all those who have a stake in it. Here, too, as the various legal and institutional reforms necessary to enforce this broadened notion of fiduciary responsibility come under discussion, the investment industry's active collaboration would be essential.

The American contribution to Catholic social teaching thus can be summarized as a quest for a new vision of the economy that for the first time is genuinely open to the aspirations and achievements, as well as the failures, of the American experiment in capitalist democracy. This vision of a participatory society that has successfully overcome the marginalization of its social and economic minorities, and insofar as it has, has also succeeded in solving the problem of "competitiveness" or declining productivity, affords a perspective in which the ethics of the investment industry can be discussed more fruitfully than it might have been discussed solely on the basis of Papal social teaching. There is more to ethics, of course, than moral vision, but without moral vision it is very difficult to establish any unifying sense of purpose that might transcend the imperatives of the immediate situation. My attempt to scrutinize the tradition of Catholic social teaching, in both its Roman and its recent American versions, is meant to show how that tradition—for all its inadequacies— might still contribute to our common search for a sense of purpose. Let me conclude this paper by pointing out some specific questions that ought to be answered by any sound ethic for the investment industry.

Toward an Ethic of Responsibility for the Investment Industry

The most accessible point of departure for an ethic of responsibility from within the tradition of Catholic social teaching is the American bishops' recognition that there is an important distinction to be made between managers' and stockholders' "responsibilities to their organizations and their responsibilities toward society as a whole." (JA, par. 118) The "ethic of responsibility" is a familiar theme in modern Christian ethics, among both Protestants and Catholics. For every H. Richard Niebuhr who has taken up this theme there is also a Fr. Charles E. Curran. While both have rightly emphasized the religious and theological significance of accepting "responsibility" for our actions before God, they have not fully developed a sufficient understanding of the various contexts in which persons as well as institutions must exercise responsibility. My colleague in various projects related to business ethics, M. L. Brownsberger, Vice-President at Organics-LaGrange, a small pharmaceutical company in Chicago, has pointed out to me how important it is to distinguish those contexts. For the task of ethics, over and above articulating a compelling moral vision, is to sort out the competing claims that may arise from various overlapping and sometimes conflicting areas of responsibility.

Without developing the theoretical underpinnings for such an assertion, let me indicate briefly that in the investment industry, as in any other aspect of business and organizational activity, one is likely to encounter three basic forms of responsibility: role responsibility, institutional responsibility and social responsibility. Catholic social teaching has very little to say about my role responsibilities as, say, a professional stockbroker, or about my institutional responsibilities to the investment banking firm which currently employs me. But it is very suggestive on the topic of social responsibility for the investment industry as a whole. The limitations of this tradition, however, consist in its inability to focus on the root problem that occasions these calls for social responsibility, except in traditionally negative terms.

That problem, as far as I am able to understand it, is another of those "externalities" often discussed by economists. Industrial pollution is a classic example of an externality: in the absence of appropriate regulation, the firm that pollutes is passing one of its unacknowledged costs of production off onto society as a whole. Unless society can discover some way to make the firm pay to clean up its own pollution, the firm will continue to pollute and make a profit by doing so. Is there something analogous to pollution currently being generated by the investment industry? I think so. The extraordinary expansion of international financial markets after the collapse of the Bretton Woods accords, based among other things on the convergence of breakthroughs in communications and computer technologies, has resulted in a new kind of volatility in financial markets, an excessive liquidity in the relationship between productive capital and finance capital, from which the investment industry has profited enormously. But this unprecedented liquidity, while by its very nature encouraging ever more risky forms of speculation, is wreaking havoc on businesses and communities that must cope with the aftermath of hostile takeover bids, both successful and unsuccessful, plant closings, and declining tax bases, not to mention new intractable forms of structural unemployment and communal demoralization. In the aftermath of Wall Street's most recent "Black Monday," some analysts were speaking without exaggeration of a tornado hitting the financial markets. That very same tornado, however, over the past several years has often hit the industrial heartland of America and turned it into a "Rustbelt." Now that Wall Street itself has been visited with a "destruction" that looks less and less "creative" with every passing day, perhaps it, too, will see that its own self-interest is at stake in recognizing the social responsibilities of the investment industry. When that happens, I suggest the investment industry consider whether excessive liquidity itself might be as serious a social problem as anything emitted from a smokestack.

If excessive liquidity is the problem, then social responsibility would require the investment industry to cooperate in finding a solution, much as the manufacturing sectors willy-nilly are having to collaborate in resolving our pollution problems. I am not competent to speculate any further as to what policies might be most effective in implementing this sense of social responsibility. What I have done here is to look to my own religious tradition in search of ethical resources. Catholic social teaching, for all its deficiencies, does possess a moral vision in which the question of social responsibility looms rather large. If, and when, the investment industry is willing and able to share that vision, it, no doubt, will find undiscovered resources in its own traditions for solving our common problems of economic development.

Ten

Ethics and Equity in the Securities Markets

Burton M. Leiser[1]

I. Fraud and the Securities Markets

In 1759 Lord Hardwicke wrote to Lord Kames:

> Fraud is infinite, and were a Court of Equity to lay down rules, how far they would go, and no farther, in extending their relief against it, or to define strictly the species or evidence of it, the jurisdiction would be cramped, and perpetually eluded by new schemes which the fertility of man's invention would contrive.[2]

Nowhere has the "fertility of man's invention" contrived more ingenious fraudulent schemes than in the securities industry. This is no doubt due, at least in part, to certain rather special characteristics of that industry, and not at all to any unique flaws in the characters of those who participate in it. Stock brokers and investment advisers are no more rapacious than their brothers and sisters in other lines of work; but it may well be that the industry in which they work provides unique opportunities for enormous profits for those who are sufficiently inventive and willing to take the necessary risks. Since creativity and risk-taking are prominent characteristics of those who succeed as investment bankers, managers and advisers, no one should be surprised to learn that those who are most successful in illegitimate activities have often been eminently successful and have made an important mark in their legitimate roles as well.

Like most complex activities in modern society, the securities markets are heavily regulated by law and administrative rules. Congressional enactments and rules promulgated by the Securities and Exchange Commission (SEC) define the rights, duties and responsibilities of persons involved in securities transactions.

Legal duties most commonly arise out of contractual commitments, as a result of legislative enactments, personal status or relationships. To a large degree, they are closely related to if not identical with ethical or moral duties. Thus, the duties parents owe to their children under the law are clearly derived from the moral duty parents have to care for and protect their children. The obligations spouses have to one another are recognized, enforced and respected by the law. The legal enforcement of duties owed by employers and employees, buyers and sellers, attorneys and clients, physicians and patients, bankers and depositors, and corporate managers and shareholders to one another is based, to a very large degree, upon a recognition that there is a moral basis for requiring fair dealing between persons so related. This is particularly true when the relationship is one in which one of the parties relies upon the other and entrusts himself, his property, or his interests to her. The person who is in a position of trust—the fiduciary—is held, both in morals and in the law, to a higher degree of responsibility than would otherwise be the case.

When one has a legal duty to disclose the fact, he can perpetrate fraud as easily by concealing the truth while saying nothing as by uttering an outright falsehood. For example, a person who gives a lease to property for a year is representing that she has the right to deal with the property in that manner and for that length of time.[3] Nondisclosure of the fact that one does *not* have the right so to deal with the property is therefore false representation. However, where there is *no* affirmative legal duty to disclose, mere silence is *not* fraud:

> However unethical it may be for one knowingly to take advantage of another's misunderstanding of facts, this is not sufficient for the crime of false pretenses unless the one has himself occasioned that misunderstanding, or because of some other unusual circumstance, is under a legal duty to disclose the facts.[4]

What is true in the criminal law continues generally to be true in the civil law as well. Tacit nondisclosure, so long as one party does not actively mislead the other, does not ordinarily lead to liability unless a fiduciary relationship exists between the parties or for some other reason there is a positive duty to disclose. Courts have in recent years moved away from the old theory of *caveat emptor* and found a duty to disclose where the defendant has special knowledge or means of knowledge that are not open to the plaintiff, and is aware that the plaintiff is acting as he is because he is under a misapprehension as to the true facts of the case. These exceptions have developed especially where latent dangerous physical conditions exist and in certain other special circumstances.[5]

The transition from *caveat emptor* in the securities markets to the recognition of certain responsibilities and the imposition of clearly defined duties upon investment bankers, insiders and traders was a long and arduous one. It was provoked by unscrupulous bankers, trustees, brokers, and financial analysts and advisers who violated the trust that was reposed upon them by an unsuspecting public.

The stock market crash of 1929 and the depression that followed in its wake led to a Congressional investigation of practices in the securities markets, and to some radical conclusions as to the necessity of protecting investors against a repetition of the practices that had led to the enormous losses which they had sustained. As the 1934 report of the House of Representatives put it:

> As a complex society so diffuses and differentiates the financial interests of the ordinary citizen that he has to trust others and cannot personally watch the managers of all his interests as one horse trader watches another, it becomes a condition of the very stability of that society that its rules of law and of business practice recognize and protect that ordinary citizen's dependent position. Unless constant extension of the legal conception of a fiduciary relationship— a guarantee of "straight shooting"—supports the constant extension of mutual confidence which is the foundation of a maturing and complicated economic system, easy liquidity of the resources in which wealth is invested is a danger rather than a prop to the stability of that system. . .
>
> . . . As management became divorced from ownership and came under the control of banking groups, men forgot that they were dealing with the savings of men and the making of profits became an impersonal thing. When men do not know the victims of their aggression they are not always conscious of their wrongs.[6]

Congress correctly concluded that no one can safely buy or sell securities without having an intelligent basis upon which to base his/her judgment as to their value:

> Just as artificial manipulation tends to upset the true function of an open market, so the hiding and secreting of important information obstructs the operation of the markets as indices of real value. There cannot be honest markets without honest publicity. Manipulation and dishonest practices of the market place thrive upon mystery and secrecy . . . Delayed, inaccurate, and misleading reports are the tools of the unconscionable market operator and the recreant corporate official who speculate on inside information.[7]

Congress also concluded that it was necessary to place certain restrictions on the activities of corporate insiders and to impose upon them affirmative duties of disclosure so that investors would have a better idea of factors that might affect the value of their investments. Members of Congress concluded that the right of corporate suffrage should be extended, because

> [i]nsiders having little or no substantial interest in the properties they manage have often retained their control without an adequate disclosure of their interest and without an adequate explanation of the management policies they intend to pursue. Insiders have at times solicited proxies without fairly informing the stockholders of the purposes for which the proxies are to be used and have used such proxies to take from the stockholders for their own selfish advantage valuable property rights.[8]

Although management is most often eager to suppress bad news, it is probably not correct to assume that management is eager to suppress *only* bad news. Under some circumstances, the selfish interests of management are probably at least as well served by suppressing *good* news as, for example, when an exciting new product is about to be introduced into the market. It is far better, under such circumstances, to keep the news away from potential competitors, even though stock prices may suffer temporarily.

Before 1900, corporations voluntarily disclosed very little financial information. Promoters frequently bought up competing plants in an industry and sold "watered stock," which was worth far less than the public paid for it. A number of states enacted so-called blue sky laws[9] in order to protect their citizens against swindlers, but were stymied when the promoters employed the mails or worked out of other states. In the absence of federal legislation, state officials were unable to reach the offenders.

Congressional determination to enact federal legislation was especially strong when investigation revealed massive frauds perpetrated upon holders of Liberty Bonds during the period following World War I. Hundreds of millions of dollars in these bonds, which were purchased by the public to help the war effort, were sold or exchanged for worthless stocks and bonds as the result of fraudulent schemes developed by unscrupulous promoters, bankers and investment counselors.

Even the most respected financial institutions withheld vital information from prospective investors. The National City Company, predecessor of today's Citicorp, for example, floated several issues of Peruvian bonds without revealing that Peru had consistently failed to honor its contractual obligations or that it depended for a substantial part of its revenue upon the cotton industry, which at that time was in a precarious state. National City's own executives had been warned in internal memos *against* lending money to Peru, but the corporation's customers were *encouraged* to do so. National City was not alone, however, for many major banks, including the Morgan bank, participated in similar schemes.[10]

In another scheme, senior corporate executives joined stock pools which hired publicists to plant stories with newspaper and radio journalists. One publicist made cash payments to reporters working for the *New York Times*, the *Wall Street Journal*, and other leading journals. These stories had no purpose other than to help the members of the stock pools make money through their trading activities.[11]

In addition to their failure to disclose other material facts connected with their underwriting activities, underwriters regularly kept their own fees and bonuses close to their vests. The chairman of National City Corporation, for example, had received "bonuses" of over a million dollars a year between 1927 and 1929 in addition to his base salary of $25,000. This was at a time when federal employees' salaries were being reduced to $1,600 per year.[12]

Management and big investors and bankers failed to disclose vital facts pertaining to the life savings of millions of citizens. They manipulated the news and the markets for their own benefit. Theoretically, management was entrusted with the duty to run a corporation for the benefit of its shareholders. In reality, they often ran it for their own benefit and concealed their operations from the shareholders.

A kind of financial cannibalism took place on a massive scale. Promoters of essentially worthless stock made promises of vast wealth and employed all the means of high-pressure salesmanship at their command. Pool operators manipulated the prices of such stocks as AT&T, American Tobacco, Gimbel Brothers, RCA and Safeway. They subsidized financial writers who touted the stocks in which they were interested. The writers not only received payment for their services, but also participated in the scheme. Market letters, publicity agents and tipster sheets helped further to whet the public's appetite for the stock, driving the prices up. Participants in the scheme then liquidated their holdings, the prices dropped, and the public was left holding the bag.

J.P. Morgan & Company set aside blocks of securities it was underwriting for leading political figures. Once the price had risen, the recipients could purchase them at the low offering price. Of course, it was expected that these politicians would express their gratitude to Morgan in appropriate ways.[13]

Such abuses led Congress to pass the securities laws which still control the markets. These laws, passed in the early 1930s, have since been supplemented by additional legislation and by court decisions that have broadened their reach. Among other things, they set standards for fiduciaries who were involved in the securities markets.

A. The Duties of Fiduciaries

When a person is a fiduciary, he has an affirmative obligation *not* to remain silent, but to reveal material information.[14] Thus, in applying the common law's principle that a person's failure to disclose material information prior to the consummation of a transaction is not fraud unless he is under a duty to make such a disclosure, American securities law now recognizes that there is a relationship of trust between the shareholders of a corporation and those insiders who have obtained confidential information by reason of their positions with that corporation. This relationship gives rise to a duty to disclose because of the "necessity of preventing a corporate insider from . . . tak[ing] unfair advantage of the uninformed minority stockholders."[15] Although the legislation was prompted by abuses against unsophisticated small investors, neither Congress nor the SEC has ever indicated that the securities laws protected *only* such investors. Fraud may also be perpetrated upon powerful and experienced investors.[16]

The fact that advice given by an investment adviser is completely truthful is not necessarily sufficient, either in law or in ethics, to establish that it is not fraudulent. Suppose a securities analyst's newsletters are completely accurate. Suppose further that her advice is quite sound. But suppose, finally, that she has purchased large blocks of shares in the corporations she recommends to her clients and fails to disclose her financial interest in the stock. Such a course of action would constitute fraud. As Justice Arthur Goldberg wrote in a case involving such an investment adviser, "a fundamental purpose common to these statutes, was to substitute a policy of full disclosure for the philosophy of *caveat emptor* and thus to achieve a high standard of business ethics in the investment industry."[17]

Thus, because of widespread abuses, Congress enacted legislation empowering the SEC to prosecute fraudulent behavior by persons involved in securities transactions, and the courts have generally upheld both the congressional enactments in this area and the regulations and enforcement measures undertaken by the SEC. Fraud, either by conveying false information or by silence, can lead to vigorous prosecution and the imposition of heavy penalties by the courts.

The duty, both moral and legal, to refrain from committing fraud, either by speech or by silence, is clear. The duty to speak out is less clear when one becomes aware of another person's fraudulent behavior.

B. Limits to the Citizen's Duty to Report Securities Crimes

Under our legal system, there are limits to a citizen's duty to report crimes of which he may have become aware. Under the English common law, citizens had *no* duty either to prevent crimes or to report them. "It is no criminal offence to stand by, a mere passive spectator of a crime, even of a murder. Non-interference to prevent a crime is not itself a crime."[18] In England, there have been some halfhearted attempts, over the centuries, to impose a legal duty on citizens to report felonies, but over a century ago, this duty was said to be virtually obsolete.[19] In the United States, Chief Justice John Marshall wrote in 1822:

> It may be the duty of a citizen to accuse every offender, and to proclaim every offence which comes to his knowledge, but the law which would punish him in every case for not performing this duty is too harsh for man.[20]

The offense of failing to report a felony, known as misprision of felony, is rarely found in state criminal codes but does exist in the United States code. It is worded as follows:

> Whoever, having knowledge of the actual commission of a felony cognizable by a court of the United States, conceals and does not as soon as possible make known the same to some judge or other person in civil or military authority under the United States, shall be fined not more than $500 or imprisoned not more than three years, or both.[21]

The Supreme Court has commented on this statute as follows:

> Concealment of crime has been condemned throughout our history. The citizen's duty to "raise the 'hue and cry' " and report felonies to the authorities . . . was an established tenet of Anglo-Saxon law at least as early as the 13th century. . . . Although the term "misprision of felony" now has an archaic ring, gross indifference to the duty to report known criminal behavior remains a badge of irresponsible citizenship.[22]

Despite the Court's *moral* condemnation of those who fail to report crimes of which they have knowledge, it has stopped short of holding that they have an affirmative *legal* duty to do so. From Chief Justice Marshall in 1822 to the most recent decisions, the Court has held that the statute provides for the punishment of those who not only have knowledge of a crime, but have engaged in "some affirmative act of concealment or participation" in the crime.[23] As other courts have put it, "mere silence, without some affirmative act, is insufficient evidence" of the crime of misprision of felony. Thus, a person who witnesses a crime violates no law if he simply remains silent.[24]

Although the statute providing for criminal penalties for failure to report a crime is rarely enforced, and then only under restrictive conditions, it is clear that British and American legal authorities have recognized that there is at the very least a strong moral obligation on the part of citizens to report serious crimes of which they become aware. This obligation may be attenuated, however, by other duties that an individual may have.

II. Ancient Sources of Corporate Ethics

The ethical problems presented by the modern securities industry are novel only in the specific forms they take and the instruments to which they must be applied. The problems themselves, however, are probably as ancient as human society, and the ethical and legal principles that might appropriately be applied to them were well formulated many centuries ago.

In his commentary on the biblical passage, "You shall not place a stumbling block before the blind,"[25] the eleventh century French Talmudic scholar Rashi,[26] drawing on still earlier sources,[27] explained that it referred to the kind of case in which a speculator, knowing that real estate prices were rising, attempted to persuade an uninformed landowner to sell his land so that he could profit from the other's ignorance. Alternatively, Rashi said, the biblical passage might have referred to those cases in which property owners knew that the value of their own property was declining and sold it to uninformed investors with the intention of buying it back at a lower[28] price. The Torah condemns such practices, and reminds anyone who is tempted to indulge in them, "You should fear your God."[29] This admonition is included, Rashi said, because "it is impossible for people to know whether the perpetrator's intentions were good or evil, for he might lie and claim that he had only the best intentions. Therefore, he is reminded that God knows all of his thoughts and is urged to bear in mind the need to revere God."[30]

Needless to say, in eleventh century France, Section 10(b) of the Securities and Exchange Act had not yet been enacted, and Rule 10(b)-5[31] had not yet been promulgated. The principles behind these provisions of our securities laws and regulations were nonetheless well established. Deception of investors or property owners by not revealing all material facts was a violation of the biblical prohibition against putting stumbling blocks before the blind, however difficult it might be for earthly courts to punish the wrongdoer.

Rashi concluded that the context justified construing this biblical passage figuratively as a reference to fraud and deception for financial gain. The text just preceding it condemns robbery, detaining a worker's wages, and the oppression of one's neighbor. The Hebrew word that is usually translated "oppression" (*oshek*) was consistently interpreted by Jewish scholars as referring to a property crime related to robbery and fraud, consisting of an attempt to enrich oneself by depriving another of the rights to his or her own property.

The prohibition against fraud is most clearly stated in Leviticus 25:14: "If you sell anything to your neighbor, or buy anything from your neighbor, you must not defraud your brother." Obadaiah Sforno, a sixteenth century commentator,[32] explained that fraud occurs whenever one of the parties is at a disadvantage, not knowing the true worth of the object, while the other party has information that he turns to his benefit at the expense of his neighbor.

Concern about such economic crimes extended throughout the history of ancient Israel, from the earliest biblical period through the later prophets and the period of the Talmud (ending about the seventh century). In denouncing the worst offenses he could think of, the prophet Ezekiel wrote, in the early sixth century B.C.E., "The people of the land have practiced fraud and committed robbery; they have wronged the poor and the needy, and have defrauded the stranger without redress."[33] The Talmud and the various codes of Jewish law[34] deal with such economic offenses at great length, both as civil and as criminal wrongs.

These ancient principles are not significantly different from those that Congress applied to the securities industry. In essence, they can be reduced to the following:

1. Buyers and sellers are bound both to speak truthfully concerning the transactions in which they engage and not to conceal material facts from one another.

2. So far as is reasonably possible, buyers and sellers are obliged to disclose all of the material facts to those with whom they deal.

3. A person who is in a position of trust should avoid self-dealing and conflicts of interest, and where he/she has any personal interest in the transaction, he/she should reveal it to the other party.

4. Misappropriation of the property of others is always wrong. This principle applies not only to tangible personal property, but also to such intangible, intellectual property as information and trade secrets.

5. People should deal fairly and equitably with one another. The principle of fair and equitable dealing may appear to be too vague and general to be of any use, since scholars generally demand clear and distinct statements with unequivocal terms and precise criteria for their application to particular cases. Courts recognize, however, that the world does not always lend itself to neat categorization. The conditions of human life, human behavior and human ingenuity are so complex and so variable that they cannot be compressed into the narrow molds of precise legal terminology. Therefore, such terms as *fairness* and *equity*, with all their seeming ambiguity, are essential to the governance of human behavior. This does not mean that they are subjective or that anyone's definition of them is as good as anyone else's. In the law, at least, such terms are well understood, and even though they cannot be defined with the precision of the word *velocity* in physics, they can be applied to particular cases in such a way as to win the assent of most of the people familiar with the facts.

III. The Principle Applied

Thus, truthfulness, full disclosure, scrupulous conduct when in a position of trust, respect for property rights—including those involving intellectual property—and fair and equitable dealing are the principal rules of conduct governing persons involved in the securities markets. The following cases will serve to illustrate some of these rules and will be useful in drawing some important ethical distinctions.

A. *Failure to Communicate the Facts: The Leasco Case*

Potential investors have a legal as well as a moral right to know what they are buying before they buy it, and what they are selling before they sell it. This does not mean that investment bankers and persons engaged in the purchase or sale of large corporations must treat shareholders as if they were third graders incapable of making responsible decisions for themselves. It does mean, however, that they have a moral duty to communicate with them in clear, precise language. This moral duty has been translated into a legal duty. Professionals in the business know, or should know, that small investors are not likely to be able to penetrate the obscure language in which prospectuses and other documents may be couched. They therefore have an obligation to see that their communications are clear and accessible to the small investor as well as the professional.

The 1971 case of *Feit v. Leasco Data Processing Equipment Corp.*[35] is illustrative of the way in which this principle has been applied. Leasco, desiring to purchase Reliance Insurance Company (Reliance), offered Reliance shareholders a package of preferred shares and warrants in exchange for their common stock.

Like all insurance companies, Reliance was required to maintain a certain surplus to guarantee the integrity of its insurance operations. However, Reliance had built up cash and other liquid reserves far in excess of those legal requirements, amounting to about a hundred million dollars. In its prospectus, Leasco made no direct reference either to the amount of these excess cash reserves or even to their very existence. The prospectus said only that Leasco intended to establish a holding company that would provide "more flexible operations, freedom of diversification and opportunities for more profitable utilization of financial resources." It added that Leasco would have Reliance provide the holding company "with the maximum amount of funds legally available which is consistent with Reliance's present level of net premium volume."

Those words meant that Leasco planned to drain Reliance's cash reserves into its holding company. Obviously, however, only a very astute investor would have understood that.

The court found that this was an example of a literary art form "calculated to communicate as little of the essential information as possible while exuding an air of total candor." "Masters of this medium," the court went on, "utilize turgid prose to enshroud the occasional critical revelation in a morass of dull, and—to all but the sophisticates—useless financial and historical data."

The court noted that the *legal* standard was that all material facts must be disclosed. It was crucial, however, to determine the persons to whom the facts were intended to have significance. The court concluded that the prospectus must communicate the material facts to the average common shareholder as well as to the sophisticated investor and securities professional. The less experienced investor is "entitled to have within the four corners of the document an intelligible description of the transaction." Consequently, the court held that the plaintiffs—investors who had exchanged their shares of Reliance for the Leasco package—were entitled to money damages because they were misled by the omission of a material fact. The court, in light of these findings, imposed liability both upon Leasco and upon some of its principal officers.

B. Self-Dealing: Affiliated Ute Citizens

In *Leasco*, the fraud was perpetrated by the buyers upon the sellers by presenting information in such an obscure way that the sellers could not appreciate its real meaning. In the *Ute Citizens* case, the violation was even more egregious, for it was committed by bankers—who are held to a high standard of ethical conduct—against an Indian tribe and individuals with whom those bankers had a relationship of trust.

The Ute tribe owned various properties, including oil, gas and mineral rights. These properties, which had been held by the United States government, were to be distributed to members of the tribe in accordance with certain procedures laid down by Congress. Under those procedures, the First Security Bank of Utah became the transfer agent for the Ute Distribution Corporation (UDC), which was authorized to manage certain rights as part of the plan to distribute shares of property to mixed-blood Utes. The UDC certificates were to bear a stamp setting forth certain restrictions on the sale or transfer of the shares the bank was holding in trust for the mixed-blood Utes, including a right of first refusal to be accorded to members of the tribe before any non-member would be permitted to purchase the shares.

Officers at the local branch of the bank prepared and notarized papers for the transfer of shares, including affidavits of the sellers stating that they were receiving not less than the price at which the shares had been offered to members of the tribe. Some of these affidavits were prepared in blank, and others did not accurately describe the sales to which they were related. The bank officers received commissions and gratuities for their services in arranging for the sales of shares to whites, and actively solicited standing orders from non-Indians for them.

The Supreme Court held that the defendants possessed the affirmative duty to disclose, among other things, the commissions they were earning for the sales they solicited, as well as their own purchases of these shares:

> The defendants may not stand mute while they facilitate the mixed-bloods' sales to those seeking to profit in the non-Indian market the defendants had developed and encouraged and with which they

were fully familiar. The sellers had the right to know that the defendants were in a position to gain financially from their sales and that their shares were selling for a higher price in that market. . . .

Under the circumstances of this case, involving primarily a failure to disclose, positive proof of reliance is not a prerequisite to recovery. All that is necessary is that the facts withheld be material in the sense that a reasonable investor might have considered them important in the making of this decision.[36]

Here the fraud was not against investors in general but against particular individuals, members of a group of people who had reposed their trust in the bank and its officers. Even if the bank had not offered the Utes its protection, there can scarcely be any doubt of the unethical behavior of the bankers involved in this scheme to sell the Indians' property at prices substantially below its market value. They were fiduciaries. They were entrusted with the responsibility of *protecting* the Indians' property. Instead, they found a way to profit personally from the ill-informed, trusting faith that the Utes placed in them. They went far beyond the mere placement of a stumbling block before the blind. They hired themselves out as protectors of the blind, and then designed and manufactured the stumbling blocks to order.

IV. Some Limits to the Principle

Professionals in the securities business and insiders have a duty to disclose facts that they believe, or reasonably should believe, would be crucial to any decision the other parties might make. But people are not necessarily obliged to tell everything they know to the world at large, to the authorities, or to other investors. There must be room in a free market system for profits derived from individual industry, ingenuity and perspicacity.

It is proper for citizens to report to the authorities crimes of which they become aware. No one, however, is legally obliged to do so. Indeed, a case may be made for the proposition that it is not ethically wrong for one *not* to do so, except in extraordinary circumstances where there is a reasonable expectation of imminent danger to other persons.[37] People in small towns are reputed to make it their business to be aware of what their neighbors are doing. One of the more endearing facts about small-town life is the concern that neighbors show for each other. One who has lived in a small town in the Midwest would not have the slightest doubt that the lady across the street who peered out of her kitchen window all day would have been on her phone instantly if she observed anything untoward happening in the neighborhood. This may be commendable under some circumstances, but it is also one of the limitations of small-town life. People feel that they are under constant scrutiny by their neighbors, and that severe social sanctions may be imposed upon them if they do not conform to local standards of behavior. The securities industry operates in a much different context. The complex deals that are arranged, the sophisticated devices that are invented almost every week, the constantly shifting and evolving structures of the markets, the swift and impersonal communications that flow across state and national borders simply cannot be compared to life in a small town. Relationships between traders are not comparable to relationships between neighbors. Traders are in a fiercely competitive relationship with one another. Such competition need not be cutthroat or indecent, and some reasonable standards of fair trading are essential to a healthy market. But such standards must be based upon an understanding of the special character of the securities industry and an appreciation of the complexities inherent in it. The principle of full disclosure to the world at large may be compared to the giving of charity. Those who give generously are deemed to have acted in a morally high-minded way, and are deserving of praise and admiration for their generosity. Similarly, traders and insiders who become aware of violations of the securities laws are to be commended for their courage when they report those violations to the authorities. But brokers, investors and other persons involved in corporate finance are not expected to be Good Samaritans, much less Splendid Samaritans. Fair and equitable dealing and living within the rules of the industry are all that can reasonably be demanded.

The *Dirks* case is the most important precedent for the principle that there are limits to an investment professional's legal duty to disclose violations to the authorities or to the world at large. It also raises some difficult ethical issues.

A. The Right Not to Disclose: Raymond Dirks and the Equity Funding Scandal

Raymond Dirks, an officer of a broker-dealer firm, specialized in providing investment analyses of insurance companies to institutional investors.[38] In March 1973, he was told by Ronald Secrist, a former officer of Equity Funding of America, that Equity Funding's assets were vastly overstated as the result of fraudulent corporate practices. Secrist urged Dirks to verify the fraud and disclose it publicly.

As a result of his own investigation, Dirks concluded—on the basis of very reliable information—that Secrist's charges were correct. Neither Dirks nor his firm owned any Equity Funding securities. During his investigation he openly discussed his findings with clients and investors. Some of these persons sold their Equity Funding shares. Among them were five investment advisers who liquidated more than $16 million in Equity Funding holdings. At the same time, Dirks unsuccessfully urged the bureau chief of the *Wall Street Journal* to write a story about the alleged fraud.

During this period, the price of Equity Funding stock fell from $26 to less than $15 per share. Soon thereafter, trading in Equity Funding shares was halted by the New York Stock Exchange, and California authorities uncovered evidence of the fraud.

The SEC found that Dirks had aided and abetted violations of various provisions of the securities acts of 1933 and 1934 and of SEC Rule 10(b)-5 by revealing his findings to investors who sold their holdings on the basis of the information he supplied. The commission reasoned that "[w]here 'tippees'—regardless of their motivation or occupation—come into possession of material 'corporate information that they know is confidential and know or should know came from a corporate insider,' they must either publicly disclose that information or refrain from trading."[39] The District of Columbia Circuit Court of Appeals affirmed, on the ground that "the obligations of corporate fiduciaries pass to all those to whom they disclose their information before it has been disseminated to the public at large," and further, because Dirks, as an employee of a broker-dealer, had violated obligations to the SEC and to the public.[40]

1. The Information Theory: Chiarella, the Printer's Assistant

On its face, this decision upholding Dirks's conviction appears to be inconsistent with *Chiarella v. United States*,[41] in which the Supreme Court had accepted the following elements as sufficient to establish a violation of Rule 10(b)-5:

1. The existence of a relationship affording access to inside information intended to be available only for a corporate purpose, and

2. the unfairness of allowing a corporate insider to take advantage of that information by trading without disclosure.

However, the Court had also ruled in *Chiarella* that not all breaches of fiduciary duty in connection with a securities transaction fall under Rule 10(b)-5, for there must also be "manipulation or deception."[42]

Chiarella, an employee of a printer who specialized in printing prospectuses and other materials connected with the securities industry, had misappropriated information concerning proposed mergers gathered in the course of his employment and used it to trade on the market for his personal financial gain. The Court overturned his conviction on the grounds that, although he had traded on inside information, he had no duty to disclose. He was not the corporation's agent, he was not a fiduciary, and he was not a person in whom the sellers of the securities had placed their trust and confidence.[43] He had therefore not violated the principle, known as the "information theory," that all traders must enjoy equal information before trading.

2. Application of Chiarella to Dirks

In its case against Dirks, the SEC assumed that a tippee "inherits" a fiduciary's obligation to shareholders when he receives confidential information from an outsider. The Supreme Court held that the "information theory" upon which the SEC apparently based its conclusion was incorrect:

> Imposing a duty to disclose or abstain solely because a person knowingly receives material nonpublic information from an insider and trades on it could have an inhibiting influence on the role of market analysts. . . . It is commonplace for analysts to "ferret out and analyze information," . . . and this often is done by meeting with and questioning corporate officers and others who are insiders. Any information that the analysts obtain normally may be the basis for judgments as to the market worth of a corporation's securities. The analyst's judgment in this respect is made available in market letters or otherwise to clients of the firm. It is the nature of this type of information, and indeed of the markets themselves, that such information cannot be made simultaneously available to all of the corporation's stockholders or the public generally.[44]

The Court acknowledged that if an insider has breached his fiduciary duty to shareholders by *improperly* conveying confidential information to a tippee, the recipient of the information must then either disclose the information he or she has received or abstain from trading on it. The Court reasoned that under the securities laws, one of whose principal purposes was elimination of the use of inside information for personal advantage, *improper* conveyance of information by an insider can occur only when the insider personally benefits, directly or indirectly, from his/her disclosure. "Absent some personal gain, there has been no breach of duty to stockholders."[45] If the insider has not breached his fiduciary duty by revealing information from which he reasonably believes he will derive some personal benefit, the person to whom he has communicated it has no derivative duty that he can violate.[46]

The result in *Dirks* was reached on a narrow reading of the securities law. The Court concluded that the tippers were motivated by a desire to expose the fraud rather than by a desire for personal gain. Therefore, neither they nor Dirks committed any breach of the securities laws or violated any fiduciary duty to the stockholders *under those laws.*

In a vigorous dissent, Justices Blackmun, Brennan and Marshall argued that however laudable Secrist's motive may have been in exposing the Equity Funding fraud, the means he chose were not. They argued further that Dirks's role in exposing the fraud did not justify his profiting from the information he received from Secrist. "A person cannot condition his transmission of information of a crime on a financial award," they wrote. "As a citizen, Dirks had at least an ethical obligation to report the information to the proper authorities. The Court's holding is deficient in policy terms not because it fails to create a legal norm out of that ethical norm, but because it actually rewards Dirks for his aiding and abetting."[47] In an acid comment on what they called the Court's "cynical view," the dissenters contended that there was no difference between the benefit Secrist obtained from his exposure of the fraud—namely, his "good feeling" and enhanced reputation—and the benefit an insider receives from giving information to a friend or relative. Moreover, they said it was reasonable to conclude that Secrist gave Dirks a gift of the commissions Dirks made on the deal. "The distinction between pure altruism and self-interest has puzzled philosophers for centuries; there is no reason to believe that courts and administrative law judges will have an easier time with it."[48]

On this point, the majority wrote:

> We do not suggest that knowingly trading on inside information is ever "socially desirable or even that it is devoid of moral considerations." [Citation.] Nor do we imply an absence of responsibility to disclose promptly indications of illegal actions by a corporation to the proper authorities. . . . Depending on the circumstances, and even where permitted by law, one's trading on material nonpublic information is behavior that may fall below ethical standards of conduct. But in a statutory area of the law such as securities regulation, where legal principles of general application must be applied, there may be "significant distinctions between actual legal obligations and ethical ideals." [Citation.][49]

Dirks had no *legal* duty either to disclose the information he had received or to refrain from profiting from his inside information or from helping his clients to do so. The members of the Court unanimously agreed, however, that Dirks had an *ethical* duty both to disclose the information he had received and to refrain from profiting from it.

This is reminiscent of Rashi's comment on the biblical prohibition against putting a stumbling block before a blind person: one may get away with it before the earthly courts, for there is no way to plumb the perpetrator's innermost intentions, but the behavior is nevertheless ethically questionable.

Despite the Court's dictum that Dirks acted unethically, closer analysis suggests that he had *no* ethical duty, much less a legal one, to report his findings to the authorities. In taking his profits and urging his clients to do the same, he may have violated no ethical norm whatever, unless he was under some special obligation to be a Splendid Samaritan.

As an analyst and investment adviser, Dirks owed no duty to the corporations whose activities and financial affairs he investigated, except the duty to be honest and truthful in his dealings with them. Nor did his obligations to the government and to the investing public go beyond those of other citizens. His principal obligation was to the firm for which he worked and to his clients, for they relied upon him to protect and further their investment interests. Those interests were both innocent and legitimate. In order to protect their investments, they retained Dirks's services. As a conscientious investment adviser, entrusted with the integrity of his clients' portfolios, he carefully investigated the financial prospects of the corporations in which his clients either had invested or might invest. It was his duty to report his findings to them in a timely manner. That is what he agreed to do, and it is what they paid him for.

An investment adviser's affirmative duty to report his findings as promptly as possible to his clients is *not* paralleled by a comparable duty to the government or to the public. On the contrary, if his research, his judgment and his advice are to be worth anything at all to the people who pay for it, they must have access to it before anyone else does. The very purpose of retaining an investment adviser's services is to make money in the market, to have an advantage over those who have *not* bought those services.

To be sure, the money Dirks's clients made on their Equity Funding shares was at the expense of the people who purchased those shares— people who were in the dark about the Equity Funding fraud and the company's precarious financial condition. Collectively, they bought millions of dollars worth of shares at $26 per share, and a week or two later were unable to unload them at $15 per share. As a sophisticated investment adviser, Dirks must have known that if his clients sold their shares before news of the fraud reached the general public, the people who bought them would face enormous losses. Those purchasers, like the blind man in Leviticus, were sure to topple over the stumbling block and be severely injured. When Dirks foresaw, or could easily have foreseen, the injury those investors would suffer, did he not have an ethical duty to rescue them?

In addressing this issue, it is important to note that Dirks did not place the stumbling block before those uninformed investors. He was (metaphorically) retained to serve as eyes for his clients, to guide them around the stumbling blocks that lay in their paths so that *they* would not stumble. He had no duty to rush to the rescue of unknown, unidentified persons who had not entrusted their financial security to his capable hands. The stumbling blocks were put in place by the principals at Equity Funding, who had participated in a massive fraud against the corporation's clients and against its shareholders. *They* breached their duty—a legal duty as well as an ethical one—to the investing public, and must bear the ultimate responsibility, in law and in ethics, for the losses suffered by those who purchased Equity Funding shares from Dirks's clients.

It might be tempting to proclaim that Dirks had an ethical duty to the investing public, and more especially to those who lost money as a direct consequence of his failure to inform them of the facts he had learned about Equity Funding. This duty, it might be said, was either to disclose his findings to the public or to refrain from disclosing them to his clients. But such an approach, carried to its logical conclusion, would destroy any incentive that Dirks and other investment advisers might have to conduct the kind of thorough investigation that Dirks conducted in the Equity Funding case, ferreting out information that others had failed to uncover. Investors were willing to pay high fees to Dirks and his employer precisely because he was diligent and tenacious enough to conduct such an inquiry and bring it to a successful conclusion. Information uncovered at great expense and personal effort does *not* become public property, in the sense that the public has a right to demand access to it, simply because the public has an interest in it. It is, however, in the public domain, for anyone who has access to it may publish it if he chooses to do so. As the Supreme Court held in 1918, information respecting current events is the history of the day and, as such, is open to all to do with as they please. "[E]xcept for matters improperly disclosed, or published in breach of trust or confidence, or in violation of law, . . . the news of current events may be regarded as common property."[50] Be this as it may, the *right* to publish does not translate into a *duty* to disclose information one has acquired through diligent effort.

3. The Misappropriation Theory: "Heard on the Street"

The decision in the case of R. Foster Winans, who wrote the "Heard on the Street" column for the *Wall Street Journal*, might seem to be a repudiation of *Dirks* because the Court upheld the convictions of Winans and his co-conspirators. However, there were crucial legal and ethical distinctions between the two cases.

Knowing that the column's comments were taken seriously by investors and often had a swift impact on share prices, Winans conspired with several friends to buy and sell shares of corporations that would be the subject of future columns. He and his co-conspirators were prosecuted for violations of the securities law by misappropriating material, nonpublic information from the *Wall Street Journal* in connection with the purchase and sale of securities, and of mail and wire fraud. The defendants argued that because they were not corporate insiders and had not misappropriated the information they used from such insiders, they had violated no fiduciary duty that would fall under Rule 10(b)-5,[51] and that they were therefore not guilty of any violation of the securities laws.

Noting that the "fairness and integrity" of conduct in the securities markets was of the utmost importance, the court construed the language of section 10(b) and of Rule 10(b)-5 rather broadly, but not inappropriately,[52] to mean that "trading on the basis of [any] improperly obtained information is fundamentally unfair." The court found that conduct constituting "secreting, stealing, purloining, or otherwise misappropriating material, nonpublic information in breach of an employer-imposed fiduciary duty of confidentiality" constituted "chicanery, not competition; foul play, not fair play." Winans "misappropriated—stole, to put it bluntly—valuable nonpublic information entrusted to him in the utmost confidence." Consequently, the court upheld the convictions. Their convictions were unanimously affirmed by the United States Supreme Court,[53] which held that even though the *Journal* was not deprived of the first public use of its information,[54] it was deprived of its right to keep the schedule and contents of the "Heard on the Street" columns confidential and to make exclusive use of that information prior to its publication. The Court compared Winans' conduct to embezzlement, noting that fraud consists of "wronging one in his property rights by dishonest methods or schemes, . . . by trick, deceit, chicanery or overreaching."[55]

V. The Ethics of the Talmud and the Securities Industry

As Lord Hardwicke said, "Fraud is infinite," and however we may legislate against it, our efforts will be "perpetually eluded by new schemes which the fertility of man's invention would contrive."[56] Neither legislation nor education will eradicate the tragedies that befall the victims of such scandals as Equity Funding and the Affiliated Ute Citizens, or, for that matter, the tragedies that befall the *perpetrators* of such schemes. We can do no more than reiterate the ancient principles that have been handed down to us—principles that have not lost their vitality over the centuries, and that continue to inspire our legislators and, we would hope, our citizens. It is still true that "the world rests upon three foundations: justice, truth and peace,"[57] for "where there is peace, there is no need for courts of law; and there is peace wherever truthfulness reigns. And therefore, all three of these foundations rest ultimately upon truthfulness."[58]

The sages of old wrote: "Among the most contemptible of men must be reckoned those who cheat and lie in their business dealings, for their lies give rise to heated arguments, to perjury, to violence, to murder, and to other violations of the law. All of these evils proceed in a causal chain from the person who accustoms himself to lying. For the lies he tells can ultimately lead him to shed the blood of the innocent person who exposes his nefarious dealings. . . . Therefore, happy is the man who keeps far from speaking falsehoods, but accustoms himself to uttering only the truth with humility and honesty. In this way he will achieve all his goals in righteousness both in this world and in the next. Let him lead the children of his household along this path and he will be spared all sorrow.[59]

The rabbis of the Talmud considered fraud, particularly against the weak and underprivileged, to be a particularly heinous crime, equivalent to murder even though it was not punishable by penalties as severe as those for violent crimes. Rabbinical courts treated business fraud with particular severity, barring or suspending offenders—especially repeat offenders—from carrying on business and, in extreme cases, confiscating their property.

Rabbi Asher ben Yehiel[60] delivered a legal opinion in response to a query about a case in which the defendant had borrowed money from the plaintiff without giving him a note or a receipt. In order to avoid repaying his debt, the defendant gave all of his property to a third party in an attempt to take advantage of a rule, similar to the British and American rule known as the Statute of Frauds, under which the lender cannot collect from a third party if there is no written agreement. Rabbi Asher invoked a rule[61] under which the court determines the intentions of the parties and then, in order to do equity, nullifies the gift. He said that it was difficult to conceive of a stronger case for nullification than this. The defendant had no intention to give away all of his property, supporting himself thereafter by begging from house to house. His intention was clearly to circumvent the law and avoid payment of his debt. "But we cannot permit his dishonest scheme to succeed. His deviousness will not help him."[62] This conclusion was derived from rabbinical precedents based upon a biblical verse that mandates doing what is "right and good." To do what is right and good, said Rabbi Asher, means that "we must use every means to thwart his [the defendant's] plans."[63] This is, of course, reminiscent of our rule requiring violators of the securities laws to remit the profits derived from their unlawful activities to the court for suitable disposition.

This rule was invoked in the case of a major investor who was noted for his good works, his support of religious, educational and cultural institutions, and his assistance to the poor and needy. Most of the money he donated to those worthy causes derived from transactions that violated the securities laws. He was compelled to disgorge his unlawful profits, and was in addition sentenced to several years in prison. Rabbi Eliezer ben Jacob, a first-century resident of Judea, expressed an opinion that seems to fit the case very well indeed: "If a man steals some wheat and makes bread from it, separates the *hallah* (a kind of meal offering),[64] and pronounces a blessing over it, his blessing is no blessing. It is blasphemy."[65]

Much the same may be said of those persons who fail to adhere to the highest standards of ethics in the securities industry. Whatever their profits may be, and however good and worthy the purposes to which they may be devoted, to the extent that they were derived from unethical practices—fraud, failure to disclose, manipulation of the markets—they are fruits of the poisonous tree. In the end, they will not suffice to bring credit upon those who gave them or spare them from disgrace when they are exposed. The credit belongs, after all, to the persons whose assets were misappropriated and given to those worthy causes.

Congress, the SEC and the courts have made enormous progress in their quest to coerce investors and professionals in the investment business to conduct their business affairs ethically. To be sure, people *can* be compelled to behave ethically. According to some views of ethics, they may not be especially praiseworthy for having to act in ways that are not fully in consonance with their true inclinations. But an ancient Hebrew maxim says that from doing the right thing for the wrong reason, people may come to do it for the right one. In the meantime, because of the laws and rules adopted by Congress and the SEC, many innocent people who might otherwise have been seriously injured are spared from the losses they might otherwise have suffered, and the people who might have taken advantage of them are deterred. Through their teachings, educators and religious leaders encourage people to behave ethically. For those who have not fully absorbed those lessons, however, the coercive power of the law is a necessary inducement.

NOTES

1. I wish to express my appreciation and deep gratitude to my colleagues, Barbara Black, Richard Creedy and Robert Keane of Pace University, as well as my colleague, Dean Janet A. Johnson—who also happens to be my wife—for their encouragement and advice.

2. Letter of June 30, 1759, printed in Parkes, *History of the Court of Chancery* (1828), 508, quoted in *Securities and Exchange Commission v. Capital Gains Research Bureau*, 84 S.Ct. 275, 283-84, n. 41.

3. *People v. Rocha*, 130 Cal. App.2d 656, 279 P.2d 836 (1955).

4. Rollin M. Perkins, *Criminal Law*, Second Ed. (Mineola, N.Y.: Foundation Press, 1969), 311.

5. See William L. Prosser, *The Law of Torts*, Fourth Ed. (St. Paul, Minn.: West Publishing Co., 1971), 694ff.

6. H.R. No. 1383, 73rd Congress, 2d Session (April 27, 1934), 11.

7. *Ibid.*

8. *Ibid.*, 13f.

9. So called because it was said that some swindlers would sell "building lots in the blue sky" to unsuspecting investors.

10. Joel Seligman, *The SEC and the Future of Finance* (New York: Praeger Publishers, 1985), 219, 223f.

11. *Ibid.*, 222.

12. *Ibid.*, 233.

13. Hillel Black, *The Watchdogs of Wall Street* (New York: William Morrow & Co., 1962), 4ff.

14. See, e.g., *Restatement (Second) of Torts*, 551(2) (a) (1976). The American Law Institute's Proposed Official Draft (1978), Federal Securities Code, 262(b), declares that "silence when there is a duty to . . . speak may be a fraudulent act."

15. *Speed v. Transamerica Corp.*, 99 F. Supp. 808, 829 (Del. 1951).

16. See, e.g., *Lehigh Valley Trust Co. v. Central National Bank*, 409 F. 2d 989, 992 (5th Cir. 1969).

17. *Securities and Exchange Commission v. Capital Gains Research Bureau, Inc.*, 375 U.S. 180, 186, 84 S.Ct. 275 (1963).

18. *The Queen v. Coney*, 8 Q.B.D. 534, 557-58 (1882), cited in Perkins, *supra*, n. 4, 514.

19. Perkins, citing Justice Stephens, 515.

20. *Marbury v. Brooks*, 7 Wheat. 556, 20 U.S. 556, 575-76 (1822).

21. 18 U.S.C.A. Sec. 4.

22. *Roberts v. United States*, 445 U.S. 552, 63 L.Ed.2d 622, 100 S.Ct. 1358 (1980). This decision concerned a defendant who had sought a lenient sentence after pleading guilty to two counts of using a telephone to facilitate the distribution of heroin. He claimed that his refusal to cooperate with the authorities in their investigation of a related conspiracy to distribute heroin in which he was a confessed participant should not have been held against him. The Court held that his refusal to cooperate *could* be held against him in setting his penalty. However, this does not imply that he could have been punished simply for his refusal to cooperate.

23. *Branzburg v. Hayes*, 408 U.S. 665, 33 L.Ed.2d 626, 92 S.Ct. 2646 (1972), at n. 36.

24. *Lancey v. United States*, 356 F.2d 407, 410 (9th Cir.), cert. denied, 385 U.S. 922 (1966); *United States v. Andrews*, 790 F.2d 663 (10th Cir. 1986); *United States v. Ciambrone*, 750 F.2d 1416 (9th Cir. 1984). In *Ciambrone*, the defendant had given the authorities *some* information about a counterfeiting operation, but refused to divulge more without a promise of a $15,000 payment for his information. The appellate court held that he was not obliged to divulge *anything*, and therefore could not be held liable for revealing *some* truthful information about the criminal acts that he had witnessed, so long as he did not lie or mislead the authorities.

25. Lev. 19:14.

26. More formally known as Rabbi Solomon ben Isaac, 1040-1105.

27. Especially the midrash *Sifra*.

28. See Rashi's comment *ad loc.*

29. Lev., *ibid.*

30. Rashi *ad loc.*

31. Section 10(b) provides that it is unlawful for any person to use, by way of any means or instrumentality of interstate commerce or the mails or any facility of any national securities exchange, "any manipulative or deceptive device or contrivance" in connection with securities purchases or sales that contravenes the rules of the SEC. Rule 10(b)-5 says that it is unlawful to use any instrument of interstate commerce, the mails, or the facility of any securities exchange "(a) to employ any device, scheme, or artifice to defraud, (b) to make any untrue statement of a material fact or to omit to state any material fact necessary in order to make the statement made, in the light of the circumstances under which they were made, not misleading, or (c) to engage in any act, practice, or course of business which operates or would operate as a fraud or deceit upon any person, in connection with the purchase or sale of any security."

32. Lived in Italy, c. 1470-1550.

33. Ezek. 22:29.

34. The Talmud, composed of the Mishnah and the Gemara, and drawing upon various other ancient biblical commentaries and legal and ethical writings, dates from about the second century B.C.E. to about the seventh century C.E.

The most prominent codifications of Talmudic law are those of Maimonides (1135-1204) and Joseph Caro (1488-1575).

35. 332 F. Supp. 544 (E.D.N.Y. 1971).

36. *Affiliated Ute Citizens of Utah v. United States*, 406 U.S. 128, 153-54, 92 S.Ct. 1456, 1472 (1972).

37. A good example of such a situation is the Kitty Genovese case. A number of years ago, Kitty Genovese's screams aroused dozens of people in her New York neighborhood. Looking onto the street from their apartment windows, they watched her being brutally attacked and repeatedly stabbed, but no one picked up a phone to call the police. She later died of her wounds. It was obvious that the harm being inflicted on her was very grave. The risk to the neighbors, to say nothing of the cost of making a phone call, was inconsequential. Under those circumstances, they were morally blameworthy, though not legally culpable, for not notifying the authorities.

38. *Dirks v. Securities and Exchange Commission*, 463 U.S. 646, 103 S.Ct. 3255, 77 L.Ed.2d 911 (1983).

39. 21 S.E.C. Docket 1401, 1407 (1981), quoting *Chiarella v. United States*, 445 U.S. 222, 230, n.12, 100 S.Ct. 1108, 1115, n. 12, 63 L.Ed.2d 348 (1980), cited in *Dirks*, 463 U.S. at 652, 103 S.Ct. at 3260.

40. 220 U.S. App. D.C. 309, 324-25, 681 F.2d 824, 839-40.

41. 445 U.S. 222, 100 S.Ct. 1108, 63 L.Ed.2d 348 (1980).

42. *Santa Fe Industries, Inc. v. Green*, 430 U.S. 462, 472, 97 S.Ct. 1292, 1300, 51 L.Ed.2d 480 (1977).

43. 445 U.S. at 232, 100 S.Ct. at 1116.

44. 463 U.S. at 659, 103 S.Ct. at 3261-62.

45. The Court held explicitly that there must be scienter, which it defined as "a mental state embracing intent to deceive, manipulate, or defraud." In this connection, it held that motivation is "not irrelevant." "It is not enough that an insider's conduct results in harm to investors; rather a violation may be found only where there is intentional or willful conduct designed to deceive or defraud investors by controlling or artificially affecting the price of securities." 463 U.S. at 663, n. 23, 103 S.Ct. at 3266, citing *Ernst & Ernst v. Hochfelder*, 425 U.S. 185, 199, 96 S.Ct. 1375, 1383.

46. 463 U.S. at 662, 103 S.Ct. at 3265.

47. 463 U.S. at 676, 103 S.Ct. at 3273.

48. 463 U.S. at 676, n. 13, 103 S.Ct. at 3272, n. 13. Citations omitted.

49. 463 U.S. at 662, n. 21, 103 S.Ct. at 3265, n. 21.

50. *International News Service v. Associated Press*, 248 U.S. 215 (1918). The Court did hold that there was a limit to what competitors in the business of gathering the news might do with information gathered from one another, but that is not germane here. See text below, at notes 52-53.

51. *United States v. Carpenter*, 791 F.2d 1024 (2d Cir. 1986).

52. See above, n. 31.

53. *Carpenter v. United States*, 108 S.Ct. 316 (1987).

54. As in the *Associated Press* case above, n. 50.

55. The courts noted that Chiarella's conviction might have been upheld if it had been based upon the misappropriation theory.

56. See above, n. 2.

57. Rabban Shimeon ben Gamliel, *Pirke Avot (Ethics of the Fathers)*, I.

58. Isaac Aboab (14th century Spain), *Menorat Hamaor*, chap. 35.

59. *Ibid.*, chap. 32.

60. Also known as "The Rosh," c. 1250-1327 (France and Germany).

61. Known in Hebrew as *umdena*.

62. *Responsum* no. 78, in Norman Lamm, *The Good Society: Jewish Ethics in Action* (New York: Viking Press, 1974), 152.

63. *Ibid.*, 153.

64. See Numbers 15:19-21.

65. Babylonian Talmud, *Baba Kama*, 94a.

Eleven

The Future of Business Ethics

George P. Brockway

Let me start with the famous peroration of John Maynard Keynes' great book:

> Practical men, who believe themselves to be quite exempt from any intellectual influences, are usually the slaves of some defunct economist. Madmen in authority, who hear voices in the air, are distilling their frenzy from some academic scribbler of a few years back. I am sure that the power of vested interests is vastly exaggerated compared with the gradual encroachment of ideas. Not, indeed, immediately, but after a certain interval; for in the field of economic and political philosophy there are not many who are influenced by new theories after they are twenty-five or thirty years of age; so that the ideas which civil servants and politicians and even agitators apply to current events are not likely to be the newest. But, soon or late, it is ideas, not vested interests, which are dangerous for good or evil.[1]

If we can assume that Keynes was wise as well as witty, we may have here a glass through which we can peer at the probable course of business practice a generation or two in the future. I hasten to acknowledge another position of Keynes's. In his *Treatise on Probability* he wrote, "Probability begins and ends with probability,"[2] He denied, as we all must, the possibility of foreseeing the future. Yet we cannot help trying.

Before trying to look ahead, we may test Keynes' dictum about practical men by examining current business practice in the light of recent economic theory. I think it safe to say that, from Adam Smith to the present, the stream of economic thought has been remarkably unruffled. There has been nothing in it to compare with Darwin or Clerk-Maxwell or Einstein or Heisenberg or even Freud. For not quite a decade, from the publication of *The General Theory of Employment, Interest and Money* in 1936 until the Bretton Woods Conference in 1944, John Maynard

Keynes seemed to have revolutionized economic thinking. But, starting as early as 1937 with J. R. Hicks's article "Mr. Keynes and the 'Classics,' " the revolutionist was gradually subdued and is now exhibited as a sideshow to the general equilibrium analysis teetering on the high wire in the main tent. Keynes' name continued to be invoked for another thirty years, but the invocations had less and less to do with his actual writings. Joan Robinson called the self-styled Keynesians of those years "bastard Keynesians," and her anathema was surely justified when Richard Milhous Nixon fatuously intoned, as he imposed wage and price controls, "We are all Keynesians now."

Adam Smith is the father of economics because of his creation of a metaphor for a proto-mechanical world. There is irony here, for Smith was Professor of Moral Philosophy at the University of Glasgow, and his first book was entitled *The Theory of Moral Sentiments*. If I were to set myself up as a moral philosopher, I would certainly dispute the notion that sentiments are the basis of morality, but the point I want to make is that Smith's famous metaphor, "invisible hand," which appears in this first book as well as in *The Wealth of Nations*, is unequivocally amoral. The message is that good economic results (how they are to be judged good is another question) can, in certain conditions, come about automatically, regardless of anyone's intention, regardless of anyone's doing, regardless of anyone's willing.

It is a biographical fact that Smith himself did not consider his metaphor universally applicable or more than suggestive. Yet it was a world-historical idea of profound and pervasive implications. It appealed to the practical world of the commercial and industrial revolutions because its acceptance invalidated the monarch's control of, or even interference in, business affairs. It appealed to the intellectual world of the scientific revolution because it offered an impersonal, *quasi*-mechanical explanation of one aspect of human behavior. It even appealed to certain members of the religious community because the invisible hand, which might be thought of as the hand of God, was an inexorable force for good. From Smith's time to the present, the steady effort of mainstream economists—and here we must include Karl Marx—has been to show how this automatic system works, to develop a scientific or "positive" economics on the model of classical physics.

Now, what do businessmen and businesswomen learn from the economists, living and dead, who have contributed to this mainstream? In brief, they learn that their mission is to maximize their material gains, that for them to have any other motive is to foul the system, that the system will likewise be fouled by political interference, that the uncontrolled market will effect the most efficient use of scarce resources, and that the market will also effect the most appropriate division of the spoils. For the past two hundred years, these lessons have been taught implicitly by the theoretical textbooks and explicitly by such popularizations as Milton and Rose Friedman's *Free to Choose.*

Those who have learned these lessons understand that neither they nor anyone else can be blamed for whatever happens in the marketplace, regardless of what anyone thinks of it. Even Marx, who seems their most censorious critic, does not blame them. In the Preface to the first edition of *Capital* he writes, "My standpoint, from which the evolution of the economic formation of society is viewed as a process of natural history, can less than any other make the individual responsible for relations whose creature he socially remains, however much he may subjectively raise himself above them."[3]

Businessmen and businesswomen caught in sharp practice express the thought a little more simply. They are not, they say, in it for their health. Accordingly, they openly—or brazenly, if you prefer—behave in the ways we have recently been hearing all too much about. We can therefore say that, at least as regards hindsight, Keynes' dictum holds. "Practical men . . . are usually the slaves of some defunct economist."

If the dictum continues to hold for the future, we must unhappily expect more of the behavior we find reprehensible unless we can revolutionize economic theory. It will do little good to lecture people on how they ought to behave so long as we teach them that they are naturally programmed to behave otherwise. As Professor John William Miller used to say, "Where everything is as it must be, nothing can become what it ought to be."

Of course, it would also do little good to try to revolutionize economic theory just because it fails to yield consequences of which we approve. There is a voluminous literature arguing whether the assumptions of conventional economics are or are not "realistic." This is an entirely proper question but one beset by quiddities. To show conclusively that conventional economics fails, we must show that it fails on its own terms, that it is self-contradictory, absurd, or otherwise fallacious. I think that such showings can be made, and in the rest of this paper I will try to suggest a few ways in which it can be done—must be done.

The Problem Is Price . . . the Solution Is Value

Most, if not all, of what I shall talk about comes from that division of economics known as value theory. The invisible hand operates through the price system, and the merest glance at the world tells us that prices jump around. In fact, most of what passes for finance concerns trying to anticipate and manipulate price movements. Nothing like this happens in science proper, where the solar system is staid and reliable. The very regularity of the auto-immune system makes its breakdown, in AIDS, understandable and, we hope, curable. But prices are erratic and cry out for explanation. Where do they come from? How are they set? Why do they change? No economic science can be built unless these shifting sands are stabilized. Value theory answers these questions by calling up underlying, fundamental and at least partially hidden forces. The problem is Price, and the solution is Value.

Several answers have been given. Let us look at four of them: supply and demand, cost, utility, and labor. They are not mutually exclusive but tend to run together. It will, nevertheless, be convenient to consider them separately.

We all learned about supply and demand at our mother's knee. If food is scarce and hungry people numerous (both propositions mean the same thing), the price of food will be high. If food production is high but food consumption low, the price of food will be low. This is perfectly obvious and understandable. It would be foolish of me to starve to death rather than pay all I could for food, and it would be foolish to pay more for food than desperate sellers would be asking.

These examples make us a little uneasy. My behavior as a starving man is rational enough, but what about the man who has scarce food to sell? He is taking advantage of my misery. He is a profiteer, and over the years many of his ilk have been lynched by outraged mobs. To be sure, he was smart enough or lucky enough to have stored food during the fat years against the lean years. Joseph did this, and turned the freeholders of Egypt into sharecroppers. We are told that the subjects of the pharaoh were grateful because otherwise they would have perished, but it is not easy to escape the reflection that he could have saved them without impoverishing them.

A more antiseptic term for a food profiteer is monopolist. While some monopolists are profiteers, many are not. There are usually substitutes available for any scarce commodity; while a stone will not serve the purposes of bread, cake may. Again, many scarce commodities are scarcely essential: thousands of philatelists would like to have one of the one hundred copies of the 1918 twenty-four-cent airmail stamp with an inverted center, but no one will die or suffer substantial distress for the lack of one.

From the point of view of the consumer, things are clearly more comfortable if monopolists are few and unimportant. When no one controls a market, no one controls either buyers or sellers. Thus, the ideal market is served by many competitors producing many interchangeable goods. To forestall cartels, producers must be able to enter or leave the market easily. There must be many consumers, too, for a monopsonist can control a market as readily as a monopolist: a manufacturer who has only one buyer for his/her product is at the mercy of that buyer—unless he or she is able to co-opt the buyer, as our arms merchants do the Department of Defense.

When many producers can supply easily substitutable goods, all have to take the price the market will bear. Even the giant oligopolies of the *Fortune* 500 are too small in relation to the total market to set their prices as they please, as the automobile companies have recently discovered. They are price takers. On the other hand, if I want to buy a car, I haven't much choice in what I have to pay. The president of General Motors does not care whether I buy one of his cars or not. There are too many like me. I am a price taker.

In a freely competitive world, every buyer and every seller—that is, everyone—is a price taker. From where, then, do prices come? They come from the reconciliation of supply and demand. The market sets the price. We have here an impersonal process, an automatic process, one that no person controls and hence all persons can enjoy. It is a Cartesian paradise.

No, it is a pathetic fallacy. A market cannot do anything. It is a place, a condition; not an agent, a doer. Of course, it is a figure of speech. No one pretends that the market literally sets prices. How could it? It cannot speak or read or write or make gestures. Yet prices are somehow set. What actual event is hinted at by this figure of speech?

The textbooks reply that there are two curves, a supply curve rising gracefully upward to the right, showing that more goods are supplied as the price is raised, and a demand curve, falling gracefully downward to the right, showing that more goods are demanded as the price is lowered. Where the two curves cross is the price that the market is supposed to set. It is said, moreover, that at this price the market is cleared; all that is brought to market is sold, and there is no incentive to bring more.

Every business person knows that this is not the way the world turns. Something like this may be imagined by market research, but the curves that predicted the success of the Edsel were scarcely objective in the sense that a graph of Boyle's Law, relating pressure and heat, is objective. In the market, what is objective is the price. Supply and demand are determined by price, not the other way around. Demand is not what I would like to have, or even what I desperately need, or even what I might buy. All that is formless and indeterminate. Demand is what I actually buy at the price offered. Supply, too, is indeterminate. A novel nobody wants to read is not, as a book, a factor in supply; it may, however, be a supply of scrap paper, and be eagerly sought after as such. In short, supply and demand are dependent variables; the independent variable is price.

Supply and demand are always equal, at any price; their equality follows from their definition. Supply is what is sold, which necessarily equals what is bought, which is demand. More important, the whole idea of market clearing is foreign to the idea of business enterprise. I want the market to be cleared if I am auctioning off my goods and chattels; but if I am in business, I want to stay in business. If I am a book publisher, I do not close up shop when I sell an edition of an ethics textbook. I look around for another book to publish; I must publish or perish, and I set my prices accordingly. In the same way, even a fishmonger, whose wares must be sold today, sets his prices with an eye to tomorrow's business.

At this point cost becomes a factor. In setting prices for a continuing business, I must consider what it will cost me to reproduce or replenish my supply. Yesterday's costs are sunk, but tomorrow's must be met. Everyone's business has the same problem, hence it seems reasonable to say that price is determined by cost. This, however, is a fallacy of composition, for my cost is my suppliers' prices, and their costs are their suppliers' prices, and so on *ad infinitum*. No supplier is without costs, which are somebody else's prices, so the regress is infinite and ultimately involuted.

The only way to stop an infinite regress is not to let it get started and, of course, this one does not get started in the real world. What actually happens, whether on the book market or the fish market, is that some person—some willful human being or corporation of human beings—for some reason names a price for some commodity, and some other willful human being accepts it. If, for whatever reason, no one names a price, or if no one accepts a price, nothing happens; the parvis of the cathedral is gaily decorated with tents and banners and filled with laughing and singing throngs, but nothing happens.

If value theory stops here, the invisible hand is impotent, and economic activity depends on the reasoning of willful human beings. No proper science could stop here; the solar system does not depend on what anyone thinks about Venus or Mars.

Utilitarianism

Thirteen years after the invisible hand had its epiphany in *The Wealth of Nations*, another world-historical idea was launched—Jeremy Bentham's utilitarianism. It sought some impersonal factor of personality, and it aimed from the start at being mathematical. Bentham developed what he called the "felicific calculus," which assigned utility values to commodities in accordance with their contribution to pleasure or to the avoidance of pain. Bentham thought his calculus objective in the same way Newton's laws of motion were objective. Of course, it was not.

What is astonishing is that the idea has hung on for so long. Even today power company lawyers talk solemnly about the "utils" of satisfaction their services afford their customers. Bentham himself pointed to a fatal weakness. "Quantity of pleasure being the same," he said aphoristically, "pushpin is as good as poetry." In other words, one man's pleasure is another man's pain, and both are private. What is useful is what provides pleasure or enables the avoidance of pain, but pleasure and pain are exquisitely subjective. As the old wheeze has it, a sadist is one who gives pleasure to masochists. It would be arbitrary for you to insist that I really derive pleasure from something I say pains me. How could you know? Pierre Dumont, who translated Bentham into French, put it baldly: "Everyone will constitute himself judge of his own utility."

In spite of its inescapable subjectivism, utilitarianism has still tantalized the 19th century mind. Independently and almost simultaneously, three writers—Léon Walras in Switzerland, Carl Menger in Austria, and W. Stanley Jevons in England—hit upon the idea of marginal utility, which seemed to them and still seems to most economists today to purge the theory of its subjective taint. It was done by means of the differential calculus.

Walras defined the role of the calculus as follows: "We may say in ordinary language, 'The desire that we have of things, or the utility that things have for us, diminishes in proportion to the consumption. The more a man eats, the less hungry he is; the more he drinks, the less thirsty, at least in general and saving certain regrettable exceptions. . . .' But in mathematical terms we say, 'The intensity of the last desire satisfied is a decreasing function of the quantity of commodity consumed' . . . . It is not an appreciable quantity, but it is only necessary to conceive it in order to found upon the fact of its dimunition the demonstration of the great laws of pure political economy."[4]

Because of this conceivable but nonappreciable quantity, it is possible for each of us to rank our utilities and to make mathematically reasonable choices. Economists tend to talk of equally (or "indifferently") desirable commodities, but if trade is to occur at all, some commodity seems at the moment of trading more desirable than all others.

In the same way, infinitesimal differences will recommend one investment over another and over all others. In each industry one firm will become strongest in resources and most successful in trading. The outcome is described by Walras:

> If, in short, at a given point, a certain quantity of manufactured products corresponds to the absence of gain and loss [that is, if price equals cost], the parties in the transaction who manufactured less take the losses, restrain their production, and finish by liquidating; those who manufactured more take the gains, develop their production, and attract to themselves the business of others; thus. . . . production in free competition, after being engaged in a great number of small enterprises, tends to distribute itself among a number less great of medium enterprises, then among a small number of great enterprises, to end finally, first in a *monopoly at cost price,* then in a *monopoly at price of maximum gain.*

As Walras comments, "This statement is corroborated by the facts."[5]

From this unexceptionable analysis, we must infer that on the assumptions of marginal utility, free competition is impossible except perhaps as a transient initial point. Since free competition is itself an assumption of marginal utility, we might expect the theory to have been abandoned at this point. Instead, the contradiction was swept under the rug, just as Adam Smith blithely continued to rely on competition and the invisible hand even though fully aware that "To widen the market and to narrow the competition, is always to the interest of the dealers . . . an order of men, whose interest is never exactly the same with that of the public, and who accordingly have, on many occasions, both deceived and oppressed it."[6]

It may also be observed that Walras did not pursue the calculus as far as it will go. Infinitesimal differences will enforce preference of one industry over all others, just as one firm is preferred within each industry. The really final end will be one firm making one product; and complete analysis might well determine that the single firm had a single owner, a single employee, and a single customer for its single product, whose sale is a single apocalyptic event.

Such a conclusion is obviously absurd, but it is not mathematically absurd. Mathematically it is elegant. The outcome is, moreover, perfectly congruent with the traditional theory of free competition, which contemplates the reduction of price to cost, the survival of the fittest enterprise, the cost-effective settling of each industry on its "best" product, and the flocking of investors to the most profitable industry. In the world we live and move in, it is an historical fact that this absurd conclusion has so far been avoided. The bright radiance of pure political economy is necessarily stained by the willful actions of us poor mortals, whose last desires satisfied are not imaginary utils but historical or biographical facts—which is fortunate, since whatever the ultimate single product proved to be, the final single consumer would either starve to death or choke to death on it, provided that he (or she) did not sooner die of boredom.

Even when not reduced to absurdity, the calculus of marginal utility did not claim to do more than rank utilities for a given individual, and that at a given moment. The pleasure Keynes derived from the ballet and the pleasure I derive from reading him cannot be compared, nor can exchanges be explained mathematically. It turns out that, on the assumptions of profit maximization and free competition, nothing happens. No exchange takes place, and so no exchange value appears.

Surprising authority for this judgment is Léon Walras himself, who writes, "What reason is there to exchange net income against net income, to sell, for example, a house yielding 2,500 francs in rentals for 100,000 francs, only to buy a piece of land for 100,000 francs yielding 2,500 francs in rent? Such an exchange of one capital good for another makes no more sense than the exchange of a commodity for itself." Then he adds, "To understand why purchases and sales take place in the market for capital goods we have to fall back upon certain crucial facts of experience in the world of reality."[7] Quite so. As Pogo might say, we have met these crucial facts, and they are us.

Walras talks only of production goods, but Carl Menger, the second of the independent developers of marginal utility, made a more general observation:

> Commodities that can be exchanged against each other in certain definite quantities (a sum of money and a quantity of some other economic good, for example), that can be exchanged for each other at will by a *sale* or a *purchase*, in short, commodities that are *equivalents in the objective sense of the term*, do not exist—even on given markets and at a given point in time. And what is more important, deeper understanding of the causes that lead to the exchange of goods and to human trade in general teaches us that equivalents of this sort are utterly impossible in the very nature of the case and cannot exist in reality at all.[8]

It is easy enough to see why mathematics is helpless to explain economic exchange. I will exchange my cow for your wheat because, for whatever reason, I would rather have the wheat; you are willing to consummate the deal because you would rather have the cow. Neither one of us considers the cow and the wheat of equal value, so the mathematics of equalities is irrelevant. But the mathematics of inequalities is bewildered, because our evaluations are and must be contradictory. $C_y > W_y = C_m < W_m$ will do as mathematical notation of an exchange embodying your and my valuations of cow and wheat, but it leaves us with four unknowns and only one equation.

There is another point to be made about utility, marginal or otherwise. Utility, we remember, was invoked to explain price. The question then becomes: How do we know what has utility, what affords pleasure or suppresses pain? W. Stanley Jevons, the third of our triumvirate (although actually the first in time) has the answer. In his classic exposition of marginal utility, he calls for increased efforts to collect economic statistics. "The price of a commodity," he writes, "is the only test we have of the utility of the commodity to the purchaser. . . ."[9] And, he might have added, to the seller, too. The theory says that price is explained by utility but, unhappily, all we know of utility is price. We are back where we started.

The same point had, indeed, been made sixty-eight years earlier by Jean-Baptiste Say who, after a brief period of disgrace during the Depression (he held that a universal glut was impossible), is again in favor. He wrote ". . . price is the measure of the value of things, and their value is the measure of their utility. . . ."[10] Although Say's observation destroyed the foundations of marginal utility nearly two hundred years ago, almost before Bentham finished pouring the footings and, although Jevons destroyed the framing even as he erected it one hundred plus years ago, this dizzily circular argument is today the leading doctrine taught in American universities, and Nobel Memorial Prizes are awarded for recondite mathematical refinements of it.

Labor Theory of Value

Almost every economist has espoused some form of the labor theory of value. Yet it is a matter of common observation that the amount of labor required to produce a commodity has almost nothing to do with its price or with its value. A house in the Houston suburbs, which was worth a quarter of a million dollars a few years ago, can be had for half that price today. It is the same house, and the amount of labor it embodies is the same, if not actually more. Or consider: It took much labor to install asbestos ceilings in classrooms; but the asbestos was worse than valueless; it was harmful and had to be removed—with the expenditure of more labor. Marx sought to get around such difficulties by insisting on socially useful labor. Socially useful labor is labor that produces a socially useful product. Thus it is not labor that is the test of value, it is value that is the test of labor. A corrupt tree bringeth forth evil fruit, but the evil fruit proves the tree to be corrupt, not the other way around.

David Ricardo thought it was an error to look for value in what labor produced or in the time it took to produce it. In contrast, he argued that value was measured by what it took to keep the laborer producing. He wrote, "The natural price of labor is that price which is necessary to enable the laborers, one with another, to subsist and to perpetuate their race, without either increase or diminution." He recognized that the market price could fall below the natural price, making their condition "most wretched," but he argued that the birth rate—or the mortality rate—would bring the prices together again. His friend, Thomas Malthus, made fun of his contention that a higher market price would cause laborers to produce more children—a crop that would take sixteen or eighteen years to ripen. Nevertheless, Ricardo maintained that the natural price of labor depends "on the price of the food, necessaries, and conveniences required for the support of the laborer and his family."[11] But the price of labor disappears into the same infinite regress that we have seen swallow up costs in general.

Finally, the recently popular version of the invisible hand that preens itself with the name of rational expectations is self-defeating in another way. The argument says that government can do nothing to regulate business because business will rationally anticipate the moves and offset them in advance. But businesses are in an adversary relationship with each other as well as with the government, and every competitive move can similarly be anticipated and forestalled. Every action of every business as well as every action of government is defeated by rational expectations. Defeat being inevitable, the thing for everyone to do is to lie back and do nothing.

Now, I can scarcely pretend even to have adumbrated the eddies of mainstream economics, but I do brashly claim that nothing will surface in any of them that will seriously upset the even course of our argument. We have seen that price, not supply and demand, is the independent variable, and that prices are set by willful men and women, not by an impersonal market. We have seen that the same is true of cost, including the cost of labor, and that the price men and women actually pay for something, which is the price other men and women actually sell it for, is the only economic evidence we have of its value to them.

If we had world enough and time we should find ourselves driven to conclude, in every case, that economics is the study of the principles whereby people exchange money for goods and services. This is a radical conclusion. The most important word in it is "people." In contrast, Adam Smith's subject was the wealth of nations, while modern schools busy themselves either with the gross national product or with a putative equilibrium of impersonal forces.

Walras, who was no amoralist, distinguished at considerable length between economics as an ethical science (which his followers today would not recognize); as an art, which taught how to achieve moral ends; and as pure science, which taught how it worked. Toward the close of the 19th century, John Neville Keynes, the father of John Maynard, made a similar tripartite analysis. In our day, Milton Friedman, perhaps indulging a puckish humor, has quoted favorably from the senior Keynes' work.

But there is no such thing as pure economics. Physics can be studied—must be studied—without regard to the willful act of any individual or any group of individuals. (This is not to deny that it takes a willful man or woman to be a physicist.) But there are no antiseptic events in economics. Walras, whose work was hailed by Joseph Schumpeter as "the only work of an economist that will stand comparison with the achievements of theoretical physics,"[12] opened his analysis, after a long introduction, with the observation, "Value in exchange, when left to itself, arises spontaneously in the market as the result of competition." But this pure proposition is immediately corrupted by willful humanity: "As buyers, traders make their *demands* by *outbidding* each other. As sellers, traders make their *offers* by *underbidding* each other."[13]

Without those traders making their demands and offers, there is no economics, pure or applied. With those traders, economics becomes inextricably immersed in questions of morals. I do not mean merely that trade is impossible unless traders abjure fraud (at least up to a point), although certainly this is true. What I mean is that demands and offers— the fundamental elements of "pure" economics—are not acts of God or events of nature but acts of human beings who necessarily define themselves by what they do, including especially what they do in the marketplace. Perhaps more to the point: Demands and offers can be *understood* only as acts of will.

Ethics and Economics

Economics is, therefore, an ethical discipline, a normative discipline, a humanist discipline, an historical discipline. It is ethical, normative, humanist, and historical through and through—not just on holidays, nor just for show, nor because of the goodwill value of an appearance of honesty. Ethics is there at the beginning, or it is not there at all.

Ethics is excluded from the pseudo-science we have studied for the past two centuries; so it is also excluded from the business practices that are based on that pseudo-science. Instead of ethics, sophists have taught a sort of prudence. You must not cheat, they have said, because the policeman on the corner will find out about your cheating, and the notoriety will hurt your business. But does anyone imagine that all cheating is found out? A merely prudent man might think it not too difficult to avoid being found out. You can sincerely want to be rich and still stop short of the splendors of Ivan Boesky. Well, ethics has nothing to do with prudence, anyhow.

Economists are always supposing, so let us suppose that we had an ethical economics. What would it be like? I can make a few suggestions. It would be concerned with people rather than with things. Its goal would be full and fair employment, not because more goods and services would be produced that way, but because more people would have more self-respect that way. It would distribute its opportunities and rewards much more evenly than we do today, because we are nearly equal in our capacities and absolutely equal in our worth.

As we explored these goals, I think we would be persuaded to try certain policies. I think we would come to agree with Keynes that demand, not saving or investment, is the key, at least in the present state of the economy. I think we would come to agree with Keynes, again, that finance should not be run like a casino. I think we would come to understand that, whether or not small is beautiful, big is ugly, not because it is inefficient, but because it reduces too many of us to automatons. I think we would come to see, with John R. Commons, that the virtue of capitalism is that its face is turned toward opportunities, toward expanding horizons, toward the future. I think, finally, that all of us have the right to participate in those opportunities, and that we can enforce that right only through ownership of the corporations which employ us; and I think that we earn the right to ownership by our labor. Therefore I propose the labor theory of right to supplant the labor theory of value.

What does all this tell us of the future of ethics in business and finance? It would be brash to expect much change because it would be brash to expect much change in economic theory. Change here is rendered the less likely because of the extraordinary popularity among social scientists of the ideas of Vilfredo Pareto, Walras' successor at the University of Lausanne.

Using a *quasi*-Greek word because he thought "utility" had unfortunate connotations, Pareto wrote: "We will say that the members of a collectivity enjoy *maximum ophelimity* in a certain position when it is impossible to find a way of moving from that position very slightly in such a manner that the ophelimity enjoyed by each of the individuals of that collectivity increases or decreases."[14] In other words, Pareto wants everyone to go up (or down) more or less together.

At first glance, Pareto's insistence on togetherness is a puzzle. Surely German society was improved by the downfall of the Nazis. He was, I think, pushed in this direction because there is no mathematical way of balancing your happiness against my sorrow. Regardless of various ingenious marginalist proposals, including Pareto's own use of F. I. Edgeworth's "boxes," the two states or situations are simply incommensurable. Of course, our situations are also incommensurable even if we are both happy; so Pareto cannot care by how much we are happier, so long as no one is unhappy.

But mark the consequence for public policy. I cannot offhand think of a policy, otherwise admittedly beneficial, that would not be to someone's disadvantage. The famous rising tide may raise most ships, not all of them, because some leak and sink. This being so, Pareto's scheme amounts to an endorsement of the *status quo*. We must look for change elsewhere.

In the meantime, we should do well to remember that ethics in economics or business is not a special problem. There has been doubt about the relevance (that memorable word) of ethics in economics but, once this doubt is resolved, the remaining problems, though knotty, are well understood. Distinguishing right from wrong in business (if it is to be done at all) is no harder than it is in marriage or public service or even sports. Nor is it any different. Ethics concerns all action. It inheres in everything we do. We perform ethical acts all the time, just as we ordinarily talk in prose, whether we intend to or not.

But I will say again that conventional economics is a world-historical idea. It is not trivial. It did not spring up casually. Economics was not split off from ethics by accident. The split would not have occurred if it had not satisfied an urgent need strongly felt by intelligent, vital and sincerely troubled men and women. The need, then as now, was for a revolution in ethics. Dogmatic moralism was no longer tolerable, but it was so domineering that the only escape from it seemed to be the denial of ethics altogether. This is where we are now.

The reform of business requires the reform of economics, and the reform of economics requires the reform of ethics. We had better get on with it.

NOTES

1. Keynes, John Maynard. *The General Theory of Employment, Interest and Money*. New York: Harcourt, Brace, 1936, pp. 383-384.

2. Keynes, John Maynard. *A Treatise on Probability*. New York: St. Martin, 1973, p. 356.

3. Marx, Karl. *Capital*. New York, Modern Library, n. d., p. 15.

4. Walras, Léon. "Geometrical Theory of the Determination of Prices," *Annals of the American Academy of Political and Social Science*, July 1892, pp. 47-48.

5. *Ibid.*, p. 57.

6. Smith, Adam. *The Wealth of Nations*. New York: Modern Library, n.d., p. 250.

7. Walras, Léon. *Elements of Pure Economics*. Philadelphia: Orion Editions, 1984, p. 310.

8. Menger, Carl. *Principles of Economics*. New York: New York University Press, 1976, p. 193.

9. Jevons, W. Stanley. *The Theory of Political Economy*, 5th ed. New York: Kelley, 1965, p. 146.

10. Say, Jean-Baptiste. *A Treatise on Political Economy*. New York: Kelley, 1971, p. 62.

11. Ricardo, David. *The Principles of Political Economy*. New York: Everyman's, 1973, p. 52.

12. Schumpeter, Joseph A. *History of Economic Analysis*. New York: Oxford University Press, 1954, p. 827.

13. Walras, *Elements*, p. 83.

14. Pareto, Vilfredo. *Manual of Political Economy*. New York: Kelley, 1971, p. 261.

Part IV

Towards an Ethic of the Investment Industry

Both the unfettered market and the welfare state approaches have proven inadequate. Missing in both is a balanced view of human reality. Although we should never lose sight of the dignity, importance and value of individual persons, we cannot ignore their life in community and human solidarity. We cannot ignore, or consider in passing—as our ideology has for the past hundred years—the common good.

> Richard De George
> from an essay in
> *The Common Good and*
> *U.S. Capitalism*

This generation of managers will be judged in large measure according to its ability to make sound ethical choices and just not for bottom-line results.

> Ronald Berenbein
> *The Wall Street Journal*
> July 15, 1988

When each citizen acts with the maximal practical intelligence that he can bring to bear upon the economic activities in which he is engaged, he adds to the degree of social intelligence available in his environment. When all other economic activists conduct their affairs with equivalent practical intelligence, then the entire social texture is rendered more luminous by the cumulative effect of all such acts.

> Michael Novak
> from an essay in
> *The Common Good and*
> *U.S. Capitalism*

Part IV consists of three essays by highly respected commentators. The first is by one of the leading scholars in the field of business ethics. Richard DeGeorge analyzes the many demands for a greater role for ethics within the investment industry. The second paper is by a former academic dean of the Columbia University School of Business and a past president of Catholic University of America. He examines the ethical climate of the investment industry and offers a negative assessment of its vitality: " . . . a long process of deterioration . . . Slowly, Surely,—but downward . . . " The final article is by the president of Union Theological Seminary in York City. Located in Morningside Heights, near Columbia University, the author has a unique vantage point to examine Wall Street's practices, achievements and excesses.

Ethics and the Financial Community

Richard DeGeorge, professor of ethics at the University of Kansas, begins his essay by examining several reactions to the current scandals that have rocked the financial world. Reactions are presented from people within the investment industry, from professors of law and business and, finally, from several political leaders. One response from the financial community was the $30 million gift to the Harvard Graduate School of Business to strengthen the study and teaching of ethics. DeGeorge suggests that the assumption with this endowment is that the scandal is not the industry's fault but more the failure of educational institutions, particularly business schools, to prepare adequately their students in ethical reflection. He finds this criticism to be wrong-headed: "They assumed that somehow a course in business ethics would have changed the actions of those people caught in their illegal insider trading." He points out that those engaged in the illegal activity knew they were committing a wrong; witness the lengths they went to cover their criminal acts. He suggests that the will to withstand the temptation to break a law cannot be provided by a course in business ethics. Although not a panacea, a course can make a contribution to a broader understanding of the social purpose of the law, thereby enhancing legal compliance. In addition, he details the need for higher standards of critical ethics:

> In teaching critical ethics, one tries to determine not only which actions are considered right or wrong, but the reasons for their being so characterized. If insider trading is unethical, and has correctly been made illegal, the task for those in business ethics is to show why these judgments are correct. When this is taught to students—or more importantly when students are taught how to make this evaluation for themselves—such understanding presumably will help motivate them to avoid such actions.

There is another chorus of reactions to the scandals, those who claim that the actions of inside traders like Levine and Boesky should not be illegal because these practices make the market more efficient. Professor DeGeorge counters the efficiency position by arguing that beyond the need for efficient markets is the need for a perception of fairness by the participants: "Unless traders in the market believe that the market is fair and that all participating in it trade on equal terms, they will not have confidence in it."

The third reaction is that of the political community arguing for a need for change. There have been many calls for new legislation strengthening securities law as it pertains to such tactics as hostile take-overs, greenmail, leveraged buy-outs, poison pills and many other disputable practices. Richard DeGeorge questions these proposed changes: ". . .we should not, without compelling reason, make actions illegal that are not unethical." For example, he believes that proponents of new legislation have not made the case that hostile takeovers are unethical. However, although he is convinced that hostile takeovers should not be made illegal, he acknowledges that there are unethical means of pursuing these takeovers and suggests that such unethical strategies be outlawed.

Richard DeGeorge's prescription for the scandal-rocked financial industry calls first for a careful examination of the changes and practices of the last fifteen years. He is not optimistic that reform will come easy:

> If deep change is necessary, it cannot be achieved without a good deal of opposition. For those in the financial industry, any change will mean that someone who is now making impressive amounts of money will no longer be able to do so in that way. Any correction of the system will initially hurt some—perhaps many—people. But the price of ethical overhaul is one worth making for the long-run good of society as a whole.

> Ethics is no panacea. Neither teaching ethics nor trying to act ethically will solve all the problems of finance. But applying ethics to finance can keep the system from going further astray, repair its present badly tarnished reputation, and help it maintain its rewon respectability. Those in finance can hardly afford now or in the future to ignore ethical norms or to avoid considering and abiding by them in their practices and dealings. The challenge of thinking and acting ethically means going beyond vested interests, short-term profits, and conventional morality to consider the investment community's role and actions from the perspective of the common good.

The Struggle for Honesty and Trust

The second essay, by Clarence Walton, a long-time member of the business faculty at Columbia University, sounds a pessimistic note; he quotes the former dean of Cornell's business school, Justin Davidson: "In the night of values, we see no star. Hard times, yet not as hard as those that may follow." He supports this view by citing the following evidence: the decline of America's industrial preeminence; the Wall Street shennanigans; and hostile takeovers, a phenomenon he views as having gone through a transition from "needed interventions" to "unnecessary invasions." He goes on to emphasize that the cracks and potholes of Wall Street reflect similar cracks in Main Street—the larger society.

For Clarence Walton, social culture is the "lived ethic" that holds a particular people—for example, U.S. citizens—together. In discussing this social glue, he refers to de Tocqueville, who said that society is held together by its mores—"the habits of the heart." Many of Wall Street's deficiencies can be traced to the larger society's cultural weaknesses:

> In the United States there is nothing intrinsically wrong in a zest for money. But the line between zest and greed is easily blurred when stakes are higher and rewards are munificent. To sum up: investment bankers, like other Americans, are interested in money; if things are somewhat askew on Wall Street, they are also askew on Main Street. Perhaps the major difference between the two is that denizens of the first have more opportunities than others and that their contributions to today's society are more suspect.

Walton argues that a complicating factor is the fact that "paper entrepreneurs" from such industries as banking, accounting and law produce little of tangible value, yet they have become the new "corporate mandarins." He claims that in 1950 only thirteen percent of America's chief executives had backgrounds in finance or law where today that figure has escalated to forty percent with the result being that they ". . .are slicing, dicing, chopping and reassembling American business and thereby accelerating the decline of U. S. competitiveness."

Clarence Walton offers a corrective based on a revitalized agency theory; if the responsibilities of owners, managers and investment bankers are based on long-term trust, then there will not be wasteful expenses and litigation. This agency relationship, relying on mutual trust, has immense implications for risk and information theory: "When insider trading and parking practices are joined to misleading rumors deliberately concocted by arbitrageurs or when appraisals of a company's worth are jockeyed to suit the occasion, the moral state of investment banking begins to look Kafkaesque." Walton focuses on the industry's fundamental human need to communicate honestly and sincerely in long-term relationships between owners and managers and between managers and investment bankers, otherwise the twin pillars of honesty and trust are shaken and the industry dies.

In a postscript, Walton proposes some questions that may spur on the cause of reform. Are investigations into the moral character of job applicants warranted and, if so, how does one so investigate? Will industry sponsored training programs be needed to raise consciousness about ethical issues? Will new and more strict codes of institutional and individual conduct be necessary? Should "audit teams" be created within firms to insure ethical conduct?

God and Wall Street

Donald Shriver is the president of Union Theological Seminary, New York City. While hesitant to write an essay titled "God and Wall Street," he was willing to discuss the affairs of Wall Street in light of Christian faith. He asks some fundamental questions. Where did the human journey originate? Where is it going? What good reasons are there to continue participating in it? These questions put Wall Street and the financial community into some kind of perspective. The dimensions of his answers to these fundamental questions can be appraised by the following story he relates:

> Just before his fall, Ivan Boesky told the graduating class of U.C.L.A. that one could be greedy and "feel good about yourself." That is one form of self interest, but in reply one has to ask what sort of self Mr. Boesky is interested in. Little in his Jewish or my Christian heritage suggests that we are destined by our Creator to enrich ourselves, without limit, at the expense of other people's misfortunes. That, by definition, is what greed is. In the Bible greed is sin. In our economic system it makes some rich while making others poor. These days Mr. Boesky is studying the Talmud across the street in my neighboring institution, the Jewish Theological Seminary. I rather hope that somewhere in that text he stumbles over some classic Jewish arguments against the ethic he propounded to those graduating seniors in California.

As a theologian, Shriver argues that a religious vision can be the horizon of human judgment and valuation. Given his background and professional commitment, there is little here that should be surprising. He advocates some criteria for the investment industry that grow out of this religious perspective. An investment is good:

—when it increases the ability of the weakest people of society to meet their basic needs,

—when profit from the investment has its origin and benefit in the work of the spectrum of people . . . who use the investment . . . and

—when the investment offers individuals and groups incentive to serve some social good beyond themselves.

Likewise, his religious vision provides indices of *misservice* to the social and common good:

—when it inflicts large penalties on any group of people without providing them either direct or indirect rewards . . .

—when its long-range harms to majorities outweigh its short-range benefit to a minority . . .

—when the major result of the investment is to make the rich richer and the poor no better or worse off . . .

Both the above positive and negative criteria are the essence of what he characterizes as "moral capitalism." Shriver believes that the religious person cannot settle for anything less, even if there is risk to profits and personal gain.

Twelve

Ethics and the Financial Community: An Overview

Richard T. De George

The Levine-Boesky and related insider trading scandals rocked the financial world in the first half of 1987. The spectacle of rich, important financial titans being led in handcuffs from their offices somewhat tarnished the glow of investment banking. The popular reaction was mixed. Some people reacted with a sense of mild amusement and pleasure at the sight of the rich and powerful tumbling. Others reacted with a cynical shrug at what they considered to be typical business behavior.

Three other reactions are especially noteworthy: that of some people in the investment community itself; that of some professors of business and law; and that of some politicians. All three of these reactions tended to focus narrowly on the scandals and from this point of view they are all conservative. They start from the assumption that the system is basically sound, and that all it needs is some fine tuning to rule out some subtle abuses.

After looking a little closer at each of the three, I shall suggest what business ethics can offer in this situation.

I

BUSINESS ETHICS HAS A ROLE TO PLAY, BUT IT IS NOT THE ROLE THAT MANY HAVE IN MIND WHEN THEY CALL FOR MORE BUSINESS ETHICS TO BE TAUGHT IN BUSINESS SCHOOLS.

The dominant chord in the reaction of those from the investment community who spoke on the scandals was a call for the teaching of business ethics in the schools of business. The chorus was led by John Shad,[1] former head of the SEC, who contributed most of a $30,000,000 gift to the Harvard Business School to strengthen the teaching of business ethics there. Such a call implicitly put the blame for the scandals on the business schools. It implied that the deficiency in the investment community was to be found in individual bad apples. And it expected the business schools either to identify such individuals and prevent them from entry into finance (perhaps by not granting them MBAs) or to reform them before granting them an MBA. This reaction implicitly exonerated the investment firms of any responsibility, and implicitly said that the system of capital financing in general was sound and ethically defensible. If only those business schools would teach ethics, everything else could be left in place and we could return to doing business as usual.

Those who voiced this reaction not only deflected attention from the financial industry, but they also made certain questionable assumptions about business schools. They assumed that somehow a course in business ethics would have changed the actions of those people caught in their illegal insider trading. Those who suggested this believed that although *they* knew the action in question was ethically wrong—whether or not they ever had a course in business ethics—somehow those caught did not, or that those caught knew the action was wrong but needed motivation to act as they knew they should, which could have been provided by a business ethics course.

To believe that the people who wrote to newspapers in this vein and that the ordinary person reading the newspaper knew that the action was unethical—as well as illegal—but that those caught did not, seems implausible. Those who acted on their inside information knew they were breaking the law. The evidence is clear from the lengths to which they went in covering up their activity. They did not simply engage in some unusual trading. Possibly they did not think of the ethics of the action, perhaps believing that ethics was beside the point, or that since "everyone was doing it" it was acceptable behavior.[2] A course in business ethics could point out to them what everyone else seems to know—namely, that the action is unethical. It is doubtful whether a course in business ethics would prevent someone who knew that an action was illegal from doing it. Moral motivation sufficient to overcome not only moral injunctions but also legal prohibitions cannot usually be provided by any course, even a course in business ethics.

One may then question the good of a course in business ethics. For either the ordinary students know insider trading of the Boesky variety is illegal and immoral, and so do not need to be told that in a course or, even if told, the telling is not sufficient to motivate them not to perform the action when the allure of millions of dollars is the alternative. The conclusion is that in either case a course in business ethics is not the solution to illegal and unethical insider trading.

The conclusion seems to me correct. We should not expect business ethics courses to do what they cannot do. Hence we should not look to courses in business ethics as some sort of panacea or as an easy answer to unethical and illegal activities in business.

Agreeing that a course in business ethics is not the solution to illegal insider trading is not the same as saying that such courses are useless. But those who call for business ethics in the business schools have a certain view of what such courses should do—a view that is both unrealistic and often based on a false idea of what such courses are or should be.

Many who call for such courses want them to teach MBA students the rules accepted by the respected members of the business community as if such acceptance made them ethical rules. In the case of arbitrageurs, the rules they want taught are the rules held by the old hands who conducted mergers and takeovers at the rate of a few a year.[3] They claim that there is only one morality, and we all know what that is.[4] They then lament that those who teach business ethics raise questions about what is right, implying that conventional morality is not right by definition.[5]

It is true that there is only one morality. Teaching ethics, however, consists not only in teaching the conventional ethical norms of a society—a task which might be incorporated into many courses in business school—but it also properly has a critical side to it. From an ethical point of view we can ask not only what does my society or my firm hold to be right and wrong, good and bad, but also is it correct? Are the system as a whole and the individual activities within it ethically defensible? If they are, such investigation at worst does no harm and at best strengthens belief in its justification. And if the analysis throws some doubt on parts of what we all believe, we have some hope of correcting our errors.

In teaching critical ethics, one tries to determine not only which actions are considered right and wrong, but the reasons for their being so characterized. If insider trading is unethical, and has correctly been made illegal, the task for those in business ethics is to show why these judgments are correct. When this is taught to students—or more importantly when students are taught how to make this evaluation for themselves—such understanding presumably will help motivate them to avoid such actions. In this sense understanding can and often does help motivate one to act ethically.

There is, however, a certain ambiguity in the desire of business to have even conventional ethics taught. Business schools tend to produce the kinds of people business wants: skilled, aggressive and imaginative individuals who are able to increase the profits of the companies for which they will work. This is what the business schools teach, and students learn this because such skills are highly valued and highly paid. To the extent businesses want people who are honest, this often means that they expect those hired to do no injury to the company that hires them.

Fifty-six percent of the executives polled in a 1987 survey[6] would hire Colonel Oliver North as an executive because he did what he thought was good for his "company" and its leader, and not for his own personal gain. This is not the same as acting ethically.

It is not clear whether many businesses want students to develop not only concern for the company but also concern for doing what is right, even when it hurts the company or goes against what the boss wants. It is not clear that business really wants ethics in business to the extent that ethics is critical: that it questions the status quo or the way business is typically done. Hence, it is not clear that an *autonomous moral agent*, which is what most of those who teach business ethics hope to produce, is the type of person that business really wants from *these* schools. Thus blaming the business schools for producing the kind of person that business has gobbled up is not altogether fair to the schools. The business schools are part of the larger environment of the business community, and if changes are required, they are required in more than just the schools.

The business schools teach the techniques by which firms can be managed most efficiently. If such techniques are two-edged swords and make possible unethical manipulation, then one possible approach is to require a higher ethic of those who go into the investment industry— where such manipulation is more profitable—than of others. Traditionally the art of locksmithing, which includes lockpicking and how to blow up safes, is carefully guarded. Apprentices are carefully screened and chosen before they are taught the art of breaching the security on which so much of society depends. Of course, some less than ethical people learn the tricks of that craft, but the profession as a whole is well respected. If the management and manipulation of finances is as sensitive and as open to possible abuse, then the same care that goes into an apprentice locksmith should go into the apprentice financier. A business school, through courses that teach moral rules and ethical ideals, can help set the stage. But the firms engaged in the most lucrative and hence most tempting kinds of transactions must take the time and effort to screen the ethical standards of potential employees and then both inculcate high ethical norms and monitor for them.

Most importantly the financial community, rather than looking to the business schools for solutions to unethical behavior in the financial industry, must acknowledge that the ethical climate on Wall Street is the responsibility of the firms there. In turn, the ethical climate of the firms on Wall Street is the ethical responsibility of top management of those companies. If that climate has deteriorated, the responsibility rests with the top management of those firms and the primary changes should properly be made by those managers in their firms. Unfortunately, thus far the public has received no sign that any of the major firms is seriously considering its activities from a critical ethical point of view. There is little visible move to change the kinds of legal, though questioned, practices in which they engage, and little sign of any internal self-policing. In the absence of any such movement or sign, the public has the right to look elsewhere for remedies to what it perceives as harm to society.

II.

PROFESSORS OF BUSINESS AND LAW HAVE DEFENDED INSIDER TRADING. THOSE IN BUSINESS ETHICS HAVE NOT COUNTERED THEIR ARGUMENTS ADEQUATELY IN THE PUBLIC FORUM, EVEN THOUGH INSIDER TRADING OF THE BOESKY VARIETY IS DEMONSTRABLY UNETHICAL.

The second reaction—interestingly enough from professors in business and law schools[7]—is that the scandals were based on a mistake, viz., the mistake of making certain kinds of insider trading illegal. There would be no scandals if the actions of Levine, Boesky, and company were not illegal. These actions should not be illegal because they make the market more efficient.

It is interesting that the defenses of insider trading have come primarily not from members of the financial community but from professors in business and law schools. This may be an indication of a discrepancy between what the business schools teach, thinking it is what the business community wants, and what that community actually wants; it may be an indication that the professors of business are less loath to present their views than are members of the financial community; or it may be an indication that it is not the students in business schools who need a course in business ethics but the professors.

Insider trading is allowed in a number of countries, such as New Zealand.[8] Is it unethical in itself; is it unethical only when abused in certain ways; or is it in fact ethical—only presently illegal in the United States?

The arguments mustered in defense of presently illegal trading all hinge on efficiency, meaning that insider trading moves the price of stocks closer to where they would be if all available information were utilized. The claim is that with all information available—that is, when it becomes available—a stock which is a takeover target will go up a certain amount. That is the actual value of the stock. Hence the purchase of the stock by people with knowledge of all the facts helps move the stock to that value, and indirectly gives the market information that is actual but not yet publicly available. To this argument are added two others.

The first draws a scenario of three traders in a stock. Trader Abel for reasons of his own is interested in selling stock Z. Trader Baker, again for reasons of his own, is interested in buying stock Z and buys 1,000 shares @ 50. Trader Charlie, who has inside information that the stock is about to be taken over, buys 500,000 shares of stock Z at the same time as Baker, and they both get the same price. According to the view that insider trading is unethical, Charlie is unethical while Baker is not, even though they buy the same stock at the same time for the same price from some anonymous source. We cannot, the argument concludes, consistently hold that the one trade is allowable and the other not.[9]

The second argument claims that by buying stock Z, Charlie does no one any harm.[10] If an action is ethically wrong only when and because it does harm, then Charlie does not act unethically. Charlie does not force Abel to sell any stock, and by placing a bid for a significant number of shares will probably raise the price of the stock, thus making the price more advantageous for Abel than it would otherwise be. Charlie's action thus increases the amount Abel receives for the stock. In this way the price is more reflective of the real situation than it would otherwise be. Hence no injury is done to Abel. As a result of Charlie's bid, the price that Baker pays for the stock might be higher than it would otherwise have been. But we know that the stock is going to go up considerably. Hence no real harm is done Baker, who is soon going to make a profit as the stock goes up. Since neither other buyers or sellers of the stock, nor those who continue to hold stock, suffer any harm, the action is not unethical and so should not be made illegal.

The arguments are deficient in a number of ways. First, efficiency is not the only important factor in the market or in ethical thinking. Fairness is central to both. Unless traders in the market believe that the market is fair and that all participating in it trade on equal terms, they will not have confidence in it. If you know a game is rigged against you, your incentive to play is certainly diminished. If the system is rigged in favor of certain players, then even if you continue to play, you can certainly prefer to play in a fair game rather than in the only one available. Hence, the alternative to an unequal, and to that extent unfair, system is a fair system. If the insider makes the market more efficient by trading on his or her privileged information, and if the gain is an increase in information, then all would benefit more and the market would be more efficient if the information, as soon as available to him or her, were made public for all to act on. Allowing information to affect the market indirectly instead of directly is to accept second best.

Second, consider the issue of fairness in another way. The market presupposes equality in the transaction between the two contracting parties. Each acts for his or her own reasons. In other markets the rule of *caveat emptor* has given way to either informed consent or other forms of full disclosure of information. Use of insider information in the stock market is in effect a return to the doctrine of *caveat emptor* and hence is unfair, as fairness is judged in other market transactions.

Third, the claim that no one gets hurt ignores the counter claims of traders Abel and Baker that they are in fact harmed by trader Charlie. Suppose the information held by the insider that a takeover is imminent and that the price of the stock will jump by ten points in two days were known by the person about to sell. Unless Abel were forced by extreme circumstances to sell, there is no doubt he would wait two days and reap his assured profit. The fact that Charlie knows of the takeover and Abel does not is the reason why Abel would claim that Charlie took unfair advantage of him, even if Abel received somewhat more than he would have if Charlie had not bought stock in company Z. Charlie is not a lucky speculator; he acts on sure information. Abel would not feel that Baker had taken advantage of him, assuming that Baker had no knowledge of company Z which was not in principle available to Abel. Fairness is a component of the total situation, not simply of the price one receives for his shares. The situations of Baker and Charlie are different, hence their actions are different from an ethical point of view, even if the result on Abel is the same.

Nor would Baker accept the assertion that he was not hurt because he still made money when the stock went up after the takeover. Surely Baker would be correct in claiming that although he made money on the stock, he could have bought the stock at a lower price, and so could have made more than he did, if Charlie had not bought Z on inside information. He would thus correctly claim that he, as well as Abel, had been done an injustice by Charlie.

The mistake of those who attempt to justify insider trading in terms of market efficiency is that they see the market as an impersonal mechanism, which does not care who gains or loses in its transactions. But clearly those who buy and sell do care who gains and loses, and they both desire and deserve a fair market.

Finally, those who act on inside information violate their fiduciary obligations to the companies they or their firms represent. They also misappropriate—and so steal—information that they properly have only in their corporate role, and which they inappropriately use in their private capacity for their personal gain. The claim that by their actions Levine, Boesky and others moved the stock in which they traded in the direction that those who paid them or their companies wanted the stock to move is beside the point. If an action is unfair to others, the fact that it produces the result one's client wants is no justification. One is not ethically allowed to act unfairly, even if it benefits one's client or firm.

The conclusion is that, arguments to the contrary notwithstanding, trading on inside information is unfair, and hence unethical.

Critical ethics can help clarify the moral status of a number of other current, new practices on the investment scene. Part of the task of critical ethics is to engage in the debate that can lead to some ethical conclusion about these practices. Teaching the conclusions, as well as the reasons for them, is part of a business ethics course. The substantive work of deciding the ethical status of the practices by analyzing their effects and the arguments pro and con are part of the research agenda of business ethics.

Business schools could incorporate business ethics more effectively into their curriculum. But to the extent that those professors of business who defend insider trading are typical, adopting critical business ethics courses will threaten the unwritten philosophy undergirding some business schools or business school courses.

III.
POLITICIANS HAVE SENSED A NEED FOR CHANGE IN THE INVESTMENT INDUSTRY, BUT THEIR PROPOSALS HAVE BEEN PIECEMEAL AND REFLECT NO COMPREHENSIVE ETHICAL POSITION.

The third reaction was the political one. Politicians sensed a potential for popular legislation, came up with a variety of proposals, and introduced several bills aimed at surgically eliminating perceived abuses. The bills traded on the fact that the actions of Levine, Boesky and others were already illegal and on the popular support for their prosecution.

It is ironic that as the insider trading laws were being vigorously enforced and a number of convictions obtained, some people objected to the existing laws because they claimed the laws could not really be enforced consistently or effectively. Hence, they said, we should not pretend that they can be enforced and we should repeal them. Of course that is one alternative; but it is one we should resist. Making the presently illegal actions legal will exacerbate the situation, since the present laws undoubtedly inhibit a considerable number of people from engaging in such practices. To rescind the laws would be to promote the unethical activity. We could also expect other illegal actions to emerge elsewhere within the system. For by the logic of the proponents of legalizing insider trading, we should then decriminalize these other actions—clearly an unending and unacceptable response. To the extent the claim of poor enforcement is correct, the better alternative is to try to improve the law and its enforcement to make them effective.

As if in reaction to the notion that one good law deserves another, legislators in both houses of Congress as a result of the insider trading scandals introduced a spate of legislation. They focused on a number of related activities: hostile takeovers, greenmail, golden parachutes, leveraged buyouts, poison pills, and other similar practices. Many of the proposals were criticized as misguided, raising more problems than they solved and protecting inefficient managers.[11]

To the extent that we treasure individual freedom of action, we should not, without compelling reason, make actions illegal that are not unethical. For instance, no convincing case has been made that all hostile takeovers are unethical. If in fact there is nothing *inherently* wrong with hostile takeovers, then they should not be legally precluded. Yet there are unethical ways of pursuing such takeovers, and such activities are legitimate legislative targets.

One type of takeover threat on which legislators have focused is the practice known as greenmail. Although some potential raiders buy up five percent of a company's stock and announce their intention to take over the company, they are willing to allow the attacked company to repurchase from them the stock they have acquired if the target company pays a higher than market price for their shares. This is not illegal. Should it be?

The argument against it is first that the declaration of the company's intent is dubious. If the intent is really to take over the company, why bargain to sell back the acquired shares? Second, the practice involves the company's paying two different prices for the same kind of company stock: one, the market price to ordinary shareholders and, the other, a premium price to the raider. The dual price system that it creates for common stock is not consistent with the usual concept of stock ownership and stock value. Third, while not legally extortion, those who wield greenmail get their higher price through threat. Whether they are more at fault than those who pay greenmail is a debatable question. This tactic of threat by a raider in order to be paid off to remove its threat either forces or induces the attacked company to buy back stock it would not have bought, and to buy it back at a premium, for which the other shareholders receive no perceptible benefit, except the continued management of the company by its present managers.

One defender of the practice counters by arguing that there are good greenmailers, and if they make a profit it should be considered payment of a consultant fee for the restructuring they proposed and the restructuring they induced management to make in self-defense. Thus the greenmail payment did not harm the other shareholders but benefited them.[12] The defense, however, is defective. For surely the practice, if considered as a consultation, is a forced one on terms set by the greenmailer, and to that extent even "good" greenmail is importantly different from a consultant's services, and arguably unethical.

Legislation aimed at preventing greenmail attempts to specify conditions for a bona fide takeover offer or attempt. One suggestion was that any raiding company be required to have available 100 percent funding to carry through any announced takeover.[13] Another required a longer delay than at present between announced intentions and vote by the shareholders on the proposal.[14] Yet another required all shares of a company's regular stock to be sold at the same price.[15] And still another prohibited two classes of stock and required one share, one vote.[16] Although there is no ethical objection to any of these, ethics does not prescribe any one rather than another of them, and a question can legitimately be raised about the need for any such legislation.

Several bills aimed at making golden parachutes illegal, even though they are not clearly unethical. Those who propose that they should be illegal argue that they do not serve the shareholders and serve only to protect possibly inefficient managers who are in danger of losing their jobs if the firm is taken over. The executives who receive them are usually highly paid, partially for taking the risk of working without job security, and for working for the interests of the shareholders, even at some possible detriment to themselves. They should not need job insurance to do what is best for the company. However, whether golden parachutes are proper and whether they should be made illegal are two different issues. And a prior question to be answered is whether legislation that precludes the practice is preferable to action taken by the stockholders themselves, who are the claimed victims.

Do leveraged buyouts with junk bonds threaten the financial stability of society sufficiently to justify governmental interference? Similarly, if a firm buys back its own stock and takes on a huge debt that it must then service in order to make itself unattractive as a takeover candidate, is it up to the government to interfere?

If the role of the government is to protect the innocent and to help keep the economy running more or less equitably and smoothly, does it properly enter into how companies run themselves, who takes over whom (unless the action violates antitrust laws), how a company defends itself, or how shareholders react to it all? Shareholders, especially large institutional investors, have forced over sixty companies to submit to them poison pill proposals. Such action by shareholders is arguably preferable to government regulation.

The role of the government is not clear in this area and is presently being debated. The difficulty is that the debates tend to be about specific proposed pieces of legislation; there is little discussion of the whole picture, of which these various practices are interrelated parts.

From an ethical point of view those actions that are unethical and threaten serious harm to the community can properly be made illegal. But they need not be. Not all harmful acts must be made illegal. Some may be tolerated if they produce more good than harm overall, or if enforcing them threatens the freedom or other values of those whose actions are controlled.

There has been too little debate about the ethics of the different practices, all of which have become equal targets for legislation. Moreover, in 1987, the issue, despite protests to the contrary, became to some extent a partisan one: the Reagan Administration opposed any legislation on takeovers,[17] and the Democrats William Proxmire (Wisconsin), Chairman of the Senate Banking Committee, and John Dingell (Michigan), Chairman of the House Energy and Commerce Committee, proposed restrictive legislation. Moreover, what legislators said and the actual legislation they proposed was often strikingly different.[18] No matter how radical their statements, their proposals tended to be conservative. This is not surprising. Politicians know the strength of the financial community and they believe that what will pass Congress and be signed by the President cannot be very restrictive or cut very deeply. The proposed legislation was reactive, piecemeal, basically conservative, and in the long run would produce little significant change in the financial community.

If deep change is needed, it can come only if the ethical issues come to the fore and the conscience of the people moves them to demand such changes strongly enough that the vested interests of the financial community can be outweighed. And here critical ethics can play a role.

IV.
ETHICS HAS A ROLE TO PLAY IN THE DISCUSSIONS OF THE INVESTMENT INDUSTRY.

Ethical analysis will not give us ready solutions to complex problems; but it can help us see what has to be remedied and why, and it can also help us—sometimes by elimination—sort out the various possible alternatives.

What ethical principles apply? Central to the market is competition, and central to acceptable competition is fairness. Fairness is the main ethical ingredient and one role of government is to ensure that the market is fair.

Some widely accepted and fundamental norms are often used to justify the free market system. In general, a transaction is fair if it satisfies three conditions.[19] First, the transaction must be freely entered into by both parties. A coerced transaction is *prima facie* unfair. This is true in all realms. Consumers should not be coerced into buying goods, nor should those who trade stocks be coerced into purchasing or selling them. Second, we assume that both parties to a transaction, since they enter freely, enter in order to achieve their own good. Each is expected to benefit from the transaction. Both buyer and seller have their own reasons for taking part in the transaction. Consumers get the products they want or need; manufacturers and retailers make a profit from selling these goods or services; and both the one who freely buys and the one who freely sells stock at the trade price expect to gain. The third condition is that both buyer and seller in principle have access to appropriate knowledge concerning the transaction. If the product has a defect, this should be known by the buyer as well as the seller. Misleading advertising violates this condition. And so does the kind of insider trading that has led to the 1987 scandals.

In addition to fairness, the market should operate to the benefit of society in general. There are many ways that a society can organize its financial affairs. The U.S. free enterprise system is only one of a number of alternatives. The justification for choosing our way is our general belief that our society is better served by this than by one of the alternative ways. Society is able to place restraints on business and is justified in doing so when it believes it will be better off with than without such restraints and when it believes it is being harmed by the lack of them. There is no unrestricted right on the part of any individual, group, or firm to make large amounts of money, and none to make money at the expense of the general social welfare. A society rightly allows people to make large amounts of money if this provides incentives for increased production, efficiency, inventiveness, risk-taking and other characteristics or results that help the general well-being of society.

These principles are not new, and have been used in the past to justify our financial institutions and practices. Yet the past fifteen years have spawned a host of new practices and new approaches to financing and takeovers. Institutional investors are now the major players in the stock market and are seeking a greater role in management decisions, as well as in takeovers, mergers, and corporate refinancing. If the old system was ethically sound and defensible, it does not follow that the new system is, and it is time for a close examination of it from an ethical point of view.

Since insider trading is unethical, one way to attack the problem it poses is head-on. The three reactions with which we started took this approach. Taking the insider trading problem at its face value and trying to treat it directly is attractive because we can leave everything else in the system as it is. We threaten no one and no vested interests, because we are simply asking how better to frame and enforce laws, some of which we already have, to catch those who do not operate properly within the confines of the system. However, this approach is primarily reactive, looking at practices only after they have been used for a considerable time and done considerable harm.

An alternative to the direct approach is to take as a working hypothesis the claim that the insider trader scandals are a symptom of something wrong not with a few individuals but with the investment industry more broadly. If there is a cancer in the investment industry, teaching ethics to MBAs will not get rid of the cancer of which the scandals are a symptom. Hence, we should not worry so much about the symptom—after all, the actions were illegal and some people have gone to jail—as about the cause. To treat insider trading as a symptom raises the question of whether there is more wrong than simply a few greedy people breaking the law. It asks what their actions are a symptom of, and if one is to cure the cause of which this is a symptom, we must open up the whole system to scrutiny, subject all its parts to ethical evaluation, and scan all the central components. In such a scrutiny, a principle of caution advises that we change as little as possible to produce the needed cure, while a radical principle calls for the overthrow of the system as a whole. A middle ground is possible.

If the system is ethically sound and its practices demonstrably justifiable, no harm will have been done it by subjecting it to ethical scrutiny. In fact, such scrutiny will quiet doubts some may have about it, and hence bolster it at a time when it can use such bolstering. If the new system is in general ethically defensible but some of the current practices ethically unsound, then we can change those practices and in the process strengthen the system. And if there are inherent in the system unremediable injustices, that is a good reason to look for an alternative system of capital financing.

Instead of simply seeking better enforcement in such cases as the Levine-Boesky scandals, can we preclude the cause? For example, we can ask: should there be positions such as arbitrageurs, in which the temptations and gains are possibly enormous? The aim of the inquiry is to get at the source of the corrupt practices, which are certainly linked to the vast sums at stake. A challenge to those in finance is to consider other structures that better preclude abuse. If, in fact, arbitrageurs perform a valuable service to the business community, we can still restructure the system so the rewards are commensurate to the service performed, while eliminating the great abuses to which they have been shown to be open. If the root of the abuses is personal greed, the system would be better off if arbitrageurs were well paid for their work by their firms but precluded from trading for themselves as one of the conditions of their employment—a condition that can be set by the firms without federal legislation. Although any such new rules would also be open to violation and circumvention, the possibility of enormous personal gain would be greatly diminished. The system would also be better off if the firms avoided even the appearance of conflict of interest, acted on a set fee for services basis, and did not trade for their own profit in any merger or takeover.

The abuses of insider trading in 1987 were related to the recent dramatic rise in the number of takeovers.[20] These in turn led to junk bonds, greenmail, and the host of defensive tactics potential takeover targets developed.

Each of these practices can be evaluated individually from an ethical point of view. Yet there is a sense in which doing so is like tackling a brush fire piecemeal. As we handle one practice another dubious practice develops elsewhere. If the proximate cause of the practices is hostile takeovers, we can profitably push our analysis deeper by differentiating between ethically justifiable and unjustifiable hostile takeovers. What is the present state of ethical discussion on this issue?

One set of ethical debates for and against hostile takeovers is between those who implicitly accept a utilitarian approach to ethics, even though they do not necessarily identify themselves by that label; a second is between those who argue in terms of justice and freedom. Debate on both sides has been biased. A third way is necessary, which gives each side its due, considers all affected, and remains cognizant of the common good.

The implicit utilitarians ask whether more benefit is achieved— both to the participants and to society as a whole—by allowing these activities rather than by outlawing them.[21] Defenders of takeovers argue primarily that they promote efficiency, and that the threat of takeovers is an incentive for managers to work harder and more productively, to raise profits for their shareholders, rather than leaving that task to a more efficient takeover manager.[22]

Those on the other side deny that the good consequences of efficiency will outweigh the bad consequences in the long run, pointing not only to the predictable plant closings, sell-offs, and displacements, but also to the growing internal debt that companies have taken upon themselves in self-defense—debt which they may not be able to service in any kind of a downturn in the economy, and which will represent enormous losses that will threaten the whole system.[23]

Moreover, the critics argue, the primary benefit achieved by the takeover frenzy has been the multiplying of paper profits. As a result of all the takeover activity we have raised the level of the market and the price of individual shares, but we have not increased productivity, created new jobs, or strengthened our economy. Since we have been building on sand, the illusion of efficiency has blinded us to the real situation, which is a weakening rather than a strengthening of our economy. Hence, overall the activities have been deleterious and since they harm society, should be seen as unethical.

Deciding between the two positions is no easy matter because the situation is extremely complex, because we have too little experience with the practices in question to be able accurately to predict what their long-range consequences will be, and because many of the supposed facts stated by one side are contested by the other. Nonetheless, whichever side is correct, it is clear that if we can preserve the good effects of takeovers while eliminating the negative effects, the situation will be better than it presently is. If the major good effect is efficiency, then eliminating those takeovers which aim simply to amass quick gains by speculators will be in the general good. Eliminating those quick gains promises to improve the situation without preventing companies interested in long-range benefits from taking over a target company. Thus focusing on short term speculative gains is more promising than precluding all takeovers or trying to legislate against specific practices.

The second set of debates focuses not on efficiency or good over bad consequences, but on freedom on the one hand and fairness or justice on the other. The benefit of this approach is that it allows us to make well-founded ethical decisions now, rather than waiting for anticipated or predicted consequences, such as the failure of junk bonds or the onset of a recession.

The issue of freedom from government regulation is a familiar one for staunch defenders of the free market. In the case of finance they argue that raiders should be free to raid, managers and corporations should be free to protect themselves, and shareholders should be free to accept or reject takeover bids. To this extent their argument amounts to a defense of the practices, which have developed without government restraint and interference, and which they claim should continue like that. The market will weed out the bad from the good, the advantageous from the disadvantageous, much more effectively than will government legislation.

The argument is valid up to a point, and that point is where freedom violates rights or justice. We are not free to do whatever we want, if what we do harms others and violates their rights or is unjust.

This line of debate, like the utilitarian one, has its merits; but neither probes deeply enough. Fairness and freedom do not necessitate short term speculative windfall profits.

The two approaches can be joined in an effort to restructure financial practices in the light of the implicit contract of finance with society. As a basis for the resulting third line of ethical analysis we can go back to the justification for the free enterprise system and the implicit contract between society and business. Society allows business to operate because it receives certain benefits—which include jobs, products, services, and taxes—from it. Business in turn stays within the rules because it can only achieve its ends in a stable, safe, well-organized society. When society no longer receives its expected benefits, or when it is hurt more than helped by the activity of business, then society is allowed and should be expected to change the rules, since the conditions justifying the original contract have changed. This is in some ways similar to the utilitarian analysis above, but joins to it the notion of implied contract and so of fairness.

The point is to look at the newly developing system as a whole, rather than simply looking at the improper motivation of the few, at changes in business school education, or at inculcation of conventional business ethics without looking at and possibly changing the system. The system has a great many vested interests built into it. Many of these are of questionable value to the system and could well be changed.

For instance, why allow the possibility of someone—anyone—making millions in a few days as Ivan Boesky did?[24] Defenders of free enterprise want people to have an inducement to take risks, to increase productivity, and to be handsomely recompensed for their efforts when appropriate to benefit the whole. Free enterprise does not need the possibility of an individual's making four million dollars in four days to achieve these ends, unless doing so is a by-product of benefiting society, and not just themselves.

The major ethical concern is not hostile takeovers, nor some of the ways that such takeovers are conducted, nor some of the financing developed to support them, nor even some of the defensive mechanisms developed to offset them. The root of the problems in the finance industry has been identified by some as greed. And the greed of a few seems to have become infectious. While executives were previously content with large salaries and stock options and with annual incomes of one or two million a year, the news of others making many times that in a few days, weeks, or months escalated the game. It seems it was not only the money but also the prestige of "keeping up" that was the driving factor.[25]

If the root of the problems in the finance industry has been correctly identified as greed, the solution is not to attempt to change people so they are not greedy or to motivate them to control their greed, but to establish structures that eliminate the temptations to which many succumb. The pernicious greed at issue is non-productive and has as its only aim the quick acquisition by almost any means of personal gain. The remedy is to preclude such gain while continuing to reward those who contribute to society's welfare through the production of goods and services. A plausible target is short-term capital gains.

In this regard Representative James L. Floris' proposal of a surtax on short-term profits from takeover attempts[26] is appealing. Even more promising is Warren Buffet's suggestion that all short term gains be taxed at 100 per cent[27]—a proposal that has not been taken seriously enough, and one that should apply to corporations and institutional investors as well as to individuals. And if the proposal sounds too draconian, it can easily be softened to tax at 100 per cent only those short term capital gains that exceed, e.g., $1,000,000, in any year. The target is not orphans, widows, and small investors. Short term gains on commodities might also be excluded, since the aim is not to preclude productive practices but counter-productive ones.

With a modified 100 per cent tax, the trades that Ivan Boesky engaged in would yield him nothing, and hence the incentive to engage in them would be eliminated. Inside trading could still be regulated by the present rules; no new legislation would be required. Eliminating short-term capital gains would preclude the benefit of greenmail, and hence remove the motive for the practice. With only long term capital gains as a source of profit, the incentive for many of the takeovers would be diminished. Takeovers would still be allowed; but those that take place would tend to be productive in a way that many now are not. Only those that were planned for long term gains would take place. Taxing short term gains at 100 per cent would preclude trading and working for the quarterly report, a practice that is frequently bemoaned but never attacked in practice.

The present and new role of institutional investors is such that they often turn out to be more speculators than investors. Under the proposed plan, institutional investors would no longer be simply speculators but would be encouraged to take greater interest in the companies in which they invest and to have more concern that those companies do well in the longer term. The pressure on management to manage effectively would come from the shareholders rather than from outside predators. Management, in turn, would not need to sell poison pills, buy back its own stock to increase its debt, or offer management golden parachutes. With large institutional investors taking greater interest in the affairs of the companies, they could be expected to vote down attempts to offer management golden parachutes.

If it is proper for executives to be well paid if they in fact contribute to the success of the companies they manage, and for the companies that contribute to the welfare of society to reap rewards, however great, then we can leave to a fair, progressive income tax the decision of how much of that income should remain after taxation. But if speculative profit, profit for profit's sake with little, if any, return to society, is the aim, then society acts within its rights to preclude such profit. One way to preclude it is to try to legislate against its being made. A second way is to take away the incentive to engage in those practices by making them unprofitable. The modified 100 per cent tax of short-term capital gains would solve this as well as a great many other problems at once.

At the least, a proposal such as this means that one can appropriately demand an argument justifying the benefits of short-term capital gains—or of such gains above some reasonable amount. The onus should be on those who wish to defend short-term capital gains, and the defense should be in terms of fairness and of the general or common good, not in terms of vested interests. In the absence of any such strong argument, the modified 100 per cent tax is an inviting solution.

Of course, this is not the only possible solution; but it is one that gets at the root of the issue. Tinkering with existing laws, closing loopholes, and pretending that the root of the problem is a few corrupt individuals will not help make the system more ethically defensible in the long run. The present situation calls for a new and radical look at the ethical justification of the existing structures and a willingness to make radical changes despite the opposition of vested interests. That possibility is the challenge raised by business ethics.

If deep change is necessary, it cannot be achieved without a good deal of opposition. For those in the financial industry, any change will mean that someone who is now making impressive amounts of money will no longer be able to do so in that way. Any correction of the system will initially hurt some—perhaps many—people. But the price of an ethical overhaul is one worth making for the long-run good of society as a whole.

Ethics is no panacea. Neither teaching ethics nor trying to act ethically will solve all the problems of finance. But applying ethics to finance can keep the system from going further astray, repair its present badly tarnished reputation, and help it maintain its re-won respectability.

Those in finance can hardly afford now or in the future to ignore ethical norms or to avoid considering and abiding by them in their practices and dealings. The challenge of thinking and acting ethically means going beyond vested interests, short term profits, and conventional morality to consider the investment community's role and actions from the perspective of the common good.[28] For only if financial practices are justifiable from that perspective do they benefit the public; and, only if the public benefits, should it accept or allow such practices.

NOTES

1. John S. R. Shad, "Business's Bottom Line: Ethics," *The New York Times*, July 27, 1987, p. A19.

2. Cf. Dr. William Criddle, "They Can't See There's a Victim," *The New York Times*, February 22, 1987, p. E5.

3. E.g., see Felix Rohatyn, "The Blight on Wall Street," *The New York Review of Books*, March 12, 1987, p. 21.

4. This position is exemplified by Irving Kristol, "Ethics Anyone? Or Morals?," *The Wall Street Journal*, September 15, 1987, p. 32.

5. The late Harvard psychologist Lawrence Kohlberg distinguished three levels of moral reasoning: the preconventional, the conventional and the postconventional, autonomous or principled level. See his paper, "The Claim to Moral Adequacy of a Highest Stage of Moral Judgment," *The Journal of Philosophy*, LXX (1973), pp. 630-646.

6. "Oliver North, Businessman? Many Bosses Say That He's Their Kind of Employee," *The Wall Street Journal*, July 14, 1987, p. 33.

7. See Paul Blustein, "Disputes Arise Over Value of Laws on Insider Trading," *The Wall Street Journal*, November 17, 1986, p. 28, which quotes, among others, Michael Jensen of the business schools of Harvard University and the University of Rochester, and Henry G. Manne, Dean of the George Mason University Law School; see also D. Bruce Johnsen of Texas A & M University, "Letters to the Editors," *The Wall Street Journal*, March 6, 1987, p. 29; and Dennis Logue, Sullivan/Dean Professor of International Business at Georgetown University, " 'Max the Insider' Isn't Always a Rat," *The Wall Street Journal*, February 10, 1987, p. 38.

8. Geraldine Brooks, "Insider Trading Thrives in New Zealand," *The Wall Street Journal*, May 28, 1987, p. 23.

9. "Scandal Primer," *The Wall Street Journal*, February 18, 1987, p. 26.

10. Prof. D. Bruce Johnsen, "Letters to the Editor," *The Wall Street Journal*, March 6, 1987, p. 29; also Dennis Logue, *op. cit.*

11. E.g., "William of the Roundtable," Editorial, *The Wall Street Journal*, April 13, 1987, p. 22.

12. Craig Forman, "Greenmail Isn't Always Blackmail," *The Wall Street Journal*, May 7, 1987, p. 30.

13. Marcia Langley and Bruce Ingersoll, "Rep. Dingell Says His Takeover Measure Will Curb Greenmail, Golden Parachutes," *The Wall Street Journal*, April 23, 1987, p. 2; Andy Pasztor, "Select Panel Is Expected to Adopt Bill to Aid Federal Antitrust Enforcement," *The Wall Street Journal*, March 12, 1987, p. 10.

14. Marcia Langley and Bruce Ingersoll, *op. cit.*

15. *Ibid.*

16. "S.E.C. Weighs One Share, One Vote," *The New York Times*, January 26, 1987, p. D2.

17. Gregory A. Robb, "Merger Bill Too Broad S.E.C. Says," *The New York Times*, June 24, 1987, p. IV, 1, reports on the testimony of Beverly W. Sprinkel, the Chairman of the Council of Economic Advisers, to this effect.

18. Joseph A. Grundfest, "Proxmire's Doubletalk on Takeovers," *The Wall Street Journal*, September 16, 1987, p. 30.

19. Richard T. De George, *Business Ethics*, 2nd ed. (New York: Macmillan, 1986), p. 128.

20. Bryan Burrough, "The Takeover Business Is Alive and Well," *The Wall Street Journal*, June 26, 1987, p. 6.

21. Jack Anderson and Joseph Spear, "Corporate Raids Spur Fears of Crash," *The Lawrence Journal World*, August 29, 1987, p. 5A.

22. "Scandal Primer," *The Wall Street Journal*, February 18, 1987, p. 26.

23. Jack Anderson and Joseph Spear, *op. cit.* See also Robert O'Brien and Richard Kline, "An Rx for Jobs Lost Through Mergers," *The New York Times*, February 22, 1987, p. 23; Bruce Ingersoll, "Labor Leaders Ask Congress to Stop Rash of Takeovers," *The Wall Street Journal*, April 9, 1987, p. 21; Walter Adams and James W. Brock, "The Hidden Costs of Failed Mergers," *The New York Times*, June 21, 1987, p. III, 3; Bryan Burrough, *op. cit.;* and Alan Greenspan, "Takeovers Rooted in Fear," *The Wall Street Journal*, September 27, 1985, p. 22.

24. Karen W. Arenson, "How Wall Street Bred Ivan Boesky," *The New York Times*, November 23, 1986, p. 8F: from May 22-29 to May 30, $4,000,000 profit on 377,000 shares of Nabisco Brands; from May 1 to May 14-15, $4.1 million from 301,800 shares of Houston Natural Gas; from February 18-21 to February 22, $975,000 on 95,300 shares of FMC Corporation.

25. Karen W. Arenson, *op. cit.*, p. 8F.

26. James L. Floris, "Disincentives Are Needed to Discourage Corporate Raiders," *The New York Times*, June 28, 1987, p. XI, 26.

27. As reported by George Will, "Keep Your Eye on Giuliani," *Newsweek*, March 2, 1987, p. 84. Since Warren Buffet has become a billionaire by long-term trading, his proposal may sound self-serving. That does not preclude its being a valuable and viable proposal.

28. For several commentaries on the concept of the common good, including my own essay, see *The Common Good and U.S. Capitalism*, ed. Oliver F. Williams and John W. Houck (Washington, D.C.: University Press of America, 1987).

Thirteen

Investment Bankers from Ethical Perspectives . . . with Special Emphasis on the Theory of Agency

Clarence C. Walton

A decade ago Justin Davidson, then dean of Cornell's Graduate School of Business and Public Administration, concluded his survey of America's basic institutions (family, professions, governments and markets) with these words: "The family is dying. The economic and social structure is hardening. Our leaders have gone away, and new ones are not appearing. In the night of values, we see no star. Hard times, yet not as hard as those that may follow."[1]

Poets of pessimism were Davidson's oracles and Robinson Jeffers was approvingly quoted when he wrote:

Lucretius felt the change of the world in his time, the great republic riding to the height
Whence every way leads downward. Plato in his time watched Athens
Dance the downpath. The future is a misted landscape, no man sees clearly, but at cyclic turns
There is a change felt in the rhythm of events, as when an exhausted horse
Falters and recovers, then the rhythm of the running hoofbeats is charged, he will run miles yet,
But he must fall: we have felt it again in our own lifetime, slip, shift and speed-up
In the gallop of the world, and now perceive that, come peace or war, the progress of Europe and America
Becomes a long process of deterioration—started with famous Byzantiums and Alexandrias,
Slowly, Surely,—but downward . . .[2]

Little imagination is needed to support the inference that the current economic situation would convince our Schopenhauerian dean that he was unerringly on target. Twenty years ago, Americans would have been incredulous if the prophets had said then that, in terms of market value, the top ranking of their large and seemingly invincible industrial giants would be surrendered to foreign firms. But the sad reality, according to Morgan Stanley Capital International Perspective's 1987 Report, is that only five—IBM, Exxon, General Electric, AT&T and Dupont—are still in the select circle of the twenty largest enterprises. Of the remaining fifteen, thirteen are Japanese. In fairness, it should be noted that on the profit side the record is more impressive—with Exxon, IBM and GE holding one, two, three position, respectively.[3] Steel is in deep trouble and the automobile industry is threatened. Whereas General Motors, Ford and Chrysler had 94 percent of the passenger auto market in 1965, thirty years later it was down to 68 percent—and with prospects of an overcapacity of 6 million passenger cars by 1990 and further declines in market share.[4]

If the scorecard on managerial performance in industry is average, the scorecard on the ethical performance of investment specialists is dismal. Wall Street shenanigans are noted, reported, discussed, dissected, but not dismissed. The stories are drab.

- In a five-year period Dennis Levine parlayed $40,000 into $12.6 million through insider trading;[5]
- Ivan Boesky, almost overnight, entered the country's folklore of rascals and rogues;
- *Wall Street Journal* reporter Foster Winans was found to have put his finger in the till more profitably than on the quill.[6]

Yet these reflect individual aberrations. More ominous are problems relating to takeovers. One is the growing temptation for one investor to "park" stocks by purchasing a large share of stock for another corporate raider who, not wanting it known that he or she is the real owner, can proceed in secret to amass a large stock portion in the targeted company takeover.[7] Boyd Jeffries, former chairman of the Jeffries Group, parked stock for Ivan Boesky and is now under suspicion of parking stock for Houston investor Charles Hurwitz who allegedly was casting covetous eyes on the Pacific Lumber Corporation.

No one denies that mediocre management was related to stock under-valuation of many corporate assets in the stock market.[8] What was initially a needed intervention, however, has become an unneeded invasion. The middlemen of the Street have traditionally played a prominent and positive role, but sophisticated participants like Felix Rohatyn and Henry Kaufman, as well as sophisticated observers, feel that the present style investment banker has assumed a new and dangerously aggressive role by moving from the "sought after" (by executives) to the "seeking after" of corporate victims. Ideas for takeovers often develop in the imaginative minds of investment bankers who stand to gain handsomely for their services. That whole world seems unreal. Investment portfolio managers can, after a few years, earn $300,000 to $1 million a year. Everywhere there is talk of money and everywhere money talks. Many feel that the epinephrine boosts are doing more damage than good for the country's financial nervous system.

Why Do We Exist?

It is, therefore, not surprising that questions and eyebrows are raised. Are investment bankers taking too big a role and too big a cut in the current restructuring process? Are competent executives diverted from the real work of managing to the less productive work of strategizing against potential raiders? Has corporate America taken on too heavy a burden of takeover related debt? Alan Greenspan, Chairman of the Federal Reserve Board, has concluded that leveraged buyouts, hostile takeovers, mergers and acquisitions have reduced equity on corporate balance sheets by $200 billion in the very short 1983-86 interval. Corporate debt has risen by a similar amount. General Motors Chairman Roger Smith commented wryly that "replacing equity with debt is a funny way to build a business . . . business, after all is more than just a money game, it's the art of providing quality goods and services and if it is to succeed in that role, that's where management's attention must be focused—on the production process."[9] Author John Brooks charged that "lawbreaking is the visible lesion that betrays the presence of possibly a deeper cancer which consists of the manipulation of money, intangible property and paper for speculation rather than for the financing of production, and its concomitant, the uncontrolled creation of new debt."[10]

So unsavory had the investment community become that *Fortune* writer Myron Magnet, commenting on the decline and fall of business ethics, noted:

. . . at least in matters concerning the vast restructuring of U.S. industry now under way—the business climate has become less ethical than it was in the relatively aboveboard period from the Depression's end until the mid-Seventies.

No place have standards dropped more vertiginously than in the investment banking trade that is presiding over this restructuring. While other areas of business are in most respects no more unethical than ever, wrongdoing in this central arena makes a crisis of business ethics seem in full swing. And with investment banking now largely manned by the young, is the erosion of ethics here an early warning of imminent trouble elsewhere in business as this generation rises to power?

Insider trading is investment banking's most widely publicized sin, and since extrasensory perception alone doesn't explain why the stock price of takeover targets regularly rises in advance of official announcement, doubtless plenty of insider traders besides Boesky's confederate Levine remain uncaught. But much more pervasive, if less heralded, is the unscrupulousness that now infects relations with clients. Says Herbert A. Allen, Jr., president of the Allen & Co., Inc. investment banking firm: "A major disquieting factor is the loss of confidentiality, well short of illegality. Important clients can find out anything about other important clients."

Formerly circumspect investment bankers now routinely trade confidential information, hoping to glean tips leading to new business. Information seeps out to other clients, too. In one example, a company preparing to go public to raise capital suddenly found itself faced with an unwelcome tender offer from another client of the investment banker arranging the stock offering. Company chiefs are becoming understandably skittish about entrusting themselves to such leaky vessels.[11]

Perhaps the punctured vessels that are beached on Wall Street are there because they lost the sense of what they are really supposed to do and how they are expected to do it. The definitional problem was illustrated in the comment by Daniel P. Tully, president of Merrill Lynch Consumer Markets, who said:

When I started my business career in New York in 1955, my friends said, "Oh, you're working for a stockbroker." Soon it became more common to say I was with a securities firm, then in the investment business, and, still more recently, the best definition is that I'm part of the financial services industry. All that time, of course, I was working for the same company.[12]

Tully's tale simply reflects the results of those cyclonic forces that have wreaked havoc in the financial service industry as a whole. In a cyclone the ship's crew can ill afford to sit complacently at the mess table while a more ominous kind of mess engulfs them. Part of the mess is due, of course, to the shift from long-range goals to short-term results. This shift was dramatically shown in the food industry, which historically was satisfied with modest returns on investment because its customers provided owners with steady demand. Once the big firms went public, the short-term philosophy took hold. Of the "big five" in 1970 (Safeway, A and P, American Stores, Food Fair and Kroger) three have been sold, one is bankrupt and the only survivor, Kroger, stays alive by selling off major divisions. Fast food chains and fast buck artists seemingly reflect the ideology and the style of the American people.

When the world encourages the short-term calculus, temptations too beguiling to resist are the results. Then the Self subdues Scripture, a shorthand way of saying that naked self-interest ignores moral precepts. Admittedly, the aberrations of the few stain the good name of the many, but this is too convenient an excuse. Reform is needed and the initiating instruments will be the government and industry—one using coercion to secure compliance and the other persuasion to assure probity. It is to this reform effort that philosophers might lend counsel. Since such advice moves necessarily from the moralist's generalizations to the expert's specifications, each has something to gain from the dialogue. A beginning is with a question: Is it not time for the investment community to ask itself what the distinguished editor of the *New England Journal of Medicine*, Dr. Arnold Relman of the Harvard Medical School, asked of hospital administrators: Why do we exist?[13] The question pained his audience because of the drift from medical care to financial profit.

In the past, investment bankers, when asked the same question, would instinctively respond: to provide sound advice to managers on a basis of strict confidentiality and to provide capital to fuel America's industrial machine—steel, coal, automobiles and the like. On this basis was built the legitimacy of investment bankers. On this basis were they trusted by corporate executives. On this basis did they prosper. On this basis did industries grow. Today's answer is different: Money is raised more often than not for the benefit of the money raisers who are the investment bankers. Of course, bankers in the past made money—big money—but that was a result of service rendered to others.

Hoping to provide theoretical inputs which improve chances for a comprehensive and realistic answer, moralists might offer a variety of provocative hypotheses. The modest goal of this paper is to present two such hypotheses and trace their equally provocative implications.

Hypothesis I

The values espoused by investment bankers mirror those of the larger culture. If culture, the "lived ethic," is marred by certain questionable qualities, the goals and methods of the investment community will also be flawed.

To suggest that the significant problems found in the investment industry are related, perhaps intimately, to those values embedded in the larger culture is to invite incredulity. Critics would charge that Big Brother (society) is being held responsible for little brother's mischief. In one sense the answer is yes; in another the answer is no. To explain the apparent contradiction first requires understanding the meaning of *culture* and an assessment of some of its present manifestations. Neither lends itself to short treatment but beginnings are helpful.

Culture is a concept so elusive that many scholars, including philosophers, shun the term.[14] But something is needed to describe those values that hold a particular people together—values that are so fully accepted that individuals act in predictable ways. One way of describing that glue came long ago from de Tocqueville, the shrewdest of foreign commentators of the American scene, who said that every society is held together by its mores, that is, "the habits of the heart."[15] Anthropologist Margaret Mead, addressing a popular audience, spoke of culture as the instrument which

> . . . enlarges and limits our imaginations, permitting us to do and think and feel in certain ways; it makes it increasingly unlikely or impossible that we should do or think or feel in ways that are contradictory or tangential to it. When we examine how any society works, it becomes clear that it is precisely the basic taboos—the deeply and intensely felt prohibitions against "unthinkable" behavior—that keep the social system in balance. The taboo lies deep in our consciousness and by prohibiting certain forms of behavior also affirms what we hold most precious in our human relationships. Responsibility and reciprocity are two basic principles of social life; without them, a community perishes.[16]

It follows quite logically that the culture which incorporates embedded and uncritically accepted values is the "lived ethic" that provides images of both ideal and actual behavior, and sets the general moral tone and direction of the community. The lived ethic must be understood before theoretical ethics can make an effective contribution. The obvious issue deals with those values that figure predominantly in the American scheme. One such value is freedom. In this culture, however, liberty has never been divorced from individualism—that "habit of the heart," to recall de Tocqueville's term, that was forged by our forefathers and now is carried possessively and proudly by their heirs.

Once defined by people like Emerson to mean the primacy of the self and freedom from involvement with others, including government, individualism was comfortable in an agrarian society; however, it went through a major transformation after the Civil War. In a country of sprawling factories and large-scale organizations, individualism came to mean the self-made man who, by dint of hard work, intelligence, and shrewdness bordering on ruthlessness, made the fictional Horatio Alger route from rags to riches a reality.[17] Downplayed was the reverse side of the coin, namely, that those who failed financially deserved their poverty. Poverty in things meant poverty in character. Fanned and fueled by the doctrine of Social Darwinisin, one strand of individualism's harsher meaning has persisted.[18] To be wealthy was to be wise. To be wise was to be virtuous. To be virtuous was to be honored.

To some this gloss may appear superficial. Yet repeated observations persuade most that it is not veneer but reality. Americans want money. The more they get, the more prestigious they become. To use a biblical thought in a perverse way: affluence and adulation do sweetly kiss. All this is by way of suggesting that the larger culture of the country reinforces the smaller culture of investment professionals. Of course, when things go wrong they are not entirely blameless, but neither are they unique in their fevered search for money-making deals. One expects no Mother Theresa in Morgan Stanley's executive suite and, were she to enter one, professionals would bail out—fast!

Complicating matters is the fact that these paper entrepreneurs from banking, accounting and law produce little or nothing of tangible use; yet from these groups have come the new corporate mandarins. In 1950 only thirteen percent of America's chief executives had backgrounds in law and finance; today that figure is forty percent—clear evidence that paper entrepreneurs have become the game's superstars. Investment bankers are slicing, dicing, chopping and reassembling American business and thereby accelerating the decline of U.S. competitiveness.[19] Today's bottom line has become more pressing than tomorrow's growth potential.

To return, therefore, to the interplay between the nation's culture and the investment world's culture is to be made painfully aware of the influence of the first on the second, and the extent to which the second has carried individualism to new dimensions. Perhaps the difference between the macro and micro culture can be illustrated best by the

"Edelman syndrome" which became a minor *cause célèbre* in mid-October 1987. Chief players in the drama were Asher Edelman, a highly successful corporate raider, and John Burton, dean of the Columbia University Graduate School of Business. As an adjunct professor, Edelman was teaching a course in corporate takeovers and told the students that their final examination would be for them to select a company that he could take over and make a presentation as to why. He added that, if the idea turned out to be one he could use, he would give the student his standard finder's fee of $100,000. The dean and faculty objected, saying that the offer somehow polluted the academic atmosphere. The incident was described by the *New York Times* as a "classic clash between the purity of the academic world and the money-making orientation of business.[20] The same paper followed its news story with a spirited editorial defense of Edelman's action by asking: "Why is the love of ideas inconsistent with a cash incentive?"[21] One notes in passing the connection between learning and earning that is presumed to go on simultaneously in a professional business school. A further intriguing point is that thirteen of the fourteen students in Edelman's class supported their professor and criticized their dean.

The purpose here is to neither support teacher nor administrator but to show, in a fairly succinct way, how subcultures within the larger culture interact. In the United States there is nothing intrinsically wrong in a zest for money. But the line between zest and greed is easily blurred when stakes are higher and rewards are munificent. To sum up: investment bankers, like other Americans, are interested in money; if things are somewhat askew on Wall Street, they are also askew on Main Street. Perhaps the major difference between the two is that denizens of the first have more opportunities than others and that their contributions to today's society are more suspect.

Hypothesis II

Correctives for a culture's malformations normally come after the lived ethic is carefully tested against an appropriate philosophical ethic and leaders are thereby motivated to undertake reforms.

Meaningful discussions of this hypothesis require some understanding of the major approaches favored by philosophers who address moral issues. Today's domain of ethics is dominated by two types. First are the deontologists who, taking their cue from Immanuel Kant, believe that rational adults can determine *a priori* what their duties are and that such knowledge can yield the so-called "categorical imperative." As a holder of rights, an individual must shoulder duties. The second set of thinkers follow John Stuart Mill who argued that the ethical person acts so as to increase the ratio of good to evil for the majority of people. This is known as utilitarianism and, while different emphases are given by different people, their common aim is to emphasize the primacy of consequences.

When, however, terms like deontology and utilitarianism are bandied about, business gets restive. Like skeptics in the corporate world, cynics in the investment world are inclined to dismiss business ethics as an oxymoron. More acceptable as counselors are those economists who, by breaking away from primary emphasis on model building, have proved they have something valuable to say about and to business. Few have greater stature than Nobel Laureate Kenneth Arrow who, twenty years ago, told business that the presence of what, in slightly old-fashioned terminology, is called virtue, plays a significant role in the operation of the economic system. He amplified the point by saying:

> . . . one way of looking at ethics and morality . . . is that these principles are agreements, conscious or, in many cases, unconscious, to supply mutual benefits . . . Societies in their evolution have developed implicit agreements to certain kinds of regard for others, agreements which are essential to the survival of the society or at least contribute greatly to the efficiency of its working. The fact that we cannot mediate all our responsibilities to others through prices . . . makes it essential in the running of society that we have what might be called "conscience," a feeling of responsibility for the effects of one's actions on others.[22]

If alive today, Kant would have approved Arrow's statement as a valid, though incomplete, reflection of deontological reasoning. While utilitarians would agree on the need for conscience, they would also insist that, while a strictly Kantian ethic might work well in a small society where interpersonal contacts are so many and so direct that the unscrupulous are easily identified, remembered and disciplined, it is not adequate for a complex world of large organizations where impersonal relations are most common. At this point the somewhat neglected theory of agency adds to our understanding of what ethics, economics and other social sciences have to offer.

The theory of agency regards all social relationships as contracts between principals and agents.[23] Lawyers act for clients. Bankers act for investors. Managers act for stockholders. Union leaders act for workers. While the courts have obviously been concerned with fiduciary relationships, the agency theory emphasizes another factor, namely, how control loss is inevitable for principals since the agent has goals not always congruent with those of the principal. The control-loss factor applies to boards of directors, consultants, regulators, accountants, fund-raising organizations, nonprofits and, very clearly, to investment bankers.[24] When the principals are driven therefore to expend resources in trying to tell the agent what to do and assuring themselves it is being done, costs are incurred. Uneasy partnerships are inevitable but they continue because it costs too much for principals to maintain full control.[25]

Since the investment bankers are agents for others it is first useful to explore in some detail the three strands of agency theory which constitute it. These subsets are known generally as (1) the theory of the firm, (2) risk and information theory and (3) sociopolitical theory. The premise of the first is that every sizable organization is built on long-term contracts between owners (principals) and managers who are their agents.[26] The risk-and-information theory (sometimes called the economics of information theory) addresses itself to two problems: (1) the "moral hazards" which arise when the principal, unable to monitor the agent, looks only at results and (2) the problem of "adverse selection" which occurs in situations where the principal can indeed monitor the agent's behavior but cannot assess the quality of that behavior as it relates to the principal's goals. The socio-political theory seeks to explain those primary incentives which determine why an agent joins, stays or leaves a particular relationship. If agency theory is used to assess the investment community, it is clear that every subset of the theory has relevance to ethicists and to investors. A brief examination of the first two can demonstrate the point:

A. *The theory of the firm* assumes that organizations are built on long-term contracts between owners and managers and between managers and investment bankers. When the assumptions fall before realities, not only is the theory barred but the ethical norms upon which assessments have been made traditionally are shaken. When corporate executives can no longer trust investment bankers, the losses are substantial and the plain fact of the matter is this lost trust means added expenses, usually litigation. Owners also lose trust in managers whose leveraged buy-backs leave them high and dry. Norms such as reciprocity, helping, giving, and the valid-agreements-should-be-kept norm are jeopardized and the whole fiduciary norm, which instructs the agent to act solely for the principal as one of the coping mechanisms, is lost.[27]

On the other hand, when principals trust agents there is less need to incur the heavy costs of monitoring; when agents trust principals the mutual loyalty that ensues reduces litigation and other costs caused by conflict; when both principal and agent trust other principals and agents there is less likelihood of intrusive government regulations and the costs that go with them.

B. *Risk and information theory*, the second element in the agency model, also has moral relevance to Wall street operations.[28] When insider trading and parking practices are joined to misleading rumors deliberately concocted by arbitrageurs or when appraisals of a company's worth are jockeyed to suit the occasion, the moral state of investment banking begins to look Kafkaesque. Bad information encourages bad risk-taking, with results tragic for a single corporation and sad for the entire society; further, when investment bankers leak information of one of their clients to another client, the consequences are severe. At this point the deontological ethical norm of truth-telling informs the risk and information theory but it is the latter that makes explicit to utilitarians the unfortunate practical consequences.

The specific issues addressed by the theorists deal with "moral hazards" and "adverse selection," respectively. Hazards arise when the principal, unable to monitor the agent, looks only to the results. If T. Boone Pickens is right that his forays into the hostile takeover bring benefit to stockholders, the principal has no concern that an on-going business might be carved up, that salvageable subdivisions are sold, that employees with long service records are terminated, that plants are closed and communities hurt. In a sense, the principal is insulated from those hard decisions that his agent has helped to bring about for the principal's advantage. Both deontological and utilitarian theorists would condemn such things and argue that, at a minimum, protective shields be thrown around those who are most defenseless.

The second problem in the risk-and-information theory deals with "adverse selection." This occurs when principals are unable to get information, except by the grapevine, on the agent's commitment to the principal and his or her expertise. At this point questions like these arise: Was the ROI fair? Has the portfolio been carefully reviewed? Does the agent keep abreast of new developments? The interesting moral question deals with the employer of generally good reputation. With the flood of business, firms may be screening job applicants too casually or paying inexperienced people too handsomely. This kind of information, of course, affects the quality of the agent's behavior, yet it is generally not known by the principal until it is too late.

The logic of the inquiry suggests that as moral questions increase, so do costs; the link, therefore, between ethics and economics becomes so visible that even skeptics are driven to admit the importance of the connection.[29] In the theory of agency, ethics is good business. There is even room for an ethic of altruism.[30] The altruistically motivated person knows that helping an important institution of which he is a part and from which he draws his livelihood does, in fact, benefit him.[31] In affairs of the world, the altruistic instinct really does matter; important institutions are preserved, freedom of choice is maintained, and the health of the economy is enhanced.

Postscript: From Thought to Act

The value of advice is measured by two things: its logic and the degree to which it is followed. The logic of ethical inquiry is susceptible to challenges by other philosophers and by practitioners who quickly separate platitude from principle. But investment bankers, once having completed their analyses, share with government joint and primary responsibility for initiating reform. One praiseworthy step has already been taken by financial regulators in New York, London, and other world centers who realize that policing the global financial markets is an absolute necessity. Regulators have become the key external agents who will greatly influence those directly involved in principal-agent relationships. The regulators' goal is agreement on common standards of control but they face a serious problem. Unlike central bankers who have had long experience in dealing with monetary policies through meetings at the Bank of International Settlements, regulators of the securities markets lack such experiences. Yet credit increasingly flows through the securities markets and much of it is beyond the purview of the bankers. The consequence is that while securities regulators seek mainly to protect investors, their counterparts wish to assure the smooth working of the banking system. This division leaves gaps in regulation, especially when banks are more and more involved in securities markets and securities firms are assuming more credit risks.[32]

Faced with problems that will take time and patience to resolve, investment bankers need nevertheless to demonstrate to themselves and to the public that appropriate action will be taken. Staunch defense of the status quo is not the answer. It is time to take the agency theory more comprehensively by making the American people the primary principal. To do so requires inspection of past experiences because—as Wall Street guru Henry Kaufman put it—the investment community's entrepreneural drive "has not been tempered by the lessons of history."[33] One of history's unnoted lessons is the role that rogues can play in reform efforts. In this instance one might, somewhat facetiously, recall the story of Boston's Joe Kennedy who put his considerable experiences to work in 1933 to discipline the investment world through the Securities and Exchange

Commission—after he himself had exploited it to his own immense advantage. While far removed from the heydays of the late 1920s (stocks are not excessively overpriced, margin borrowing is relatively modest, the SEC is a watchdog), the speculative use of debt and other forms of leveraging is rampant. The result is what Susan Strange of the London School of Economics has called "casino capitalism," by which she meant an increasingly unstable financial system which has added very substantially to its power over political and monetary authorities.[34]

If Kennedy's "shady" experiences were used to good advantage over fifty years ago, could the last fifty weeks' experiences of Wall Street's shady figures be put to equally good use? Perhaps needed is a Purple (penitential) Ribbon Commission (consisting of Ivan Boesky, Dennis Levine, Martin Siegel, Robert Wilkes, Randall Cecola and other conspirators) to address the central question: how can their shenanigans be made less likely in the future? Comfortable quarters at one of the better federal prisons could be provided at taxpayers' expense. Helping to produce a "polished" report is journalist Foster Winans. Six months would be allowed the Panel to complete its work, after which (in the fashion of some medieval monasteries) food would gradually be reduced until the work was finished. The panel would add to its own agenda such other questions as these:

(1) Should the "Dotterweich doctrine" be applied to senior executives of investment firms? (Dotterweich was president of a Buffalo pharmaceutical firm whose employees unwittingly introduced adulterated drugs into interstate commerce. Dotterweich was unaware of wrongdoing, participated in no fraud, committed no violation and did not authorize a violation by others. Yet the Supreme Court found him guilty on the theory that those at the top were captains of the corporate ship and therefore responsible for the behavior of their subordinates.)

(2) Should the growing practice of hiring respected lawyers to keep brokerage firms in line be encouraged? If so, what *special* codes of conduct are necessary to specify appropriate behavior for their *special* kind of work? This is necessary because, to lawyers, the client comes ahead of society.

(3) Are investigations into the moral character of job applicants warranted? If so, how should they be conducted and evaluated?

(4) Are intensive industry and company sponsored training programs necessary to raise consciousness for ethical issues?

(5) Do hostile raids increase temptations for investment bankers? If the answer is yes, can such temptations be reduced by prohibi-

tions against taking or giving greenmail, requirements that both raider and target make public their plans for restructuring (downsizing),etc.? Should these be evaluated for the public by disinterested outside experts independent of the Federal Trade Commission? The resultant slowing of the takeover/merger process may be a small price for society to pay.

(6) Are new and tougher codes of institutional and individual conduct necessary?

(7) Should ethical audit teams (patterned after instrumentalities used by major accounting firms) be created within each firm?

Purple prose may be evident in the purple ribbon group's final report. That it would be provocative is clear. It might even help. From emphasis on institutional controls it might be inferred that personal integrity is relatively unimportant. The truth of the matter is that individual character is most important. It is hard to get good performances from bad performers. Too often during the applicant's interview and investigating processes, class standing is stressed and "class" character is ignored. Even so, the importance of sound institutional structures is essential.

Two centuries ago James Madison wrote that "as long as the connection subsists between a man's reason and his self-love, institutional controls are always needed." Since neither enlightened leaders nor enlightened clients provide the total answer, one must conclude with Madison that ultimately "in the extent and structure of governance will be found the practical answer to individual greed and group ambitions.[35]

NOTES

1. H. Justin Davidson, "The Top of the World is Flat," *Ethics for Executives: A Harvard Business Review Reprint Series*, Part II (1977) p. 22.

2. *Ibid.*, p. 13.

3. *The Wall Street Journal*, September 18, 1987, p. 28D.

4. Roger Smith, "A New Era in Competition," Ann Arbor: University of Michigan, Major Management Briefing Seminar, August 5, 1987, p. 3. Unpublished.

5. Douglas Frantz, *Levine and Company: Wall Street's Insider Trading Scandal*, New York: Henry Holt Company, 1987.

6. Like many mischief makers, Foster Winans hastened into print with his book, *Trading Secrets: Situation and Scandal on Wall Street*, New York: St. Martin's Press, 1986.

7. *The Wall Street Journal*, October 5, 1987, p.3.

8. John Brooks, *The Takeover Game*, New York: E.P. Dutton, 1987.

9. Remarks by Roger Smith to the Advertising Council in New York City, November 20, 1986, p. 5.

10. Quoted in *Business Week* (September 21, 1987), p. 174.

11. Myron Magnet, "The Decline and Fall of Business Ethics," *Fortune* (October 8, 1986) p. 65.

12. Daniel Tully, "Financial Services—A Changing Industry Where the Consumer Can Only Win," *Review of Business*, St. John's University, Summer, 1985.

13. Arnold S. Relman, "What Are Hospitals For?" The Roger G. Larson Memorial Lecture at the Annual Meeting of the American Hospital Association (Atlanta, Georgia, July 27, 1987). Unpublished.

14. "Thinkers," *Philadelphia Inquirer*, August 27, 1983, pp. 4C and 8C.

15. Alexis de Tocqueville, *Democracy in America*, Garden City, NY: Doubleday American Books, 1969, Ch. 4. Edited by J.P. Mayers.

16. Margaret Mead, "We Need Taboos on Sex and Work," *Redbook Magazine* (April 1978) p. 31.

17. John William Ward, "The Ideal of Individualism and the Reality of Organizations," in Earl Cheit, ed., *The Business Establishment*, New York: John Wiley, 1964, pp. 37-76.

18. Richard Hofstadter, *Social Darwinisin in America*, Boston: Beacon Press, 1955.

19. *Business Week* (November 24, 1986), p. 86.

20. *The New York Times* (October 14, 1987), p. 1.

21. *The New York Times* (October 17, 1987), p. 30.

22. Kenneth Arrow, "The Economics of Moral Hazard: Further Comment," *The American Economic Review* (June 1968), p. 538. See also *The Limits of Organization* (New York: W. W. Norton, Inc., 1974), pp. 26-27.

23. See the seminal article by Armen Alchian and Harold Demsetz, "Production Information Costs and Economic Organizations," *The American Economic Review* (December 1974), pp. 777-95. Barry Mitnick of the University of Pittsburgh has been identified as a major expositor of this theory. Of his many papers this author found two most illuminating: "Agents in the Environment: Managing in Boundary Expanding Roles" which was presented to the 1982 meeting of the Academy of Management in New York, and "Agency Problems in Political Institutions" which was presented to the 1984 annual meeting of the Midwest Political Science Association in Chicago.

24. Wanda Wallace of Texas A and M University has explored the effects of the agency problem for the nonprofit sector. "Agency Theory and Governments and Nonprofit Sector Research" (College Station, TX: Texas A&M, 1986). Unpublished.

25. Barry Mitnick, "The Theory of Agency and Organizational Analysis." Paper presented at the 1986 annual meeting of the American Political Science Association, August 29, 1986.

26. Chester Barnard's old classic, *The Functions of the Executive* (Cambridge: Harvard University Press, 1938) in this mold.

27. Mitnick, "The Theory of Agency and Organizational Analysis," *loc. cit.*, pp. 27-28.

28. The source of this theory has been traced to Frank Knight, *Risk, Uncertainty and Profits* (Boston: Houghton-Mifflin, 1921) and updated by Kenneth Arrow, "Uncertainty and the Welfare Economics of Medical Care," *The American Economic Review* (December 1970), pp. 941-73.

29. Eric Moreen, "The Economics of Ethics: A New Perspective on Agency Theory" (Seattle: University of Washington, 1986). Unpublished.

30. Altruism's weakness resides in the fact that too much is expected of the altruists. If individuals are less than perfect in deciding on their own interests, it follows that they may be less than effective in deciding the fortunes of others. For these reasons most economists and many philosophers prefer utilitarianism where compliance with rules usually works to the advantage of the individual and others. Thomas Schelling, "Game Theory and the Study of Ethical System," *Conflict Resolution* (1984), pp. 33-49.

31. Hirshleifer, "Economics from a Biological Viewpoint," *The Journal of Law and Economics* (April 1977), pp. 1-52.

32. *The Wall Street Journal*, September 18, 1987, p. 20P.

33. Henry Kaufman, "History Lessons We Failed to Learn," *The New York Times*, October 25, 1987.

34. Susan Strange, *Casino Capitalism*, London: Basil Blackwell, 1986. Anthony Bianco called ours a "casino society" where almost everyone, everywhere (Tokyo, London, Frankfurt) is investing with other people's money. *Business Week* (November 9, 1987), p.46.

35. James Madison, *The Federalist*, No. 10.

Fourteen

Ethical Discipline and Religious Hope in the Investment Industry

Donald W. Shriver, Jr.

The title originally assigned to this paper was "God and Wall Street." Some would say that such a title was not only provocative but also oxymoronic, that is, a contradiction in terms. Our culture continues to make room for the term "ethics" in most discussions of public affairs; but it is shy about room for religion. And hardly anyone thinks about God and Wall Street.

An implicit exception to this rule occurred on the evening of Friday, October 23, 1987, in the program "Wall Street Week in Review," hosted by Louis Rukeyser. Four days had passed since "Bloody Monday." Introducing the program, Mr. Rukeyser said something like this: "The sun came up today, the members of your family still love you. The world is still there, you are alive, and much else you count on has not 'crashed.' That is a lot to be thankful for, in spite of what happened to the world on October 19." This is as close to "religious reflection" as public television is likely to get. Mr. Rukeyser was not far from confessing: "Thank God, the world is not really under the control of the stock market. All may not be right with the world, but God being in 'heaven' makes a difference to our much buffeted humanity." In the same program, John Templeton, a Presbyterian and a frequent guest on this series, was the image of serenity. "Long-range," he said, "stocks will continue to be your best investment."

Whether "ethics" requires religious faith as its root and ground remains a question of great dispute among philosophers, culture-critics and ordinary Americans. Hardly disputable, however, is the religious "trace" still visible in the chemistry of much ethical thinking about economics in modern American society. I think, for example, of George Brockway's summation[1] of what he believes would be the elements of truly "ethical economics": Such an ethic would be founded on the principles of (1) the worth of "people rather than things," (2) self-respect fortified by a sufficiency of work and things, (3) the "absolute equality" of human beings to each other whatever may be their inequality of capacity, and (4) a more even distribution of economic opportunities and rewards than those presently obtaining in the world. These great principles activate in me the memory of how some of them came to be in Western culture. How could we be so sure of the "worth" of human beings without the religious stories that suggest our worth to the Power that created us? Why would we expect the material side of our existence to reflect and fortify our own worth, unless we refused that religious option which splits the human world between "spirit" and "flesh"? William Temple said once that Christianity was the most materialistic of the world's religions, and Rabbi Leiser was pointing to the Hebrew roots of that Christian materialism when he commented, "The Seder meal, in the Passover, is part of our holy human work." And as for "absolute" anything in human life, it would be difficult to conceive of some absolute human equality outside of some "ideal observer" or other *viewpoint* distinct from ourselves. The user of such language as Brockway's does not have to be personally religious, but terms like his resound with the historical overtones of the religious ground-bass in the music and cacophony of our culture. H. Richard Niebuhr once commented that, if we believe in God, we have views of the Absolute but no absolute views. Religion in this mode is not a platform for imposing one's own absolutes on other people but a faith that we all live in a Presence which, in power and in goodness, transcends "all that we ask or think."[2] Religion in this mode is not the root of human pride and domination but a rebuke to the same. As Kierkegaard pointed out, it is an invitation, not to pose as Director of the human drama but as actor on a stage whose Audience is God.

Only in this sense would I ever consent to write an essay on the topic, "God and Wall Street!" Like any trained ethicist, I try to do my intellectual bit in identifying various assumptions and principles that shape this and that human action in the world. Like economic historians, I am aware that some of the concepts which make our economic system "work" are concepts refined out of the fires of ancient cultural controversy. Some of those concepts I will use below in calling attention to certain ethical issues in the modern investment industry: the ethical justification of interest, or rent on money; just prices and market-determined prices; social justice as a society's active provision for the needs of its poorest members; and the like. All of these concepts lie deep in the alluvial layers underlying the rivers of economic life that swish and swirl around us everyday. Or, to shift the image a bit, the economic "ships" which we navigate over the waters of our history come equipped with production capacities, inertias forward and sideward, and (especially) charts which tell us something about the purposes and meanings of the voyage itself. One reason we have such a problem talking about religion in relation to shipboard economics is that we seldom stand back to ask those large questions which are the very substance of religion: Where did the human journey originate? Where is it going? What good reasons are there to continue participating in it? All such questions, in a specific sense, are the *dramatic* questions of human life: they concern the nature of the whole plot, the whole drama in which we humans act. Religion is far more concerned with reasons for journeys than with the equipment or even the ships necessary for undertaking them. People of religious faith dare to believe that they know something about those reasons, something about the nature and meaning of the journey as a whole. But they are not bound by their faith to believe that they know everything about these things. Quite the contrary: they are alerted by their faith to their ignorance. Thus it is that an ethic specifically religious, such as Christian ethics, acknowledges two kinds of boundaries at the very start of its thinking about human action in the present: It acknowledges what we know, and that we do not know.

That second boundary, our ignorance, comes to prominence on our visual horizon once in a while, and comes sometimes with the force of a sudden gale. Such was the event of October 19, 1987, in the stock markets of the world. Had this conference been held on October 9-11, 1987, our consciousness of this boundary would not be so stark for all its participants as, in fact, it was on November 9-11, 1987. Two days after October 19, the head of a major investment firm on Wall Street commented in a meeting at Trinity Church, "The loss of *money* is not the great tragedy of the current crash, but the loss of *confidence.*" One dimension of the confidence-loss is the courage of anyone to believe that he or she can understand, predict, and cope with the "behavior" of world capital markets. Something happened to millions of people on Black Monday that took almost all of them, even the most professional, by surprise. Leaders of a system based on concepts of economic rationality, reasonable risk, and fair competition do not like to be taken by large, negative surprise. We no more like it than we like to be overtaken by other tragedies—death, illness, war, and earthquakes.

That we should make such analogies shows how very present is the boundary of ignorance in our attempts to be ethically reasonable about large economic dynamics. Below, I intend to try to be ethically reasonable about a number of sub-principles that seem to flow from the three notions above, basic to the capitalist system and basic for the operation of the investment industry: interest, fair prices and justice. But the exercise has something of the quality of "cultivating your own garden," so wisely recommended by Voltaire through Candide but so unwisely recommended, too, for it is not easy, or even rational, to cultivate a garden in the midst of a hurricane. Or, to change the image, Hamlet ordered up from the visiting players a play that fitted into the drama current in Elsinore Castle and into Hamlet's own sense of role in that drama. When one is not sure—has no right to be sure—of what the large drama is, one has difficulty knowing how to construct the smaller plots in which one might be able to play a role. My use of this image allies me with philosophers like Alasdair MacIntyre and theologians like H. Richard Niebuhr who contend that human affairs, and ethics in those affairs, are more like discerning large plots and figuring out your own small roles in them, and less like the working out of rational deductions from principles and the calculation of foreseeable results of this or that human action. What if you live in a time when the principles are in great need of revision? And when much that used to be foreseeable is no longer so? Then you may be left with an effort to stumble, with your neighbors, into some new role-playing. As you do so, you will search for north-star-like direction from something ethically more relevant than the principles of a market system. You are open, as not in "normal" times, to something like the large dramatic contexts of religion.

I have not been asked to portray those contexts in any comprehensiveness. I turn instead to some normal, normative principles that seem to be in the ethical stratum of the daily operation of the investment industry. But I hope that this analysis will help raise the curtain on larger dramas in which we all may need to play. I cannot help hoping that the very inadequacy of this analysis for comprehending, coping with, and being *religious* in relation to investment in our society will be all the more evident now that we meet in early November of 1987 rather than in early October.

I have divided the rest of the paper into two sections: first a set of corollaries to the three principles of rent, justice in information-pricing, and need; and second some questions that such principles and corollaries ought to raise in any analyses of three pertinent cases of ethical import in the contemporary investment industry: insider-trading, corporate takeovers, and the purchase of stock-index futures. At the end, I return to raise again the question of what the economic perturbations of the American economy in 1987 should mean for the *religious* redirection of the economic thinking of Americans.

Some Corollaries of Rent, Informational Freedom, and Need in Investment Transactions

1. *Information and its costs: In a market with many competing buyers and sellers where information costs are low, interest rates (rents*

on money) will be adjusted to supply, demand, and level of risk; but information costs, when high, diminish effective market competition.

One of the more appealing features of Adam Smith's market of small-scale business operators was that it assumed the availability of information about products and competitive sources of supply. Modern economic systems, almost paradoxically, have raised and lowered the cost of information about innumerable products, including objects of investment. Technical details must now be filtered to investors through experts and trusted advisers. "Comparison shopping" for some products is very difficult in some market sectors. And *long-term* profitability may be intrinsically impossible to predict—which means that there is nothing in market signals to guide an investor except his or her tolerance for risk and confidence in personal hunch. With the advent of electronic communication and computer-driven stock transactions, however, information costs for some participants in the market have fallen on a global scale. In an era when huge amounts of information are quickly available to larger numbers of investors than ever before, one may even ask if this very availability does not inexorably push investors and producers towards shorter and shorter-range profits. This is a debatable assumption. Does the information revolution benefit or threaten the innovative enterprise that requires long years to mature? How can anyone these days build a business carefully and persistently when competition for scarce capital and quick profit constantly threaten both the care and the persistence? Behind the takeover "industry" lies an impatience with long-delayed profitability, which in matters of economic change may not be the only signal of the future worth attending to.

2. *Regulation and responsibility: In a complexly organized, large-scale society, various forms of monopoly on information, relevant to investment opportunity, are inevitable. The investment industry will require at least regular self-policing of these monopolies, or society through government will have to do the policing. But neither will eliminate a role for plain personal responsibility for fair-play in the distribution of information.*

When the leaders of giant corporate organizations, such as General Motors, begin to think about some major shift in their resources, they have already in their hands enormous power for benefiting their own economic interests. Long ago, through both internal corporate norms and external political controls, our society sought to prevent the gross misuse of such power for such benefits. But the ability of anyone, inside or outside a particular investment decision, to keep open a "free market" among all possible beneficiaries, is very limited. Someone will always be at the head of the line among those who buy a particular stock, and the benefit of knowing which line to head will always accrue to those who have some level of "inside" information. I discuss this at more length below. Here it is important to observe that self-control, even to the point of forgoing large economic benefits, may be indispensable to the working of "informational fair-play" in the market system. And the persons who must be in control of their own economic ambition include everyone from the finance committee of the corporation to the youngest stock broker in investment firms.

Just before his fall, Ivan Boesky told the graduating class of U.C.L.A. that one could be greedy and "feel good about yourself." That is one form of self-interest, but in reply one has to ask what sort of self Mr. Boesky is interested in. Little in his Jewish or my Christian heritage suggests that we are destined by our Creator to enrich ourselves, without limit, at the expense of other people's misfortunes. That, by definition, is what greed is. In the Bible greed is a sin. In our economic system it makes some rich while making some others poor. These days Mr. Boesky is studying the Talmud across the street in my neighboring institution, the Jewish Theological Seminary. I rather hope that somewhere in that text he stumbles over some classic Jewish arguments against the ethic he propounded to those graduating seniors in California.

3. *The well-off and the poor: A market system is unlikely to serve effectively to express or meet the needs of the neediest persons and groups in a society; and large aggregates of economic power, like majorities in politics, are likely to influence markets in their own favor to the neglect of the interests of minorities.*

One can blunt the force of this corollary by pointing to the statistics of increasing numbers of equity-owners in modern American society and by assuming that in our modern "mixed" economy we are all agreed that government must effect transfer payments to the truly unfortunate. The problem with this reply is that the bulk of government transfer-payments are *not* to the "truly unfortunate" in American society but to the middle class. The large blocks of stock owned by pension plans, after all, represent the interests of people with the best-funded pension. Of course, while they may not be effective participants in markets yet, one argument for government welfare programs may be the equipping of poor people for participation in markets. This is Milton Friedman's argument for the so-called Negative Income Tax.

As humane and hopeful as such arguments may be, they still do not address the weak link between what markets "say" in response to money and what they say in response to the needs of total populations. The rise in proprietary hospitals, for example, is a response to the ability of some population segments to pay for quality medical care, and one result of this innovation is greater pressure upon the facilities of non-profit and public medical facilities. In the same industry, cost-lowering H.M.O. care probably depends less on market opportunity for producers and more on the willingness of some physicians to put caps on their annual incomes in the form of salaries. Here, again, personal responsibility may intervene as a response to needs to which a market will not respond.

4. *Doing justice and doing well: Social injustice is probably inevitable when no one has any economic incentive to tend to the needs of the economically weak members of society. Investments that supply such incentive have strong ethical warrant, therefore. But economic incentives for integrity and law-abiding in the industry are no substitute for sanctions of power, inside and outside the firm, pushing society towards action on behalf of the truly poor.*

The Federal "war on poverty" was widely criticized for providing jobs for middle class residents of the ghetto while not helping the employment of many of their poor neighbors. It was further criticized (in its extension into the C.E.T.A. program, for example) for giving people "busy work." If such programs have a flaw, however, it is not the start on employment which wages offer every worker. It is rather the difficulty of finding a way to use short-range income benefits to some poor people to enhance the possibility of longer-range benefits to them and others. That, apparently, is what has happened in the Head Start Program, in which simple tasks performed by adults in day care centers have significantly boosted children's capacity to take later advantage of schooling. In a just economic order, government might collaborate with business to be sure that poor people get paid to do things that are good for them in the short run and good for needy others in at least the long run. Here, again, conflict between short-run profit and long-run human benefit may be severe. The conflict exists for investors, too. Many of us stand to benefit from a more skilled national labor force, a decline in unemployable people, and a decrease in the alternative employment system that is crime. But executives honed to the discipline of quarterly reports and brokers alert to customer profit before the end of the tax year are not likely to think hard about such social costs and benefits. Such costs and benefits affect the corporation as well. In the *long* run, a deteriorated educational system, like a deteriorated natural environment, undermines the economic system itself. Here, the "corporate responsibility movement" among stockholders may have the task of convincing fellow stockholders that it is better for their company to invest in the technical and social integrity of the next generation of workers than in the quickest way to raise the market value of the stock. Perhaps all ethical conflicts can be reduced to argument about short and long ranges of proposed human benefit. More to the point of justice, however, is the conflict between benefit for the current participants in the social system and benefit to those—the poor and the unborn—who cannot participate in markets. Some may say that this is not a "rational" economic concern, for it takes account of preferred time-spans that have nothing to do with the calculation of benefit itself. Others may say that it is up to government, through taxes, to make it cost-effective for corporations to take longer rather than shorter time-spans of social benefit seriously. In any event, both as creatures and as sinners, human beings always have some preferred time-spans, and usually some calculable receivers of benefit are left out of the calculations. It is a great ethical leap to put the good of the next generation on a par with that of your own, and a greater leap yet to suffer damage to one's own economic class in preference to the interests of the poor.

To speak of these justice-concerns, of course, is to touch on responsibilities which no one may be able to exercise chiefly in his or her investment decisions, either as investor or employee of an investment firm. But one of the freedoms that a democracy provides for citizens is the freedom to pursue in other subsystems of society (government, religion, the voluntary association) versions of justice that the economic subsystem may serve poorly. Another version of this freedom—individual entrepreneurship inside the investment firm—may not be so promising, however. Knowledgeable people in firms like E.F. Hutton and Solomon Brothers have said that individual account managers, often young and upwardly mobile, are only too free to cut ethical and legal corners, and they sometimes do so with the implicit encouragement of senior managers. As one such senior manager said recently in a conversation, "The word from top management is often, 'Get results, don't get us in legal trouble and, if you are courting such trouble, at least don't let us know it.'" The analogy to the President's directives to Oliver North here is exact.

The observance of law and ethics in any organization has as much to do with the power and supervisory responsibility of managers as with the integrity of the character of individual employees. And, of course, when the leaders of an industry—those with the great reputations for "success"—set an example of bribery, lawbreaking and apparently infinite rapacity, the effect on the neophytes in the industry is likely to be demoralizing. Fear of being caught may now substitute for fear of economic failure, and other noneconomic sanctions may now come to bear upon everyone's ordinary workday. But ethics in this event has taken a backseat to cynicism and fear, which will not soon cease to dominate the spirit of the investment workplace.

Three Questions of Ethics in the Contemporary Investment Industry

1. *Insider Trading*
A. What is just, fair or beneficial about full and equal disclosure of information to potential buyers of securities?

For disclosure to be full and equal, it must be "public," and such publicity has at least two ethically admirable benefits: it gives equal opportunity to many potential buyers to serve their self-chosen economic interests; and it also expands the opportunity for buyers to implement their other, nonprofit interests as well. This second argument for disclosure is often neglected, because popular economic rhetoric seems to assume that self-interest in economics is the same as economic self-interest. Again, much depends on what kind of self one is interested in. It is a variety of economic determinism to assume that the pursuit of "mental income" has no force in the marketplace. (And, since humans can get "mental income" from a huge array of putative goods and evils, the notion of *economic* determinism, in both socialist and capitalist theory, never seems to acquire convincing specification. *Everybody* likes "bread and roses.") Promoters of the six-year boycott of the Nestle Corporation counted on such force among customers and also among Nestle managers. They assumed that Nestle would do something about infant-formula marketing, not only from market share considerations, but also from worldwide reputation considerations. One of the arguments for at least the ideal of a "free" market in a democratic society has to be that, since human beings do not in fact live by bread alone, such freedom gives them scope to deploy their resources in the direction of a great variety of combinations of wants and needs.

B. What is unjust about insider-trading?
The answer is implicit in much that is written above. Insider trading expands and (literally) capitalizes on unjust distributions of power *already in place* in the society; it corrupts that side of the competitive system which exerts some control on the power of the most powerful to impose their will on the least powerful; it undercuts even the power of majorities to protect themselves by putting their interests second to the interests of a secretive minority; it is a greedy misappropriation of a form of wealth—information—more vital to the economic relations of huge aggregates of people than ever before in history; and it is an attempt to subvert and bypass legal controls that express something of the ethical wisdom of political democracy, especially its fear of the inclination of the few to connive against the interests of the many.

Walter Rauschenbusch wrote: "The strong have enough power to pursue their just interests and enough power left over to pursue their unjust interests as well." Reinhold Niebuhr was describing the same theologically-tutored anthropology when he wrote: "The human capacity for justice makes democracy possible; the human inclination to injustice makes democracy necessary." Adam Smith's famous disdain for business people who combine their interests under the facade of achieving "some public good" stems from this same suspicion. Insider trading is a conspiracy of the few against the many.

Obviously, this very concept of "insider trading" is a creation of law and political philosophy, external to the efficiency of markets. Indeed, the demand for certain controls, ensuring more or less equal information for potential investors, always involves costs to implement. Such costs may retard efficiency. Democrats argue that the costs are worth paying, but the argument has rough going in a world market, some of whose powerful actors have no such costs imposed on them by their governments.

Perhaps the most troubling question here concerns the specification of insideness in trading. Particularly troubling is the question of insider *non*-trading, which can be as profitable a response to scarce information as its opposite, insider trading. When some investors, following market signals, behave rationally by trading, others stand perfectly still in the markets because they know better what is coming.

In any event, "full" disclosure equally accessible to all the public, is at best an ideal and at worst a myth of the investment system. Profit-relevant information is never fully, equally and justly distributed. Full information remains a privilege of the privileged, the well-placed, the quick and the strong. The very use which most investors make of a broker embodies the limits that most of us have for taking advantage of information that would be available to us if we but had world enough and time. If and when a limited issue of promising stock comes on the market, what is illegal about our broker putting himself or herself at the head of the line of buyers? Or relatively far up in line? More difficult, yet most likely, are those occasions when, in the normal course of some investors' associations, they acquire information that heightens their ability to predict where some profits are on the horizon. If the chairwoman of the board cancels her regular golf game with you and you find out that she has gone on a quickly-arranged trip to Zurich, do you have in your possession the materials for an educated guess that an international merger is in the offing? What if you happen to have a close business association with persons, leaders in government or the investment industry, who have excellent track records for sensing shifts in the market? Was it only personal hunches or a superior place in the market informational network that enabled some Americans to bail out of the stock market into cash the week before October 19? The questions are more easily asked than answered, but they all come up against the measure of the "blameless" person described in Psalm 15:4, "who swears to his own hurt and does not change." (For ethical analysis of modern investment, that particular Psalm is troubling, for it continues the description with a fifth verse: "who does not put out his money to interest, and does not take a bribe against the innocent." A footnote in my edition of the Bible saves us here: "The prohibition of interest has reference to charitable loans made for the relief of distress rather than to the purely business type of loan which became common in a later commercial age." But someone should remind that footnote-writer that the Bible knows very little about human transactions that are "purely business.")

2. *Corporate Takeovers*

In the past four years, some 12,000 mergers and acquisitions, valued at about half a trillion pre-October 19 dollars, have taken place. Controversy over the effects of these transactions upon the Crash of 1987 will continue for many years. The ethical part of the debate may center on two contrary claims. Takeovers and the threat of takeovers put corporate management on their mettle, challenging them to greater efficiency, imagination, and competitive zeal. (That would be the view of a Carl Icahn and Boone Pickens.) No, say the critics, the majority of takeover targets have been well-run companies suffering temporary economic adversity but on their way to greater prosperity, which others now want to purchase for themselves at no extra benefit to anyone except to stockholders, whose moral interest in a company is only pecuniary. (That would be the view of an Anthony Solomon, president of the Federal Reserve Bank of New York.) Add to this the economic burden which new internal borrowing puts upon a company trying to protect itself against a takeover, or the effect of some takeovers on the destruction of jobs and company cultures, and one has a case for saying: corporate takeovers manipulate money and promises of future profit to stockholders, with little or no consideration for new, real production for the benefit of a larger society.

This argument had become more or less conventional among takeover critics before October 19. Now they have assigned to takeover specialists a significant role in the Crash and have persuaded a number of Congress members to consider a law that would take some of the profits out of takeovers financed largely through huge borrowing on small margins. Said *The New York Times:* "It is ironic that takeover fever almost produced a market 'meltdown' . . . because it was the explosion in merger and acquisition activity that had made this such an astoundingly lucrative, and unsettling, era before Monday."[3]

It seems simplistic in the extreme to elevate takeover transactions to the status of first-cause of the market meltdown, not to speak of the status of moral evil; but the moral dimension of what "unsettled" some observers of these transactions, even before Bloody Monday, should be identifiable. This writer is poorly equipped to be sure precisely where the evil is located. My best surmise is that of many another relatively naive observer of this most speculative side of stock markets: somewhere in their rise to wealth, speculators cross a line between offering something for the money and offering very little of anything. Hidden in these transactions are two matters of moral concern, old in the culture of the West but unavoidable, apparently, in the culture of capitalism: greed and the unjust price.

It is easy to score greed in the aims and the behavior of many arbitragers; it is not so easy to speak anymore about "a just price" in an economy built on the theory that prices are just when people voluntarily agree to pay them. To revert to the old notion that money stands for some "real" value inherent in the thing being sold, is to raise the ghost of an ethic long thought dead. In fact the spirit of the just price may still be with us, if only in a certain common sense, among a mass of investors, that one cannot morally or empirically for long make something out of nothing. The first seller to glimpse this truth about a specific investment makes money; the last to glimpse it is left holding an expensive empty bag. *Economic* transactions, insofar as they have anything to do with ethical integrity, ought at least to have a distinction from gambling.

3. *Stock Index Futures*

As a case of advanced offense against the same principles that raise questions about the takeover business, there is the purchase, through borrowed cash, of options to buy stock whose possible future worth will be many times the borrowed sums—or many times less. Again, as the *New York Times* puts it: "These high-powered new securities, which allow an investor to make a bet in the direction of the overall market without having to buy or sell dozens of individual stocks, and with only a tiny down payment, have been interacting with the stock market explosively for three years—but never so much as Monday" the nineteenth of October, 1987.[4] The descriptive language here is that for gambling, raising not only the question of how much reward any human should get for successfully risking his or her own resources but why they should get notably rewarded at all for risking mostly the resources of other people, that is, loans. It is a routine in the investment business, of course, that one borrows money invested at low risk and low interest to invest in higher risk and higher return. How high is it legitimate for this process to go? What is the point at which investment in something "real" effectively disappears, to be replaced by . . . . a bubble? Presumably the economy of the United States is now protected against some of the bubble-phenomena of the nineteen-twenties; but what about this presumption? The question makes more sense now than before the October 1987 crash.

Investment in the Service and Misservice of Social Good

Whether one speaks of ethics as the matching of collective behavior to certain stipulated principles of right, such as justice, or as the shaping of collective behavior to serve certain goals for defining the good society, the question of doing right or doing good *socially* is bound to occur in any ethical discussion of economic systems. Classic capitalist theory externalizes this discussion, asking the disputants individually to enter their particular notions of the right or the good for society into the system through competitive market transactions. In recent years the "corporate responsibility" movement has taken this theory at its word, calling supporters to use their collective market power (analogous to the collective market power of business corporations) to shape economic benefit to various classes of people. Members of this movement are compelled by their ethical commitments to enquire into a variety of facts that market prices do not always reveal—such as how their investments help or harm these classes of people. Like other investors, they are sometimes unable to be sure of the (future) facts, so they are likely to repair to principles such as justice with high symbolic meanings remote from mundane economics. An alternative ethical style or mood is one that draws from experiences like Bloody Monday of '87, an experience of surprise, shock or reorientation in a crisis. As I commented at the beginning, from such experiences humans sometimes derive new perceptions of their life-stories and act in roles different from any in which they have acted before.

Whether by religious vision that centers on the plight of the world poor, a commitment to democratic "liberty and justice for all," or a new awareness of the finitude of planet earth, a sizable number of investors and other constituents of corporate responsibility movements believe that, if they are to be investors, they must do so for social purpose as well as for their own profit. Here at the end of this paper, I will not attempt to assess the state of the argument between those who expect the market to do well by them and those who expect the market to do good as well. But I will conclude with a précis of the ethic which many, if not all, in the movement seek to implement.

For them, an investment is most likely to serve the social good:

—when it increases the ability of the weakest people of society to meet their basic needs.

—when profit from the investment has its origin and benefit in the work of the spectrum of people (managers, workers, suppliers, customers) who use the investment. (That the profit should be produced from only one of these groups, or in disproportion from any of them without proportionate reward, is exploitation. To include customers in this list is again to suggest that there is still something resembling a just price in market transactions).

—when the investment offers individuals and groups incentive to serve some social good beyond themselves.

By the same token, an investment is most likely to *misserve* the social good:

—when it inflicts large penalties on any group of people without providing them either direct or indirect rewards, (some plant closings, some workload increases, and some early retirements.)

—when its long-range harms to majorities outweigh its short-range benefit to a minority. (The case of some divestments in South Africa, where compensations for jobs lost to some non-white workers may be impossible to supply by the divestor. When the latter situation occurs, a serious conflict between this pair of principles arises. Divestment may in fact hurt some black workers, but long-range hope for nonviolent political change in South Africa may be served by such economic strategy.)

—when the major result of the investment is to make the rich richer and the poor no better or worse off. (The case of some efficiencies that follow corporate takeovers, some of the unemployment resulting from plant closings, and some investments in elite-controlled poor countries is a key principle in the writings of John Rawls on justice.)

Are markets, especially investment markets, poor servants of social justice? Set up to offer individuals a chance to compete economically with other individuals, can markets do much more than tame the acquisitive instinct of some by forcing them to compete with others? Given unequal resources with which to compete, can markets do other than reflect or magnify this inequality? The answer to this last question would seem to be that there are only two ways in which markets can serve the interests of people who participate least in markets: (1) external regulation or re-distribution by government, applying its own standards of justice; or (2) internal dynamics generated by investors who insist that their money serve social justice as well as their profit, even if this insistence means that profit must diminish if justice is to flourish. Probably the "bottom line" of the social-responsibility-in-investment movement is some version of this latter, multi-valued choice: less profit with justice, in preference to more profit without it. This is clearly the policy of the Ecumenical Develop-ment Cooperative Society (E.D.C.S.) organized by the World Council of Churches. This organization specializes in small loans to farmers and vil-lagers in the Third World who cannot command the attention of large investors or central governments. The pay-back record of these loans so far in the ten-year history of the E.D.C.S. has been remarkable. The principal of its investment funds appears quite secure, but no dividends have yet been paid. A moral capitalism may require its participants to be willing to set aside some of their capital for below-market rate loans to the poor.

Postscript: To Return to Larger Stories

Reflection on ethics in the investment industry in modern America moves the reflector inexorably beyond that industry to the ethics of the American public itself. Many of the ethical questions inside the industry arise from the history and culture of the American people. As well, any of the grave problems now facing the industry cry out for new readings of that history, new recovery of old cultural wisdom, and the devising of new practical collective commitments that are the stuff of political pol-icy, political history and political story.

I know of no more powerful recent diagnosis of and prescription for this larger picture than the long article by Peter G. Peterson in the Octo-ber 1987 issue of *The Atlantic*, "The Morning After."[5] It made riveting reading in the month after its publication. Peterson's analysis has as much to do with the psychology of collective blindness to historic fact as it does with forgetfulness of economic and ethical wisdom. It has to do su-premely with what American politicians will have to start telling their constituents if governmental policy is to address the facts of "investment failure" in the country as a whole. ("Fact" here might best be translated as "event," an important truth which rears up in our social consciousness, having been avoidable for a long time. In and as an event, it now compels our attention.)

In fact, says Peterson, "we have managed to twist the global economy into the most lopsided imbalance between saving (foreign) and spending (American) ever witnessed in the industrialized era. In the process—as we all know—we have transformed ourselves from the world's largest creditor into the world's largest debtor." Quoting David Hale, Peterson adds: "The U.S. is a debtor nation with the habits of a creditor nation while Germany and Japan are creditor nations with the habits of debtor nations."

In fact, the superior economic position of these two countries relates directly to the high levels of investment they have sustained during all the years since the 1950s. During the past twenty years, Japan's total net investment as a share of GNP

> . . . has fallen from 22.6 percent to 16.1 percent; the latter figure, however, is still three times larger than the equivalent U.S. figure for the 1980s (5.3 percent) . . . It is a spectacle that ought to shock Americans: a population half the size of our own living on a group of islands the size of California, is adding more each year to its stock of factories, houses, bridges, and laboratories—in absolute terms— than we are to ours. And Japan still has savings left over, about $80 billion in 1986, to lend to thriftless foreigners. (About $50 billion of that sum was lent to us.) Between the two countries, therefore, the 1986 disparity in net savings ($380 billion in Japan versus only $125 billion in the United States, a six-to-one per capita difference) was even more lopsided.

In fact, the American government itself has set the example to its citizens in living beyond its annual income and borrowing huge resources from the future, not as an investment in future wealth but to fund current consumption, especially in national defense and Social Security for the elderly. "Our government's function as an investor, a steward of our collective future, is small and shrinking. Its function as a consumer, a switchboard for income transfers, is large and growing." The majority of those transfers, through various entitlement programs, do not pass the test of justice for the poor but instead go to sustain those in our society who are middle class or above. As for the poor, probably no more than 20 percent of the half billion of benefit programs now goes to them. "The rest represents income transfers from non-poor taxpayers to non-poor beneficiaries (and, increasingly, to non-poor purchasers of federal debt)." Meantime, federal investment in education, job skill training, environmental preservation, research and infrastructure (roads, bridges, parks and buildings) "has plummeted."

Thus, in fact, the great human injustice building up here is not to be suffered by anyone in contemporary America. Given the same trends, it will be suffered by generations to come. The time has come for old wisdom—native to investment ethics in both the socialist and capitalist systems—be reasserted in policy: ". . . if the flow of invested endowment from each generation to the next has ceased—and if each generation instead insists on its 'right' to consume all its own product and part of the next generation's as well—then we can count on a meager and strife-torn future."

What are the political policies to be derived from this economic-ethical wisdom? Most of the answers involve some form of hard collective discipline for Americans all. Such discipline has failed to get any American president elected in recent decades: a really tamed federal budget deficit, a limit on entitlements for the middle class and the rich, new taxes on either income or consumption, and new tax incentives for increasing the rate of private saving. To advocate such stringency for all living Americans will call for rare political courage on the part of new coalitions of politicians. It will require them to tell us things we wish were not true, but which are true. Above all, Peterson says,

> True vision requires the forging of a farsighted and realistic connection between our present and our future. It means recognizing in today's choices the sacrifices all of us must make for posterity. America's unfettered individualism has endowed our people with enormous energy and great aspirations. It has not, however, given us license to do anything we please so long as we do it with conviction.

To end this essay with this postscript is simply to confess *where* the real, colossal, public discussion of investment ethics has to happen in the near future of the United States of America: not merely in the investment industry, but among us all. We are told by the pollsters that over ninety percent of Americans believe in God. If we believe in One resembling the God of the Bible, we believe in that Presence who lures us into a future more hopeful than our present. In the Bible the doors of the future swing on the hinges of repentance, and collective repentance at that. Saving and investing more money is not likely to be the only or the chief step of a repentant body politic in America, but it is bound to be one of the steps, if only as a token of our corporate willingness to serve human causes that will outlast our own generation. That remains one specification of the great divine law of society, that we are to love our neighbors as human beings like ourselves.

NOTES

1. See the essay by George Brockway, "The Future of Business Ethics," in this volume.

2. Ephesians 3:20.

3. *New York Times*, October 26, 1987.

4. *Ibid.*

5. All quotations from Peter G. Peterson, "The Morning After," *The Atlantic*, Vol. 260, No. 4 (October 1987), pp. 43-69.

Contributors

G. Robert Blakey is O'Neill Professor of Law at the University of Notre Dame School of Law. He received his A.B. and L.L.B. at the University of Notre Dame. He is the author of *Techniques in the Investigation and Prosecution of Organized Crime*, and was the principal author of the Racketeer-Influenced and Corrupt Organization Act (RICO).

George P. Brockway is an economist, president of the Yale University Press and former chairman and director of W. W. Norton and Company. He received his undergraduate degree from Williams College and did postgraduate work at Yale University. He is the author of *Economies: What Went Wrong and Why and Some Things to Do About It*, a columnist for the *New Leader*, and an honorary member of the Society of American Historians.

Richard T. De George is a University Distinguished Professor of Philosophy at the University of Kansas, vice president of the International Federation of Philosophical Societies and past president of the Society of Business Ethics. He received his Ph.D. from Yale University and has been visiting professor at Santa Clara University and the University of St. Gallen, Switzerland. He has written widely in the field of business ethics, and is co-editor of *Ethics, Free-Enterprise and Public Policy*, and the author of *Business Ethics*. Professor DeGeorge has been the recipient of numerous fellowships, including National Endowment for Humanities, Ford Foundation and Fulbright.

Kirk O. Hanson is a management consultant and a senior lecturer in business administration at the Stanford University Graduate School of Business. He received his B.A. and M.B.A. from Stanford and was a Rockefeller Fellow at Yale University. He has been a consultant on corporate public policy, ethics, and business practices, and served as an expert witness in trade secret legal cases. He is chairman of Stanford University's

251

Commission on Investment Responsibility and has developed ethics workshops and seminars.

John W. Houck is a professor of management in the College of Business Administration at the University of Notre Dame and co-director of the Notre Dame Center for Ethics and Religious Values in Business. A former Ford and Danforth fellow, he has earned both a liberal arts and J.D. degree from Notre Dame, an M.B.A. from the University of North Carolina at Chapel Hill, and a master of law from Harvard. He has lectured and conducted workshops on the role of religious and humane values in business. He has co-edited *Matter of Dignity: Inquiries Into the Humanization of Work*, and *The Common Good and U.S. Capitalism*, and co-authored *Full Value: Cases in Christian Business Ethics*.

Gregg A. Jarrell is director of research and senior vice president for The Alcar Group, Inc. and former chief economist for the Securities and Exchange Commission. He received his B.A. from the University of Delaware and his M.B.A. and Ph.D. from the University of Chicago. He has taught at the University of Rochester and worked at the University of Chicago's Center for the Study of the Economy and the State. While at Chicago, he served as consultant on antitrust matters with the Federal Trade Commission's Advisory Panel on Tender Offer Policy. He has authored numerous articles on the economics and regulations of tender offers and has had considerable experience serving as an expert witness in securities litigation and antitrust cases.

Burton M. Leiser is Edward J. Mortola Professor of Philosophy at Pace University. He studied at the University of Chicago, Yeshiva University, and received his Ph.D. from Brown University and a J.D. from Drake University. He has taught at Fort Lewis College, SUNY, Sir George William University in Montreal, and Drake University. He is the author of *Custom, Law and Morality, Justice and Morals*, and *Values in Conflict*. He has authored many articles on topics ranging from archaeological discoveries to capital punishment and terrorism in such journals as *International Journal of Ethics, Standard Review of International Law, Judaism*, and *The Journal of Business and Professional Ethics*. Professor Leiser is also a practicing attorney, having been admitted to the bars of Iowa and New York, as well as the federal courts.

Dennis P. McCann is a professor of religious studies and director of the Center for Study of Values in Modern Society at DePaul University. He received his St.L. from the Gregorian University in Rome and his Ph.D.

from the University of Chicago Divinity School. He has published *New Experiment in Democracy, Christian Realism and Liberation Theology* and is co-author of *The New Messiah? A Future for Practical Theology.*

Alfred (Pete) C. Morley is concurrently president and chief executive officer of the Financial Analysts Federation and president and chief executive officer of the Institute of Chartered Financial Analysts. He received his undergraduate and graduate degrees from West Virginia University. He was formerly the managing partner of the Wainwright Organization, vice president and investment officer of the Security Trust Company, and president and director of the Frank Russell Investment Management Company. Mr. Morley has provided testimony on security and investment industry matters at SEC hearings.

Patricia A. O'Hara is an associate professor of law at the University of Notre Dame School of Law. She received her B.A. degree *summa cum laude* from the University of Santa Clara and was awarded a Kiley Fellowship and attended the University of Notre Dame Law School, graduating *summa cum laude.* She practiced law in San Francisco with Broebeck, Phleges and Harrison for six years before returning to Notre Dame where she teaches and writes in the area of corporate and securities law. Professor O'Hara has published articles in the *UCLA Law Review* and the *Georgetown Law Journal.* She is a member of the California State Bar, the Federal Bar for the Northern and Central Districts of California, and U.S. Court of Appeals for the Ninth Court.

John J. Phelan, Jr. is chairman and chief executive officer of the New York Stock Exchange. He received his undergraduate degree in business administration from Adelphi University and was awarded an honorary doctorate from Hamilton College. He serves as director of Securities Industry Automation Corporation and is past chairman of the board of the New York Futures Exchange. The trustees of Adelphia College elected him the chairman of the board. He was decorated Knight Sovereign Order of Malta and Knight Sovereign Order Holy Sepulchre and was appointed to the Cardinal's Committee of Laity. Mr. Phelan has been awarded many honors for working with the youth of New York.

Frank K. Reilly is Bernard J. Hank Professor of Business Administration at the University of Notre Dame. He received his undergraduate degree from Notre Dame and his Ph.D. from the University of Chicago. Professor Reilly is a Chartered Financial Analyst, a member of the Council of Examiners and Grading Committee of the Institute of Chartered Financial Analysts. He was president of the Financial Management Association, the Eastern Finance Association and is currently chairman of the Board of Trustees of the FMA. He has served on the editorial board of *Financial Management, The Financial Review, Journal of Financial Education,* and *Quarterly Review of Economics and Business.* His published articles, monographs and papers number well over 100. He is the author of *Investments, Investment Analysis* and *Portfolio Management.*

Donald W. Shriver, Jr. is president of Union Theological Seminary. He has studied at Davidson College, Union Theological Seminary, Yale University and received his Ph.D. from Harvard University. He is an internationally-recognized scholar and spokesman in the field of Christian ethics and is a past president of the American Society of Christian Ethics. Professor Shriver teaches "The Public Accountability of the Business Corporation" at the Columbia School of Business Administration. He has written over 60 articles and nine books, including *An Introduction to Christian Ethics for Young People, Rich Man/Poor Man, Medicine and Religion, Redeeming the City, Spindles and Spires: A Study of Religion and Social Change in Gastonia* and *The Lord's Prayer: A Way of Life.* Long active in the World Council of Churches, he has just completed a term as a member of the Governing Board of the National Council of Churches of Christ.

William B. Smith is a senior member of management for Dean Witter Capital Markets. He received his B.B.A. from the University of Notre Dame and his M.B.A. from the Wharton School of Business. He began his career with Paine Weber Capital Markets in the Investment Banking Department in 1967. In 1982, Mr. Smith joined Dean Witter and is presently the director of investment banking.

Paul E. Tierney, Jr. is chairman of Gollust, Tierney and Oliver and a partner in both Coniston Partners and Sabre Associates. He graduated *magna cum laude* from the University of Notre Dame, after which he spent two years with the Peace Corps in Chile. In 1966 and 1969, he was a Baker Scholar at Harvard University. Mr. Tierney was the founder, principal, and vice president of Inter Link Corporation, vice president and founder of Starwood-Geneve Corporation, general manager of Continental Illinois Limited, and vice president of White, Weld and Company.

Clarence C. Walton is the former president of Catholic University and currently the Charles Lamont Post Professor of Ethics and the Professions at American College. He studied at the University of Scranton, Syracuse University and received his Ph.D. from Catholic University of America. He has taught at Duquesne University, University of Scranton, Columbia University, University of California at Berkeley and Oregon State University. Internationally, he has taught in Switzerland, Finland and Argentina. Professor Walton has written and published extensively, including *Corporate Social Responsibility, Big Government and Big Business* and *Ethos and the Executive.* He is the editor of *Ethics of Corporate Conduct* and *Inflation and National Survival.* His most recent book is *The Moral Manager.*

John G. Weithers is chairman of the board of the Midwest Stock Exchange. He graduated from the University of Notre Dame and received his M.B.A. from DePaul University. He served as a U.S. naval officer for two years. In 1958, he joined the Midwest Stock Exchange as an examiner and was subsequently promoted to secretary, senior vice president and executive vice president. Mr. Weithers was appointed president and chief operating officer of the Exchange in 1980 and chairman and chief executive officer in 1983. He is a member of the Board of Trustees of DePaul University, a director of the Chicago Association of Commerce and Industry, and a director of the Federal Life Insurance Company (Mutual).

Oliver F. Williams, C.S.C. is an associate provost at the University of Notre Dame and co-director of Notre Dame's Center for Ethics and Religious Values in Business. He teaches and researches in the field of business, society and ethics. He holds a Ph.D. in theology from Vanderbilt University and has had the experience of a research year at the Graduate School of Business Administration at Stanford University. Father Williams is the chair-elect of the Social Issues Division of the National Academy of Management and has published articles on ethics and religious values in business in journals including *The Harvard Business Review, The California Management Review, Theology Today,* and *The Journal of Business Ethics.* He is the co-editor or author of several books, including *The Apartheid Crisis: How We Can Do Justice in a Land of Violence, Full Value: Cases in Christian Business Ethics,* and *The Common Good and U.S. Capitalism.*

Robert K. Wilmouth is president of the National Futures Association and has served in this capacity since the organization began operations in 1982. Prior to that, he was president and chief executive officer of the Chicago Board of Trade. Mr. Wilmouth was in the banking industry for

27 years. As senior vice president of the First National Bank of Chicago, he was responsible for the construction of the bank's present headquarters in Chicago. He was elected executive vice president in 1972 and named to the bank's Board of Directors in 1973. He is the former president, chief administrative officer and director of Crocker Bank of San Francisco. He is a member of the Board of Trustees of the University of Notre Dame and is chairman of its Investment Committee.

Index